DIGITAL DIDACTICAL DESIGNS

As web-enabled mobile technologies become increasingly integrated into formal learning environments, the fields of education and ICT (information and communication technology) are merging to create a new kind of classroom: CrossActionSpaces. Grounding its exploration of these co-located communication spaces in global empirical research, *Digital Didactical Designs* facilitates the development of teachers into collaborative designers and evaluators of technology-driven teaching and learning experiences—learning through reflective making. The Digital Didactical Design model promotes deep learning expeditions with a framework that encourages teachers and researchers to study, explore, and analyze the applied designs-in-practice. The book presents critical views of contemporary education, theories of socio-technical systems and behavior patterns, and concludes with a look into the conceptual and practical prototypes that might emerge in schools and universities in the near future.

Isa Jahnke is Director of Research for the Information Experience Lab and Associate Professor of Information Science and Learning Technologies at the University of Missouri, USA. She was Professor of ICT, Media and Learning at Umeå University, Sweden, and Assistant Professor at TU Dortmund University, Germany.

DIGITAL DIDACTICAL DESIGNS

Teaching and Learning in CrossActionSpaces

Isa Jahnke

Routledge
Taylor & Francis Group

NEW YORK AND LONDON

First published 2016
by Routledge
711 Third Avenue, New York, NY 10017

and by Routledge
2 Park Square, Milton Park, Abingdon, Oxon OX14 4RN

Routledge is an imprint of the Taylor & Francis Group, an informa business

Library of Congress Cataloging-in-Publication Data
Jahnke, Isa.
  Digital didactical designs : teaching and learning in CrossActionSpaces /
Isa Jahnke.
    pages cm
  Includes bibliographical references and index.
  1. Internet in education. 2. Computer-assisted instruction. 3. Tablet
computers. 4. Educational technology. 5. Teachers—Training of.
I. Title.
  LB1044.87.J33 2016
  371.33'44678—dc23
  2015009778

ISBN: 978-1-138-92848-0 (hbk)
ISBN: 978-1-138-92849-7 (pbk)
ISBN: 978-1-315-68170-2 (ebk)

Typeset in Bembo
by Apex CoVantage, LLC

CONTENTS

List of Figures and Tables   *ix*
Preface   *xi*
Acknowledgments   *xiii*

1   Introduction: The Internet in Our Pockets and Handbags;
    ICT Is More Than Just a Tool   1
    1.1   Classrooms of the Future—Learning in CrossActionSpaces   4
          1.1.1   Spaces   6
          1.1.2   Communication Spaces   6
          1.1.3   Co-expanded Communication Spaces   7
          1.1.4   Multi-Existing Co-expanded Communication Spaces   7
          1.1.5   The Character of Human Action in Such
                  Communication Spaces Is CrossAction   8
          1.1.6   A First Summary, CrossActionSpaces   9
          1.1.7   What Does This Have to Do With Teaching
                  and Learning?   9
    1.2   Teaching Practice Turns Into Digital Didactical
          Design—Teaching Is Process Design for Learning   12
    1.3   The Broader Context—Different Levels   15
    1.4   Book Organization   16
    1.5   References   19

2   From Sociotechnical Systems to CrossActionSpaces   22
    2.1   The Sociotechnical Paradigm—Social and Technical Systems   25
    2.2   What Is a System? Differences Between Technical and
          Social Systems   28

2.2.1   The General Concept of a System   29

2.2.2   Different Forms of Systems—Structures and Processes   30

2.2.3   Technical Systems   31

2.2.4   Social Systems—Grounded on Communication   34

2.3   Elements of Social Systems: Communication Leads to Expectations and Roles   35

2.3.1   Communication Is Interpretation—The Basic Element of Social Systems: Easy and Complex   35

2.3.2   Communication, Behavior, (Inter)Action, Cross-Actions   38

2.3.3   Characteristics of Social Systems   39

2.3.4   System Theory for Designing Teaching and Learning?   41

2.3.5   Structures of Social Communication Systems: Made of Expectations While Making Connections   43

2.4   Sociotechnical Systems Turn Into CrossActionSpaces   45

2.4.1   What Is a Sociotechnical System? (A Definition)   46

2.4.2   From Sociotechnical Systems to Co-expanding Communication Spaces   47

2.4.3   Educational Institutions: From Systems to CrossActionSpaces   48

2.5   Social Bots as New Forms of Sociotechnical Agents? Antisocial Media   50

2.6   Summary   54

2.7   CrossActionSpaces Linking Systems, Networks and Communities   55

2.8   References   62

3   Dynamics of Roles in CrossActionSpaces: Enabler and Hinderer   68

3.1   Roles—The Interactionism Point of View   72

3.2   Roles—Structural-Functionalism Perspective   74

3.3   Roles in Technology and Software Development (Roles in CSCW)   77

3.4   What Makes Human Behavior Into a Role? Multiple Dimensions   78

3.5   Summary—Roles Enable and Hinder MultiCrossActions in Relations   84

3.6   Teaching, Learning, Roles—Problems in Teachers' Roles and Students' Roles   86

3.7   Role Mechanisms—Assigned and Taken Roles   92

3.8   Different Types of Roles—Informal, Implicit and Formal, Explicit   98

3.9   Summary: Human Interaction Is Evolving Toward Multi-Cross-Action—Roles as Paradox, They Enable and Limit Cross-Action   104

3.10 References   106

4 Learning as Reflective CrossAction: The Example of
   Learning Expeditions   109
   4.1 How Education Has Been Understood for Many Years   110
   4.2 Beyond the Concept of the Classroom   114
   4.3 Who Learns? We All Do! And Who Has Knowledge?
       We All Have—It Depends on the Situation   117
   4.4 From Course-Based Learning to Learning Expeditions   117
       4.4.1 A Candidate for Learning Expeditions: Research-Based
             Learning Situations (Inquiry-Based Learning)   119
       4.4.2 No Learning Expedition Without Creating Conditions
             for Creativity   121
       4.4.3 Beyond Courses—Thinking of Learning Expeditions
             in Groups and Communities   122
       4.4.4 Schools and Universities of the Future—Beyond
             Courses Toward Learning Expeditions   124
   4.5 References   126

5 Teaching Creates Conditions for Learning as Reflective
   Cross-Action: Digital Didactical Design   130
   5.1 Digital Didactics—Three Interwoven Layers   132
   5.2 The Middle Layer—Digital Didactical Design (Theory and
       Process View of Triangle 2)   135
       5.2.1 For Empirical Studies—Transforming the DDD Into a
             Five-Layer Pentagon   139
       5.2.2 A Typical Example From Our Classroom
             Studies—Process Design View   143
       5.2.3 Design for Teaching Aims and Learning Intentions   147
       5.2.4 Design for Learning Activities (Individual,
             Collaborative, Community Learning)   149
       5.2.5 Process-Based Assessment as Guided Reflections,
             Feedback and Feed*forward*   153
       5.2.6 Social Relations and Roles—Designing for Social
             Relationships   155
       5.2.7 Interactive Media: ICT Is More Than Just a
             Tool—Design Thinking in Education   158
   5.3 It Is Not Technology or Didactics—Emergence of New
       Digital Didactical Designs   166
   5.4 References   167

6 Projects and Empirical Studies Toward Reflective
   CrossActionSpaces   172
   6.1 #InPUD—Example of an Early Form of Co-expanded Spaces
       in Higher Education   173
       6.1.1 Technology-Embraced Informal-*in*-Formal Learning
             Fosters the Conative Level of Learning   174

	6.1.2	Anonymity as Duality	175
	6.1.3	InPUD Organizes the Jungle of Information for Learners	175
	6.1.4	InPUD Is an Example of an Early CrossActionSpace	176
6.2	#PeTEX—Remote Lab Learning in Engineering Education	177
	6.2.1	Learning Expeditions Designed as Reflective Cross-Actions	178
	6.2.2	Reflective Cross-Actions for Different Learning Levels	179
	6.2.3	Intertwining the Technical, the Pedagogical and the Social Dimension	180
6.3	#DaVinci—Creating Conditions for Creativity of Learning Expeditions	182
6.4	#IPM—An Example of Challenges When Designing for Learning Expeditions	185
	6.4.1	Why Didn't Students Use the Mobile Devices?	185
	6.4.2	The Potential of Mobile Devices—Access to Collaboration at Any Time, Anywhere	187
6.5	#Tablet-Mediated Learning Expeditions in Schools	187
	6.5.1	Classroom Studies—Learning Through Reflective Making?	188
	6.5.2	Range of Learning Expeditions	195
6.6	References	198

7 Conclusion and Looking Forward . . . — 201
7.1 Empowering Teachers as Collaborative Designers—Organizational Change! — 202
7.2 Lessons Learned—Designing the Future — 203
 7.2.1 Our World Is Full of Co-expanded Spaces—CrossActionSpaces — 205
 7.2.2 Learning Cannot Be Delivered—Traditional Designs Neglecting Designs for Partnerships — 205
 7.2.3 Learning Is Reflective Multi-Cross-Actions in Relations — 205
 7.2.4 Designing Conditions for Sociotechnical-Pedagogical Processes—Teaching Is Process Design — 206
 7.2.5 Schools and HE Need Practices That Design for Learning Walkthroughs and Learning Expeditions — 206
 7.2.6 Not All Learning Can Be Measured — 207
 7.2.7 ICT Is More Than Just a Tool — 208
 7.2.8 Learning Analytics Is a Method and an Instrument to Control Students and Their Behavior—a Provoking Look — 208
 7.2.9 There Are No Simple Step-by-Step Models for Digital Didactical Designs — 209
 7.2.10 More Design-Oriented Research and Formative Evaluation Studies — 210
7.3 References — 211

Index — 213

FIGURES AND TABLES

Figures

1.1	Moving toward CrossActionSpaces	6
1.2	Communication spaces and cross-actions are based upon an ongoing process of affecting each other's development/ emergence = CrossActionSpaces	10
1.3	Three layers of challenges in designing for learning	16
5.1	Digital Didactical Design layers in educational institutions— obstacles and spaces for negotiation and development	133
5.2	Digital Didactical Design—elements and relations	137
5.3	Teachers' and students' views on the Digital Didactical Design	139
5.4a	Example A of a Digital Didactical Design	139
5.4b	Example B of a Digital Didactical Design	140
5.4c	Example C of a Digital Didactical Design	140
5.5	Digital Didactical Design of classroom ID11 from the process design view	146
5.6	Kember's model of teachers' teaching concepts informing different levels of the learning quality	152
5.7	Examples of digital media and its different functions (crossovers in reality)	163
6.1	Six facets of how teachers conceptualize student creativity	183
6.2	Learning language skills by using digital paintings, student voice recordings and text	189
6.3	Screencasting app for documenting and reflecting math strategies	190
6.4a	QR codes outdoors for improving grammar language skills	192
6.4b	QR codes outdoors for improving grammar language skills	193

6.5a Media tablets for collaboratively creating, documenting and
      reflecting physics experiments   194
6.5b Media tablets for collaboratively documenting and reflecting
      physics experiments   195

Tables

2.1   Toward a sociotechnical society   48
3.1   The interactionism perspective   73
3.2   Structural-functional perspectives on role concepts   76
3.3   Four dimensions of roles that constitute MultiCrossActions
      in Relations   80
3.4   A fictional example of teacher and student roles 100 years
      ago—*exaggerated*   88
3.5   Why the teacher role suffers (with the example of history
      and future)   90
3.6   Effects in a networked world   91
3.7   From modifications and changes of human behavior to the
      emergence of roles   95
3.8   Support and nature of role mechanisms in social and technical
      systems   96
3.9   Descriptive categories of roles   99
3.10 Types of sociocultural roles with examples (Roles Type 1)   99
3.11 Types of assigned and taken roles; formal/informal roles
      (Roles Type 2)   100
5.1   Using the DDD for empirical studies (researchers) and for reflecting
      learning practices (teachers and learners)   141
5.2   Matrix for designing the quality of learning   153
5.3   Applying design thinking in education—teachers are designers
      for learning   160
6.1   Exploring types of learning expeditions—from surface,
      individual learning to deeper, group learning   196

PREFACE

For 10 years we have had the same problems:
ICT is not integrated enough in education.

(A teacher at a conference in Norway, Oct. 2013)

There is a shift away from the separation of digital media and education towards co-expanded settings where mobile technology becomes part of the classroom; both merge into new communication spaces. This situation affects teaching and learning in different ways. The research I have performed in recent years makes a contribution toward research-based teaching practices and student learning in such emerging multiexisting communication settings—technology-enhanced designs for learning and tablet-mediated designs for learning.

Since starting as a researcher in this field in 2001, I have seen change in technologies. We went from almost no Internet in the 1980s to Web 1.0 in the 1990s; now we work with Web 2.0, Industrial Revolution 4.0 and the Internet of Things. The guiding questions have always been the same: To what extent is it possible to support learning by interactive technologies, and what kind of learning quality does teaching support with interactive media? What are the potentials for teaching and learning with web-enabled technology that is not possible without? "How do you know that students are learning and have learned?" A simple question by Thomas Reeves (2006) that I put it on the table once again for discussion. I intend to bring these issues of *teaching, learning, quality and design* together and take them to the next level: what *is* learning in the era of a digital networked world, when access to information poses no difficulty whatsoever?

The main assumption of the book is that it is not information design or content that need our attention. Designs for teaching and learning, which use materials and content, require both detailed reflection and a cultural change. This perspective, and the activities it embodies, is called Digital Didactical Design.

Not wishing to disappoint the reader, I will be clear at the outset in saying that I do not have all the answers to the questions that this perspective poses—indeed, I pose many new ones myself. Asking the right questions takes us halfway toward designing the future, and it is my hope that these questions may be useful when reflecting on our current understanding of education, teaching and learning.

The book could have borne many subtitles, each of them quite different, and it was not easy to choose only one of them. An alternative option to the one that I have chosen is *Learning Expeditions in Arena X* (Jahnke & Norberg, 2013). This stresses the unknown situation of higher education in the future. Instead of focusing too much on new technology-driven designs or content design, the challenge is to develop Digital Didactical Design so as to enable meaningful and deep learning.

Actors in educational settings such as teachers, designers, educational developers, researchers and policy makers, but also learners themselves, can easily restrict learning; but do we know how to support learning in order to help learners to grow in their learning progress? The enablement of learning, and creating opportunities for learning, are at the heart of this book. The challenge is to design learning in educational institutions where not only ICT-supported resources are at the center of teaching but also new forms of Digital Didactical Design, which unfold an evolution toward a diversity of learning expeditions.

ACKNOWLEDGMENTS

This book could not have been written without reflection and help of my colleagues, and members of our research team in Sweden, to whom I am very deeply grateful: to Anders Norberg (for his critical eye, challenging perspectives and inspiration on time-blended learning), Lars Norqvist (for his creative view on pedagogical attitudes), Andreas Olsson (for his engagement in iPad-classrooms and conducting workshops for university teachers), Eva Mårell-Olsson (for her exciting studies in higher education with GoogleGlass) and Peter Bergström (for his rich contributions of process-based assessment and power relations)—all from Umeå University in Sweden. You are very creative and reflective design-based researchers—thank you!

I would also like to pay deep thanks to my mentors, friends and co-reflectors across work boundaries, in online spaces and from different communities; special thanks go to three outstanding professors: Thomas Herrmann (IMTM, University of Bochum, Germany—InPUD, DaVinci projects), Gerhard Fischer (University of Colorado at Boulder, USA) and Johannes Wildt (TU Dortmund, Germany—DaVinci, PeTEX projects). They have always challenged my thinking and that is what excellent researchers do. Thanks so much!

Over the last few years, I met researchers from different countries and together we walked partly similar trajectories, we discussed and reflected about Mobile Learning (is learning mobile or wearable?), Educational Technology, CSCL at the Workplace, and I hope we continue working together; in particular, I thank Swapna Kumar (University of Florida, USA), Sean P. Goggins (University of Missouri—thanks a lot for co-chairing ACM Group '14 with me; wow, that was awesome!) and Julia Liebscher (Duisburg-Essen, Germany).

In this book, I refer to some of our research projects such as InPUD, DaVinci, PeTEX and Digital-Didactics. The success of these projects refers to a team—research is teamwork. In InPUD (2001–2010), I collaborated with Volker Mattick and Hans Decker (both TU Dortmund, Germany). Thank you for making InPUD rich of experiences. DaVinci (2008–2011) would not be successful without Tobias Haertel (TU Dortmund, Germany). Thank you Tobias for your multi-perspective thinking and pluralism! The project was funded by the German Ministry of Education (BMBF). PeTEX (2009–2011) was a European project (in the Lifelong Learning Programme) and its success was driven by Claudius Terkowsky, Christian Pleul, and A. Erman Tekkaya (TU Dortmund, Germany). Many thanks go to the teams at Palermo University (Italy) and KTH/Stockholm (Sweden). It was a pleasure working with you.

For three years, from January 2012 to the end of 2014, we studied tablet-classrooms in Denmark. It is an amazing 1:1 media-tablet-program and school project in the municipality of Odder. Dear Lise Gammelby in Odder, thank you so much for opening the doors for us and "Tusen Tack" (many thanks) to all teachers who do a great job of designing for learning. Thank you very much that you let us in and become a part of your tablet-classrooms. I also want to thank the head-masters and all teachers in Sweden, Finland and Norway that open their classroom doors for us researchers. The Swedish project was funded by the Swedish Research Council (Vetenskapsrådet), 2014-2016. Thanks to Marko Kuuskorpi for inviting us to Kaarina (Finland) and thanks to Erling Gronlund for inviting us to Oslo (Norway) – tablet-classrooms integrated into the curriculum on the move! In 2012, I visited the P.K. Yonge Developmental Research School at the University of Florida. Thanks go to Julie Henderson and Swapna Kumar for creating this great opportunity.

My research is also inspired by my colleagues when I was a PhD student and later a post-doc researcher at IAW-IMTM, Ruhr-University of Bochum (until 2008), especially, I am grateful and want to thank deeply, Kai-Uwe Loser (our discussion on Anti-social Media) and Gabriele Kunau (for her crucial reflections on Sociotechnical Systems) – I liked very much (although sometimes exhausting) our Luhmann readings in the evenings; thanks go to Rainer Skrotzki for his nice humor useful to reflect on existing routines. Thanks to the IAW-IMTM team!

Andrew Hossein Ordoubadian has my gratitude for comments on an earlier version. I deeply thank Anthony Scully for providing his knowledge of proofreading and critical commenting.

Unfortunately, I cannot mention all people that accompanied me during my research path; there are many more who inspired me, for example, guest professors who visited me in Umeå, and people who I met at conferences such as the GMW, European EUNIS and EC-TEL (thanks to Ilona Buchem for co-organizing great workshops and special issues!), E-CSCW (thanks to Michael Koch for 'Web 2.0 goes Academia', 2009), COOP (thanks to Wolfgang Prinz, Aurélien Bénel, Jean-Pierre Cahier, Manuel Zacklad for supporting the Web 2.0 workshop, 2008) the International ICED, CSCL and ACM Group (thanks to Pär-Ola

Zander for co-authoring a nice paper), on Social Media and in discussions, after presentations and keynote speeches.

However, there is one person who is very important. Without the support of my husband Ralf, I would never have finished this work; he has always supported my desire to go beyond my own horizon. We are living together for how many years now? The answer will always be, "Not enough!"

Isa Jahnke
March 2015, Umeå, Sweden

1

INTRODUCTION

The Internet in Our Pockets and Handbags; ICT Is More Than Just a Tool

I went to a highly ranked college where all the professors came from excellent universities. . . . But all they did was read from their textbooks. Then, I quit.

(M. Prensky, 2001, p. 3)

In the era of web-enabled mobile technology, one factor has changed that has enormous impact on our current understanding and definitions of the nature of teaching and learning in education. It has an effect on how schools and universities, teachers, students and decision makers approach teaching and learning. This changing factor is ubiquitous access to information through mobile devices and wearable technology (e.g., media tablets, smart glasses). It is the omnipresence of online presence, independent of where we are. More people have better access to information with easy-to-use mobile devices, anytime and anywhere; we potentially have all information always at hand via our media tablets or web-enabled phones. Such a simple-sounding development has tremendous impacts on learning. Whether we like it or not, mobile technology has already affected the way we learn: discussions and learning strategies have changed. If the learner does not know about Subject X, she merely has to search for it online, instantly. In the digital age—in an Internet-driven, networked world—constant online access supports the Homo Interneticus in searching immediately for solutions to a question or a problem. This technology-mediated social action takes place as an individual person or as the individual engages in contact with her groups and learns in collaboration.

Unlike informal learning outside educational institutions, traditionally Information and Communication Technology (ICT) was segregated from the normal teaching classroom, for example, in computer labs (Henderson & Yeow, 2012). This has changed with the advent of smaller, flexible devices. Differences between laptops and small, easy-to-handle multimodal Web-enabled devices are discussed in other literature (e.g., Johnson et al., 2013). There is a shift from separating ICT and education to co-located settings (De Chiara et al., 2007) where mobile technology becomes part of the classrooms; both the offline and online worlds have merged into new forms of co-located communication spaces. These new spaces are the expansion of the traditional classroom boundaries—in short, CrossActionSpaces.

CrossActionSpaces provide various offline and online 'rooms' for social interaction and communication within one physical location at the same time. For example, imagine a lecture hall with 100 students in the traditional setting, where the teacher asks an open question; only one student is able to answer at any one moment. With mobile technology, all students are able to contribute and become active agents—it is the expansion of the established communication space. Traditionally, communication was limited to the physical lecture hall, and only those people that were part of the physical room could interact. With web-enabled technology, learners can consult their online networks, such as social networking sites and micromessaging services (e.g., Twitter, LinkedIn) for different reasons. Some want to find an answer to a question or solution; others want to engage in discussions about the lecture content. Such cross-actions of learners expand the given physical room to many spaces. It is the extension from those who attend in the physical location to new and other participants elsewhere. These spaces are connected to other spaces. The learner in the lecture hall and classroom interacts with her networks and these members have access to other networks, and so on.

A person is in a physical place but at the same time in two or several other online spaces; she reads information, she contributes actively in discussion boards, she shares photos about presentation slides, she searches for solutions on how to build a product such as a solar energy item at home. And other people do this, too.

PROBLEMS

Technology has not only the advantage of supporting learning and sharing information; the use of technology can shift learning to a direction where humans and learners are more and more disconnected from the social environment.

There are side effects. In a ubiquitous, digital-networked world, information, all information, seems always to be with us, in our pockets and handbags. Does this make everything perfect? No. Easy access to information does not necessarily make learning easier; access to content does not necessarily mean that a person learns. No learning progress takes place without reflection—and a smartphone, a media tablet or a laptop itself cannot make the user reflect (Jahnke et al., 2012).

Another problem emerges. The digital networked world consists of humans but also social bots, automated software programs. It is not a social media world we inhabit; humans and bots have together created an asocial media world.

Social bots, for example, copy and paste the existing content in huge amounts within a short time. In the name of its programmer, the bots influence the opinion of the human participants, for example, in politics. It is known from psychology research that the more often we hear and read the same sentences, the more readily we believe in them, even though the message might contain false information. Bots did influence, for example, the political opinions and actions of those using Twitter in the Iran election in 2009 and using online communities in the Ukraine crisis in 2014 (read further in "Twitter Bot Influences Real Americans," NBR, 2011). "The Bot Traffic Report" from 2013 showed that 61% of all networked communication had been initiated by bots. According to Alexis C. Madrigal, senior editor of the *Atlantic*, he flooded Twitter with thousands of automatically generated 'auto tweets' and caused 100,000 visits to a single web page, in such a way that no one noticed that they were generated from the same Internet address. The networks of bots and other forms of intelligent computer machinery are part of our Internet-driven world—often with malicious purposes, such as collecting human online profiles and human patterns of activity (Boshmaf et al., 2011; Chu et al., 2010; Wagner et al., 2012).

In addition to such invisible technical mechanisms, there are also hidden social mechanisms. When humans communicate and interact, they create new expectations, and expectations of expectations, and so forth, which create boundaries, intended or not intended, implicitly or explicitly. In the Internet world, such boundaries are, for example, online role structures (Jahnke, 2010b). To take one instance, in online courses, teachers and students have many different roles to perform. Teachers are structure givers, creators of scaffolds, experts, process mentors, designers and colearners in the workplace. Students are learners, consumers, knowledge constructors, creators, feedback givers and sometimes teachers for their peers. This role complexity is like a burden; it is difficult to juggle with the complexity of role expectations—sometimes these are contradictory and cause behavior conflicts. For example, sometimes teachers know that they are in different roles, such as that of a designer, but they do not know how to handle all the different expectations. Sometimes, students do not know that teachers expect them to act as creators; they think the consumer role is the norm. Some students expect that the teacher has the right answer and that s/he tells the student what to learn. In such cases, students will not use web-enabled technology—except where the teacher has designed for its use. This means that the teacher creates a design for learning that fosters social actions by students in such CrossActionSpaces.

These social and technical mechanisms make our environment appear to be an open world. It is not open; we only think it is open. We wish it so. Terms such as 'open world' have often been used in recent years, but what does 'open' mean? Do all people have access to all information? Is all information open? Are all people open-minded? Is everyone able to learn what and as they wish? CrossActionSpaces are communication spaces in which humans perceive a new quality, a tension between openness and role constraints.

The theories of social roles and social system theories form the basis for this thinking; they remind us that our world is made of social system boundaries in which learning is constrained by the role performance. It is not only the technical system that codes and recodes boundaries; it is human communication that enables but also restricts our way of communication and learning. Learning in this book is understood as a form of reflective communication.

Developing the approach of CrossActionSpaces further, it leads into a new model of how we think about learning, which helps to turn the given learning restrictions into learning opportunities. It also informs new types of learning technologies. In a networked world full of big data, learning is emerging from traditional role performances into multiple-role connections that can be seen in various interactions across established boundaries of systems. A person using her web-enabled devices is at several spaces, sometimes at the same time, physically and online. Cross-actions in relations are emerging. CrossActionSpaces are evolving.

This brings new questions to the agenda: how do humans learn in a digital, interactive, social and antisocial or asocial networked world, especially in such co-expanded spaces? What is the purpose of teaching and how to design for learning? What is the relationship between them?

The book discusses new forms of innovative pedagogy. More specifically, it initiates reflections about relationships of learning, teaching, pedagogy and ICT/tablets in education. What is the new normality? Challenges and unexpected factors will be illustrated. I argue that one answer can be called Digital Didactical Designs for Learning Expeditions (Jahnke, Norqvist & Olsson, 2014), which supports Inclusive Learning Spaces and education for all that does not only rely on access for all but on reflective learning for all.

1.1 Classrooms of the Future—Learning in CrossActionSpaces

In this book, I argue that the digital networked world is neither one space nor several social or sociotechnical systems; rather, it can be also understood as CrossActionSpaces. These spaces are emerging through interactions of humans using web-enabled technology. Human behavior in such spaces does not only rely on interactions but also on multiple actions across established boundaries of traditional organizations and institutions. Spaces are constituted through the cross-actions by humans.

For example, a group of people is chatting; during the discussion, open questions arise such as 'how far away is city X' or 'why do so many bees die in the winter'. They use their online networks to find solutions. Another group is learning about automobile mechanics and uses the Internet to find solutions on how to fix an automobile. People are searching for information online, they are using their online networks, they make Do-It-Yourself products offline, and they are part of the maker-movement culture, on- and offline. While acting in such flexible ways, the off- and online worlds are merging into new spaces. Cross-actions by humans are the creators of these new spaces.

When human action is changing toward such cross-actions, and when learning takes place under the conditions of spaces, then the question is: how to design for learning? What is learning in such a world?

The traditional classroom has been organized around textbooks and a physical location in which to learn. Schools and universities practice teaching and learning as if there existed one right answer. However, the world in the digital age does not work in that way. First, there are always many different answers available to a specific problem. Second, when schools and universities do design learning in such a way where one right answer is available, then learners just can go into CrossActionSpaces and google for the right answers and ask their online networks. Who would not ask the Internet, when we would know the right answer is available there? When we have the Internet in our pockets and handbags everywhere at any time, why shouldn't we use it? This means that schools and universities need new designs for teaching and learning. Instead of creating learning designs where a right answer is available, more complex problems are required where students solve problems together and become makers connecting to real-world experiences. Bring the world, and the world's problems, into the schools and universities by using CrossActionSpaces.

The future classroom will be organized around 'access to' content and, moreover, access to social capital (Huysman & Wulf, 2004). Social capital is the knowledge that people have and communicate: what is not in the textbooks, nor explicitly available otherwise. Social capital can be on the Internet. It is 'in' the social networks; it is also in massive open online courses (Daniel, 2012); it is in Twitter and in all other forms of communication spaces, which create access to these kinds of knowledge.

Figure 1.1 illustrates how the traditional offline classroom and online clouds are merging into new CrossActionSpaces by the expansion of communication beyond the physical walls.

The future classroom will be organized especially around interaction and cross-actions. Teachers will create designs for learning that enable cross-actions conducted by students in groups, sometimes at the same location and sometimes in different places and spaces, to solve a problem in collaboration. The key design factor will be the 'process.' The logic of the future course design will be the process at center and not the location. Teachers design for processes first, and the locations are second. A course in schools and universities is then characterized by processes that enable student activities and cross-actions over time.

CrossActionSpaces can be described as multi-existing co-expanded communication spaces in co-located settings of online spaces and offline places that are made by cross-actions and human communication. I describe this step by step in the next sections.

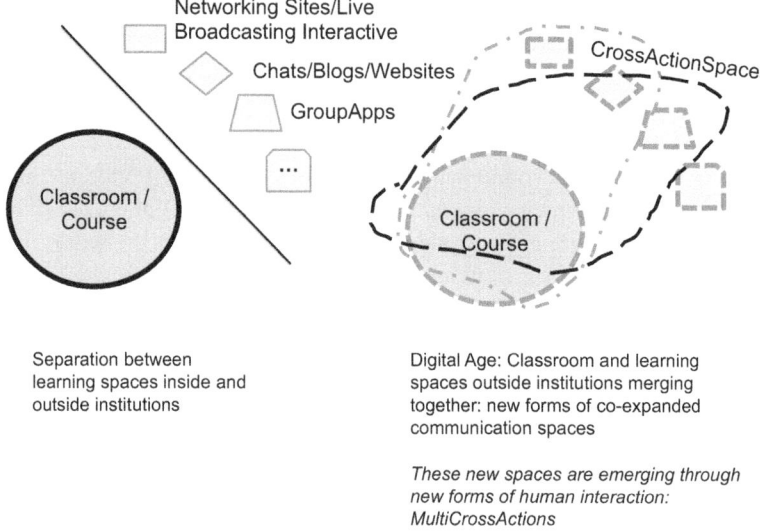

Networking Sites/Live Broadcasting Interactive

Chats/Blogs/Websites

GroupApps

CrossActionSpaces

Classroom / Course

Classroom / Course

Separation between learning spaces inside and outside institutions

Digital Age: Classroom and learning spaces outside institutions merging together: new forms of co-expanded communication spaces

These new spaces are emerging through new forms of human interaction: MultiCrossActions

FIGURE 1.1 Moving toward CrossActionSpaces

1.1.1 Spaces

Over the years, the classroom has been constructed as a social system (Chapter 2) in which teacher and learners meet. Designs for learning often followed an Instruction-Response-Evaluation structure (Mehan, 1979) in which students reacted to questions by teachers. In the digital age, the old classroom, however, is changing toward a more open space, especially when the teachers and students use digital media and web-enabled technology. In our tablet-classroom studies, we saw such new spaces (discussed in Chapter 6). Students use the media tablet to search for information on the other side of the classroom walls; they are makers of new products, they upload their products into a school Vimeo channel, and they even invite an audience from outside schools to join them in their learning processes. The classroom wall and the construct of the traditional social system are blurring; new spaces evolve. We can call this the system or space perspective.

1.1.2 Communication Spaces

The space metaphor does not rely on location but on communication. The space is not constituted by places but by communicative actions of people, learners and teachers. Learning is no longer restricted to the classroom location as a physical place; it is rather the emergence of new spaces for communication where offline places and online communication spaces are merging. The traditional concept of a classroom as a social system is evolving into such communication spaces. These new spaces are not limited to 'just more' offline places or offline locations; rather, these spaces offer new forms for and new ways of communication for learners during their learning processes.

1.1.3 Co-expanded Communication Spaces

Learners use web-enabled technology to contact the world outside the classroom, for example, to connect to their world and their experiences. In doing so, the learners collaboratively co-expand the traditional classroom boundaries. Suddenly, the classroom is no longer the only place for learning. Co-expanding means that the offline room for communication by learners and teachers is enlarging into the world of all information, the "InfoSphere" (Floridi, 2014), and into the world of other learners and their expertise, knowledge, experience and their networks. An example is a platform for teenagers who are broadcasting their activities in real time, live, and they see on their screen via chat function the written questions and comments by other users, to which they react with oral communication. They can even sing in their rooms and invite some friends. However, they expand their space for communication with others when they use such a technical platform. For example, instead of sitting at the marketplace and playing guitar, teenagers sing or play piano at home and have hundreds of visitors, chatting with them and getting feedback; others discuss issues such as not fitting into the societal standard look, and others show short dancing performances. In our tablet-classroom observations, we also saw how teachers and students (8th and 9th graders) used media tablets to extend the traditional classroom communication toward CrossActionSpaces. They created new experiments in the fields of physics and chemistry; they planned, conducted, and video-recorded them; and they used the video to reflect about the failed experiments (if these failed). They then uploaded the videos into a school video channel and engaged in a chat with university students about the experiments and results.

1.1.4 Multi-Existing Co-expanded Communication Spaces

Terms such as InfoSphere emphasize that offline and online settings are interwoven and intertwined with each other. There is no longer a clear difference between whether we are online or offline. However, there is not 'one' big InfoSphere or space—rather there exist multiple communication spaces besides multiple other existing social systems, networks and communities. Therefore, the term 'multi-existing' emphasizes that we do not have just one space for communication; rather, we have many multiple spaces that are co-expanding. Whenever we are in meetings and use our tablet to search for information, to check what the lecturer tells us or what a retailer wants to sell us, we create such a new space; when we are sitting in a classroom or lecture hall and chatting about the lecture content with others online, a new space has been created. Wherever communication is involved that is technology mediated, a new form of co-expanded space has been developed. These spaces differ with regard to their duration (for how long the space exists), topic and numbers of participants.

Surprisingly, such spaces are not totally open. They are limited by their creation of social boundaries. Wherever humans meet, they build expectations and assumptions toward the others that limit communication and learning experiences (Chapter 3). There is a new quality of tension between openness and closeness. From the viewpoint of a person, he or she cannot access the entire world of data. He cannot access all information that is on the Internet, and he cannot enter all of the billions of communication spaces. This is only a theoretical possibility. In practice, the person makes a decision due to time and resource restrictions. She decides what to read online, what kind of networks to attend, what kind of spaces to enter and not.

1.1.5 The Character of Human Action in Such Communication Spaces Is CrossAction

When such new spaces are constituted by communication, how can we characterize human action there? It is a form of social interaction enabled and mediated by technology. A person acts, she interacts, she communicates and, even more, I argue, in the digital age, she conducts several cross-actions. She is in an offline conversation; she takes photos, puts them online on Twitter or elsewhere, and comments on the entries of others. For example, imagine about 300 participants at an international conference in a huge hall, with people listening to the keynote speaker on the stage; some of them are discussing facts and sharing opinions about it online at the same time, using a Twitter hashtag. Even those people that are not part of the conference hall participate in the Twitter hashtag discussion. This is an example of a CrossActionSpace and how it has emerged. At the end of the speech, some of the questions that came up in the CrossActionSpace are asked to the keynote speaker. While people conduct such cross-actions, they are part of such spaces; they create new ones or they are participating in existing ones. In such situations, people interact off- and online—chatting with the person beside them, listening to the keynote speaker and chatting via media tablets.

Instead of using the traditional term of 'social interaction,' I have chosen *cross-actions* to stress that human action in the networked world is distributed 'across' traditional boundaries that take place in usual or even unexpected spaces in different online and offline contexts, settings and situations. Interactive, web-enabled media affects the expansion, dissolves and redefines, codes and recodes new and existing boundaries of social, socio-technical systems and co-expanded spaces. The terms 'multi-' and 'multiple' cross-action are used to emphasize that human action is more diverse and flexible than before the Internet era. Multiple cross-actions are possible at the same time in different settings using mobile technologies and interactive media applications. A person acts in a set of different online settings, not with his or her physical body but with the capability to communicate in written forms as well as nonverbal and verbal forms. Even when a person seems to be offline, s/he is always online at the same time. Why? Because she can get notifications on her mobile phone or via email when other people want to connect or communicate with her in the digital space. Offline and online spaces are smelting together. In that way, there is no separation between offline and online any longer. We live in CrossActionSpaces.

1.1.6 A First Summary, CrossActionSpaces

CrossActionSpaces are those multi-existing co-expanding communication spaces. They are characterized by dynamic multi-layers, overlayered spaces and 'rooms' that are made of human communication, linking both physical and online places that connect existing sociotechnical systems, networks and communities—such spaces are based on communication as social practice takes place in and across those spheres using web-enabled technology. It is the expansion of communication beyond the physical walls and emphasizes the dynamic processes of human interaction across established boundaries in today's networked world. The term 'co-expansion' emphasizes that communication connects to another communication that is already linked to a third one, and that one is related to another one, and so forth; it spreads in cocreation. Those communication spaces are not constituted solely through human or social *inter*action but through crossing interactions, in short *cross*-actions. However, this does not mean that everything is connected and open; instead, such communication or CrossActionSpaces create boundaries built upon human behavior expectation patterns and individual and group assumptions. In practice, boundaries are built by the person who makes a decision on what kind of spaces to enter or not—due to different reasons, such as time and resource restrictions. The boundaries are discussed in detail in Chapters 2 and 3, argued from the view of sociotechnical systems and behavior expectation patterns as enablers for, and hindrances to, CrossActionSpaces.

Figure 1.2 illustrates how communication spaces (system view) and crossaction (action view) refer to each others' development.

1.1.7 What Does This Have to Do With Teaching and Learning?

What has happened with ICT is that the classroom walls have eroded; some students contact the world outside (learning contact or simply entertainment, social or other contact) with or without a plan constructed by the teachers. This means that the classroom no longer works in the same way. We can try to revert the situation by turning off Wi-Fi and forbidding Internet access, so as to build up the walls again, but this repaired patchwork will probably not survive. Thus, how do we use classrooms in schools and universities in the future, not to isolate

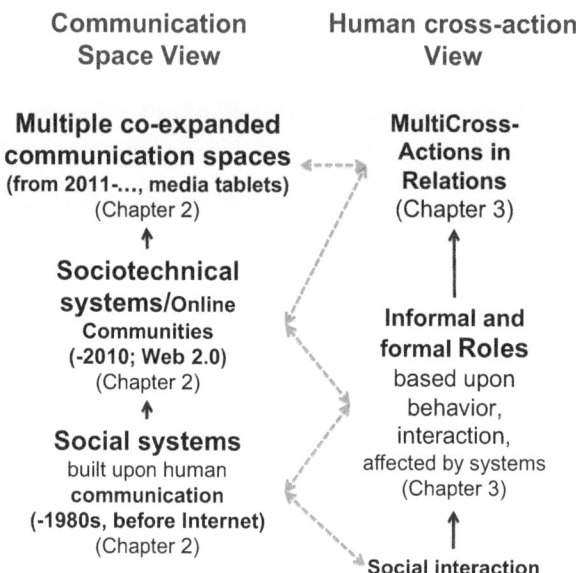

FIGURE 1.2 Communication spaces and cross-actions are based upon an ongoing process of affecting each other's development/emergence = CrossActionSpaces

them from the world, which does not work any longer in the same way as before due to digital media richness, but to communicate with it?

In our big data world, learning is a form of reflective communication that proceeds through the reflective doing of cross-actions. The classroom turns into a social meeting spot for learners, where teachers are learning companions and didactical process designers in order to enable different opportunities for learners to learn together, such as mastering X, exploring Y and understanding the implications of Z (Norberg & Jahnke, 2014). Learning is not dependent only on traditional human action and interaction; rather, learners perform several actions across existing spaces. They even create new spaces—some of these disappear, while other spaces are sustained over time. In a digital networked world, human interaction turns into multi-cross-action, and learning is then a reflective form of multi-cross-actions.

CrossActionSpaces provide different opportunities for designing teaching and learning, such as:

- Supporting the learner in changing her role from the exclusivity of consuming content toward reflective makers in groups;
- Connecting the classroom with the world outside schools and universities (communication to a real audience);

- Designing learning technologies by seeing the world through the eyes of a learner; and
- Enabling learning as reflective making of multi-cross-actions.

Over the last years, schools and universities have been understood as the location where all information was gathered. Learners went to schools, libraries and universities to access to this information; but today, almost all information is all around us. There is no need to go to school only in order to receive information, but there are other reasons. The diverse functions of schools range from socialization, reflecting societal values, creating social relationships and cultural innovations to developing social and methodological skills (as discussed in many other books).

In the classroom of the future, students do not only learn to memorize what is in the textbook but what they can learn from the textbook or other material to solve a problem creatively with a team of learners. The classroom of the future is organized around cross-actions, for example, in the form of learning expeditions using tablets or web-enabled devices. Learning expeditions focus on problem-solving skills. To solve the problem, students use different resources: they use content from textbooks and different sources on the Internet, and they use Internet access to gain benefits from multiple forms of social capital across established networks and organizations and across different offline rooms and online spheres. The learners create new networks in different contexts and in different relations. To solve a problem, students become co-designers of communicative reflections in multilocated spaces; they become reflective actors that support their learning progress. The range and intensity is open and depends on a learner's age, situation and context. The design of old-fashioned, course-based learning moves into designs for multi-cross-actions; one example is called learning expeditions (Chapter 4). Teachers develop designs for reflective multi-cross-actions (Chapter 5).

The central question remains: When teaching, learning spaces and mobile web-enabled technologies are merging into CrossActionSpaces, what designs for learning are useful and powerful under those new conditions? Derived questions are:

- Do educational institutions, schools and university teachers use the potential of these new spaces; if so, in what ways? What is the purpose of teaching in multilocated settings, and how is teaching conceptualized and practiced in a networked world? What designs for teaching and learning are useful and related to the new conditions of our networked world?
- In CrossActionSpaces, how can actors in educational institutions link teaching and learning? In what ways do actors in schools and in universities design for teaching and learning practice for enabling multi-cross-actions?
- What quality of learning (surface to deep learning) does (and should) teaching address in an Internet-driven world conceptualized as CrossActionSpaces?

The ambition to reflect on teaching and learning is not new at all. Barbara McCombs wrote in 2000, "This paper argues that it is time to think differently about assessing the role of educational technology in the teaching and learning process. . . . What is learning?" I agree with her: we have moved forward, but there is still (or again) the same question on the table. In our networked world, what is learning, and, moreover, what is the perceived value of learning?

In this argument, teaching practices and pedagogical designs are needed where students are able to become reflective makers of multi-cross-actions (they are not merely consumers but also active agents and producers) and 'learnerpreneurs' to help them to grow in their learning progress toward becoming critical problem solvers, fostering intellectual development and "conceptual change" (Kember, 1997). Conceptual change is a process of learning where the person changes and develops her existing concepts of a subject toward a new understanding (Roschelle, 1992). When learning is reflective multi-cross-action, how and which designs for learning are required that support such learning?

One possible candidate of such learning is shown by do-it-yourself (DIY) cultures, both DIY and do-it-with-others, that Hatch (2013) illustrates as "maker movements" and "maker cultures." In such maker cultures outside educational institutions, learners at home and in their garages make new products, learn while doing this, and share their ideas and products. The idea of one maker is used by another maker; she uses parts of the idea and transforms it for her problem so as to find an appropriate solution. The question for schools and universities is whether this kind of learning and its characterization of highly motivated learners can be transferred to education. How would school and higher education look if this learning approach were used? What kinds of designs for teaching and learning are required then?

1.2 Teaching Practice Turns Into Digital Didactical Design—Teaching Is Process Design for Learning

When learning in our digital networked world can be understood as reflective multi-cross-actions, then the question is, what is the function of teaching? How can teaching be designed so that it supports reflective multi-cross-actions?

I use the concept of design thinking that has the potential to construct and study teaching and learning from the different angles of a design. Planning and conducting of a teaching practice moves away from a common routine activity and turns into a design project. The word 'design' focuses on specific actions and parts of activities by the teachers in schools and universities. Designing is the act of giving a form; moreover, it is the act of modeling the teaching and learning practice—the designing action shapes a focus and key points. A design focuses on certain elements but does not take all of the reality into consideration. A design has both a planned component and an operative doing—teaching is process design.

When teaching means creating conditions for learning, then teachers in the digital age create designs of sociotechnical-pedagogical processes to enable students' learning. This embraces the planning and application of the design in practice: what we can call 'design in action.' Such a design has two aims: 1) it helps the teachers to reflect on their practice *in situ* and points to improvements for learning, and 2) a design links teaching activities to students' learning expeditions. We call these 'digital didactical designing for learning' (Chapter 5).

The word *didaktik* (didactics) comes from a Greek term that denotes the theory of teaching and learning—the linkage of teaching processes to learning processes. The European approach of *didaktik* not only includes the methods of 'how to' teach but also embraces the question of 'what to' learn (curriculum and content), 'why,' 'when/where,' and in what kinds of situations. *Didaktik* argues that the cultivation of social partnerships and learnerships is central in learning.

This view on both didactics and design puts teaching and learning into a new light—teaching is not only a tool for achieving the cognitive dimension but is also an activity-driven design to enable learning as activity for critical-reflective knowledge coproduction instead of knowledge consumption (Hauge & Dolonen, 2012).

In an ideal ('dream') world, the teachers create a process design for learning that integrates the following components toward a new form, the Digital Didactical Design or DDD (addressed in Chapter 5):

- Co-aims: teaching aims are formulated as intended learning outcomes (ILO; learning intentions): the teacher makes clear the intended learning outcomes (content and skill aims), asks her students about their aims (co-aims) and their expectations, and matches them to her design so as to create a new design.
- Learning activities in a process: complex problem-solving challenges, which are linked to the world outside the school/university and linked to the students' experiences and their worlds and contexts—designs for learning expeditions—this is the maker layer.
- Process-based assessment such as guided reflections for all to support a learning progress (Bergström, 2012; Daudelin, 1996): milestones during the course, to adjust/improve the DDD dynamically—this is the reflection layer.
- Social relations and roles: the teacher designs for different roles purposefully over time with regard to aims and co-aims, and with regard to the different activities over time, in order to help the students to shift in their roles from being passive to becoming active and critical-reflective agents (Jahnke, 2010a)—teachers and students perform many different roles and explicitly reflect on them.
- Mobile web-enabled technology provides access to multi-located, overlayered communication spaces to enhance learning expeditions (such as several online networks, online communities, specific apps, interactive content, using and creating videos, audio files, recording one's own voice, and so forth).

These five elements are constructively aligned to each other to foster student engagement and quality learning. A "constructive alignment" (Biggs & Tang, 2007) is like a house with building blocks or pieces of a larger puzzle that fit with the other pieces so as to create learning opportunities. The assumption is that the better these five elements align to each other, the higher the likelihood that the students learn. In a way, the five design elements coevolve together, and the design as a whole requires a reflection, a new balance, and a new adjustment when one of the elements changes. This can be called a new form of constructive alignment.

The dream world differs from teaching practice; in our research, we have studied the difference between this dream world and the reality. In detail, we have studied the teachers' applied Digital Didactical Designs for learning in co-located spaces, for example, when using media tablets (Jahnke, Svendsen, Johansen & Zander, 2014). In the 16 of 24 observed classrooms, we have found designs that created CrossActionSpaces. Students from preschool class to Grade 9 across all subjects, e.g., math, language, science, geography, music, history, religion/ethics, were makers of learning products individually or in groups; they created, for example, MathStrategy screencastings, book trailers, short videos and interactive lessons (Chapter 6). They designed sociotechnical-pedagogical processes for learning.

CrossActionSpaces create two new requirements: 1) they "require teachers to undertake more complex pedagogical reasoning than before in their planning and teaching" (Webb & Cox, 2004), and 2) when teachers turn their classroom from traditional teacher-led concepts to learner-centered, 'reflective maker' approaches, where learners produce new knowledge and do not repeat textbook content, then teachers face a wider 'unknown' situation (Bergström, 2012).

The design element of social roles is crucial, as the learning-centered paradigm argues that meaningful learning is "an active process of constructing rather than acquiring knowledge" (Duffy & Cunningham, 1996, p. 171)—the student learns when s/he is active and engaged. Jonassen, Howland, Moore and Marra (2003) provide a nice overview of what active meaningful learning is "when students making meaning" (p. 6). The five attributes are active, constructive, cooperative, authentic and reflective. Active learning is also related to the role of the learners; they are not consumers but also active agents and producers: *pro-sumers* (Johnson et al., 2013; Fischer, 2011, 2013); furthermore, they become makers. Existing educational concepts claim that students should be able to become co-designers of their own learning. In research, it remains unclear how the teacher actively designs this opportunity so that it supports students in dynamically changing their different roles. How do the teachers design for the dynamics of roles in their classroom and course practice? In what ways can the role concept be an explicit part of the design?

I call this a digital didactical design because, in the Internet age, didactical designs are always technology based, but they range from a low extent to a high extent of support for different forms of learning, where the quantity and quality of the technology integration vary. For example, the sharing of documents, slides and literature via Intranets is one manner in which to use technology. A low extent is defined as a low or nonadded value of using mobile devices in the classroom situation, or when the value of the use is not evident; for example, the media tablet is a substitute for pen and paper or a printed textbook and does not use the potential of ICT. A medium extent is assigned when the mobile devices are a substitute for other existing technologies that could also have been used, for instance, a computer, laptop or digital camera. A high extent is defined when the use of the mobile technology shows special characteristics or new functions and features that no other device can offer at present, for example, special apps, a one-in-all device, or a multimodal device (Selander & Kress, 2010). McCormick and Scrimshaw (2001) made a useful distinction between 1) ICT as "efficiency aid" (to make learning faster within a special time frame), 2) ICT as "extension device" (to extend learning such as having access to material on the Internet), and 3) ICT as "transformative device" that turns learning into new forms, for example, learning expeditions. Web-enabled ICT and tablets provide a new 'room' for communication: it is more than just a tool; it provides the possibility for creating co-expanded communication spaces made by social interactions, social relations and roles—CrossActionSpaces.

1.3 The Broader Context—Different Levels

The innovation of mobile technology, such as the media-tablet boom (Kaganer et al., 2013), leads to a new situation in educational institutions on different levels. The classroom is not isolated in a vacuum; a classroom is rather embedded in different social contexts and social systems influenced by this, but also shapes them.

The adoption of such devices affects many layers of education, stretching from how humans act in the classroom, content in courses, activities and agendas, which take place inside and outside the university, to decision-making, both locally and nationally. The new situation affects three layers of designing for learning: 1) the relation among teachers, students and content, 2) the Digital Didactical Design (middle layer), and 3) the didactical conditions such as curriculum design (including exams), institutional strategies and academic staff development for teachers, leaders, IT- and media technologists, educational developers, instructional designers and students (Figure 1.3).

Broadly, the book contributes to the different layers of education. Through our research, focused on the middle layer but not limited to it, the qualitative changes and challenges within and between the layers will be made clear and visible.

This emerging research field of CrossActionSpaces informs interdisciplinary studies. This book makes a significant contribution toward research-based quality teaching and learning practices in an Internet-driven world. It also contributes

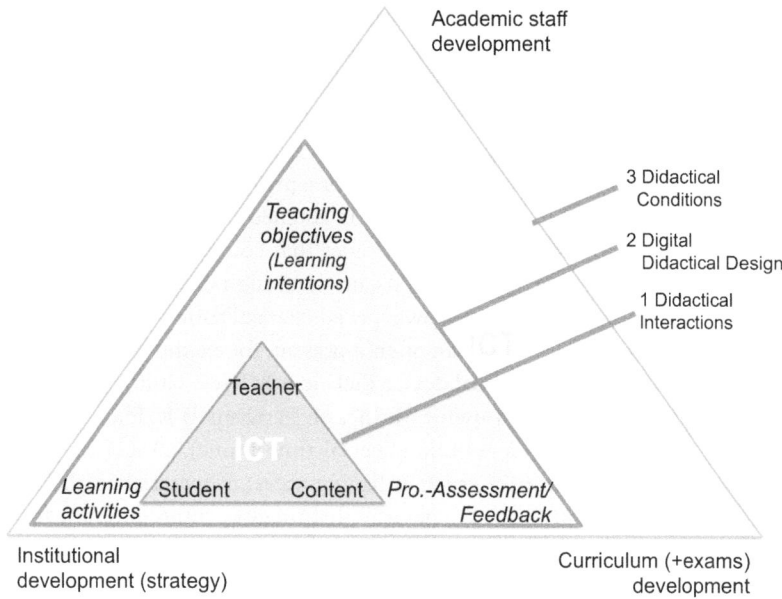

FIGURE 1.3 Three layers of challenges in designing for learning (from Jahnke et al., 2014)

to the theoretical conceptualization of approaching first, a new thinking of the digital networked world as CrossActionSpaces; second, a new thinking toward learning, as reflective multi-cross-actions; and third, a new thinking of how to design for learning.

The approach of Digital Didactical Design makes visible how teaching and learning designs can be linked toward learning expeditions. It is grounded on my different interdisciplinary and empirical research studies, with different levels of participation, in particular, creativity in higher education (DaVinci Germany), remote-controlled laboratories in engineering education (PeTEX, a European project in Sweden, Italy and Germany), technology-enhanced Informal-in-Formal Learning (InPUD, Computer Science education), and didactical designs for the use of media tablets in education (Denmark and Sweden, funded by the Swedish Research Council) and cooperation with schools in Finland.

1.4 Book Organization

The object of my recent studies, and this book, is tablet-mediated design for teaching and learning, especially technology-enhanced designs for learning. Writing this book has been a journey that started with the motivation to understand learning in the digital networked world. In common with many other researchers, I could see the fundamental difference between learning inside and learning outside institutions, schools and higher education using both informal and formal learning (Jahnke, 2012).

Outside educational institutions, people learn because they want to learn, rather than having to learn what schools or universities tell them to learn. Of course, this is not valid for all people; however, a characteristic of schools and universities is that learners assume that the teachers tell them what to learn. Outside such institutions, people use the Internet to solve problems; they are highly motivated; they search for information online; and they share their lives, photos and short messages, reply to each other or forward information. They are makers; they learn and share their ideas and products, as is seen in the Do-It-Yourself cultures, where people build products at home or in their garages. They share and use ideas of others that Hatch (2013) identifies as "maker movements." In spite of challenges such as data privacy, ethical concerns and online bullying, humans engage with the online world around them.

Within education, teachers try to motivate learners; in tablet classrooms, they motivate students to use the Internet, while attempting to connect them to the course content. Teachers use collaboration models, problem-based learning approaches and many other designs. However, it seems that nothing is really being done to close the gap between designs for learning inside and outside institutions; they are still separated and seen as two different worlds instead of designed for informal-in-formal learning (Jahnke, 2012). The "pedagogical attitude" still shows an isolation of those worlds rather than an integrated view, as shown in the empirical study by Norqvist, Leffler and Jahnke (2015).

From this thinking, new questions came to my mind. What if we had started creating designs for learning at the wrong end? Before we are able to design for learning in schools and universities, we first need a better understanding of our digital networked world and what it really is, how it is socially constructed. When I read Floridi's (2007) argument that we were probably the last generation that makes a difference between the offline and online worlds, I became convinced that an alternative understanding of our networked world would have a huge impact on designs for learning.

In this book, I argue first of all that the digital networked world is neither one space nor several systems but rather can be understood in terms of many communication spaces that are co-expanding—in short, CrossActionSpaces—they emerge through human/social interaction and communicative cross-action. Everything is built on communication. Learning is reflective communication. The underlying knowledge of what communication is, how communication organizes itself in social systems, and how they differ from technical systems is discussed in Chapter 2. The chapter especially shows the historical development, how social and sociotechnical systems are changing and evolving toward Cross ActionSpaces; such spaces are characterized by 1) system boundaries created of people, groups, communities, networks and infrastructures and 2) a higher tension between openness and constraints than in the nondigital world.

Second, human behavior builds such emerging spaces but does not rely only on social interactions; it also relies on social actions across established boundaries. A group of learners is online and offline, sometimes at the same time; they are searching for information and reading; they use their online networks, share photos, and want to express their opinion. The group members search for all kinds of problem solutions, such as how to improve swimming style, how to trade, how to organize house moving, and many other issues; some of them are part of the maker-movement culture in on- and offline settings. Such multi-cross-actions are new forms of communication; however, they are not totally open. Humans make decisions every day about what space to enter or not; in doing so, they create boundaries, excluding some while they include others. Another boundary in such spaces is built through their established patterns of communication, assumptions and expectations, which are called social roles. Roles enable and hinder learning in CrossActionSpaces.

We all have expectations, and we all more or less make assumptions. Whenever people meet, they develop expectations that stay implicit or become conscious, or old ones are intensified. All humans and groups create those behavior expectations. It is a matter of reflection whether and how humans break through their typical expectations. The various established behavior patterns, known as roles, that enable but also restrict communication are discussed in Chapter 3. Especially in a digital networked world, such traditional role patterns provide the framework and pathway for dynamic multi-cross-actions; they enable cross-actions, but they also hinder them. I call them MultiCrossActions in Relations to emphasize that they depend on, and are affected by, the context and space in which they happen.

Third, when human action changes toward multi-cross-actions, then we can ask what learning is. I argue that learning is communication in the form of reflective performance of multi-cross-actions. In Chapter 4, I illustrate what learning as multi-cross-action requires and how it can be understood. I use the example of learning expeditions to clarify reflective multi-cross-actions, how they can be used in classrooms and how to design for these learning expeditions.

Fourthly, when learning takes place in such dynamics of CrossActionSpaces and learning is reflective multi-cross-action, then the question is what the purpose of teaching is and how to reorganize teaching so that it supports learning as reflections of multi-cross-actions. I argue that teaching under such conditions of multi-existing spaces requires itself a design perspective. Teaching is creating conditions and designs for learning. Teaching is no longer limited to the speech of an expert. I introduce the concept of Digital Didactical Design, which points to a new understanding of how to design for teaching and learning, in Chapter 5. This design view is not only a matter of science or researchers; it also claims that teachers need to become reflective designers and teacher education needs to integrate this new view into its study programs, a view we can call 'teaching and learning as design science.'

The understanding of the networked world as CrossActionSpaces informs and leads to new technology-enhanced designs for learning, tablet-mediated designs for teaching and learning, and new forms for sociotechnical-pedagogical prototypes. Some of the empirical studies and prototypes are shown in Chapter 6.

A conclusion and a look into the future are presented in summary in the final chapter (Chapter 7).

This book explores the characterization of the digital networked world, and I suggest seeing it as CrossActionSpaces built upon co-expanded communication spaces. The book illustrates how the Internet-driven networked world, viewed from the perspective of CrossActionSpaces, is influencing teaching and learning. Under the premise that the digital world is such a new form of multiple-emerging communication spaces, the book argues that human action in such a world is not only grounded in *inter*actions, but rather on multiple *cross*-actions within and across such spaces. What is learning then, when the digital world is multi-cross-actions in CrossActionSpaces, and what is the function of teaching? The book uses the concept of *didaktik* (didactical designs) and design thinking from other disciplines, such as that of interaction design and design schools, and explores how this model can be transformed and used to change teaching and learning practices in schools and universities.

This book understands teaching and learning as didactical process designs, and is useful for teachers, learners, educators, instructional designers, educational technologists, educational developers, pedagogical actors and leaders as well as decision makers in educational institutions, who obtain a framework for initiating design thinking so as to develop teaching and learning from the perspective of Digital Didactical Designs and develop learning as reflective multi-cross-actions. Researchers and students in the interdisciplinary nature of the learning sciences, instructional design and education, and actors in schools and universities receive a framework with which to study the practice and new forms of innovative pedagogies for teaching and learning.

1.5 References

Bergström, P. (2012). *Designing for the Unknown. Didactical Design for Process-Based Assessment in Technology-Rich Learning Environments.* Umeå, Sweden: Umeå University Press.

Biggs, J. & Tang, C. (2007). *Teaching for Quality Learning at University*, 3rd ed. New York: Open University Press.

Boshmaf, Y., Muslukhov, I., Beznosov, K. & Ripeanu, M. (2011, December). The social-bot network: when bots socialize for fame and money. In *Proceedings of the 27th Annual Computer Security Applications Conference (ACSAC '11).* Technical report: http://lersse-dl.ece.ubc.ca/record/272

Chu, Z., Gianvecchio, S., Wang, H. & Jajodia, S. (2010, December 6–10). Who is tweeting on Twitter: Human, bot, or cyborg? In *Conference ACSAC '10*, Austin, TX.

Daniel, J. (2012). Making sense of MOOCs: Musings in a maze of myth, paradox and possibility. *Journal of Interactive Media in Education*, 3.

Daudelin, M. (1996). Learning from experience through reflection. *Organizational Dynamics*, 24(3), pp. 36–48.

De Chiara, R., Di Matteo, A., Manno, I. & Scarano, V. (2007). CoFFEE: Cooperative Face-2Face educational environment. In *Collaborative Computing: Networking, Applications and Worksharing, 2007 Conference*, pp. 243–252. doi:10.1109/COLCOM.2007.4553836

Duffy, T. M. & Cunningham, D. J. (1996). Constructivism: Implications for the design and delivery of instruction. In: D. H. Jonassen (Ed.): Handbook of Research for Educational Communications and Technology. New York: Simon & Schuster Macmillan, pp. 170–198.

Fischer, G. (2011, May–June). Understanding, fostering, and supporting cultures of participation. *Communications of ACM Interactions*, 18(3), pp. 42–53.

Fischer, G. (2013). A conceptual framework for computer-supported collaborative learning at work. In: S. Goggins, I. Jahnke & V. Wulf (Eds.): *Computer-Supported Collaborative Learning at the Workplace (CSCL@Work)*. Heidelberg: Springer, pp. 23–42.

Floridi, L. (2007). A look into the future impact of ICT on our lives. *The Information Society: An International Journal*, 23(1), pp. 59–64.

Floridi, L. (2014). *The Fourth Revolution. How the Infosphere Is Reshaping Human Reality.* Oxford: Oxford University Press.

Hatch, M. (2013). *The Maker Movement Manifesto: Rules for Innovation in the New World of Crafters, Hackers, and Tinkerers.* New York: McGraw-Hill.

Hauge, T. E. & Dolonen, J. (2012). Towards an activity-driven design method for online learning resources. In: A. D. Olofsson & O. J. Lindberg (Eds.): *Informed Design of Educational Technologies in Higher Education: Enhanced Learning and Teaching.* Hershey, PA: IGI Global, pp. 101–117.

Henderson, S. & Yeow, J. (2012). iPad in education: A case study of iPad adoption and use in a primary school. In *System Science (HICSS), 45th Hawaii International Conference*, pp. 78–87. doi:10.1109/HICSS.2012.390

Huysman, M. & Wulf, V. (2004). *Social Capital and Information Technology.* Cambridge, MA: MIT Press, pp. 355–399.

Jahnke, I. (2010a). A way out of the information jungle—a longitudinal study about a socio-technical community and informal learning in higher education. *International Journal of Socio-technology and Knowledge Development*, 4, pp. 18–38. doi:10.4018/jskd.2010100102

Jahnke, I. (2010b). Dynamics of social roles in a knowledge management community. *Computers in Human Behavior*, 26(4), pp. 533–546. doi:10.1016/j.chb.2009.08.010

Jahnke, I. (2012). Technology-embraced informal-*in*-formal learning. In: A. Ravencroft, S. Lindstaedt, C. Delgado Kloos & D. Hernandez-Leo (Eds.): *21st Century Learning for 21st Century Skills. 7th European Conference on Technology Enhanced Learning.* Berlin: Springer, pp. 395–400.

Jahnke, I., Bergström, P., Lindwall, K., Mårell-Olsson, E., Olsson, A., Paulsen, F. & Vinnervik, P. (2012). Understanding, reflecting and designing learning spaces of tomorrow. In: A. Sánchez & P. Isaías (Eds.): *Proceedings of IADIS Mobile Learning 2012.* Berlin: IADIS International Association for Development of the Information Society, pp. 147–156.

Jahnke, I., Norqvist, L. & Olsson, A. (2014). Digital Didactical Designs of Learning Expeditions. In: C. Rensing et al. (Eds.): *Open Learning and Teaching in Educational Communities.* The 9th European Conference on Technology Enhanced Learning, EC-TEL 2014, Graz, Austria, September 16–19, LNCS Vol. 8719, pp. 165–178.

Jahnke, I., Svendsen, N.V., Johansen, S.K. & Zander, P.-O. (2014). The dream about the magic silver bullet—the complexity of designing for tablet-mediated learning. In *GROUP '14, ACM Conference Proceedings*.

Johnson, L., Adams Becker, S., Cummins, M., Estrada, V., Freeman, A. & Ludgate, H. (2013). *NMC Horizon Report: 2013 Higher Education Edition*. Austin, TX: New Media Consortium.

Jonassen, D.H., Howland, J., Moore, J. & Marra, R.M. (2003). *Learning to Solve Problems With Technology: A Constructivist Perspective*, 2nd ed. Upper Saddle River, NJ: Merrill, Prentice Hall.

Kaganer, E., Giordano, G.A., Brion, S. & Tortoriello, M. (2013). *Communications of the ACM*, 56(11), pp. 68–75. doi:10.1145/2500494

Kember, D. (1997). A reconceptualisation of the research into university academics' conceptions of teaching. *Learning and Instruction*, 7(3), 255–275.

McCormick, R. & Scrimshaw, P. (2001). Information and communications technology, knowledge and pedagogy. *Education, Communication and Information*, 1(1), pp. 37–57.

Mehan, H. (1979). *Learning Lessons. The Social Organization of Classroom Instruction*. Cambridge, MA: Harvard University Press.

NBR (2011). Twitter bot influences real Americans. Retrieved April 14, 2011, from http://www.noonehastodietomorrow.com/tech/the-Internets/2881–2881

Norberg, A. & Jahnke, I. (2014). "Are you working in the kitchen?": European perspectives on blended learning. In A.G. Picciano, C.D. Dziuban & C.R. Graham (Eds.): *Blended Learning—Research Perspectives*, Vol. 2. New York: Routledge/Taylor & Francis, pp. 251–267.

Norqvist, L., Leffler, E. & Jahnke, I. (2015). Sweden and informal learning—towards integrated views of learning in a digital media world. A pedagogical attitude? In: T. Burger, M. Harring & M. Witte (Eds.): *Handbook for Informal Learning*. Weinheim/ Munich: Juventa.

Prensky, M. (2001). *Digital Natives, Digital Immigrants. On the Horizon*. Vol. 9, No. 5. Lincoln, NE: NCB University Press.

Roschelle, J. (1992). Learning by collaborating: convergent conceptual change. *Journal of the Learning Sciences*, 2(3), pp. 235–276.

Selander, S. & Kress, G. (2010). *Design för lärande—ett multimodalt perspektiv* [Designing for learning—a multimodal approach]. Stockholm: Norstedts.

Wagner, C., Mitter, S. Körner, C. & Strohmaier, M. (2012). When social bots attack: modeling susceptibility of users in online social networks. In *Proceedings of the WWW*, Vol. 12.

Webb, M. & Cox, M. (2004). A review of pedagogy related to information and communications technology. *Technology, Pedagogy and Education*, 13(3), pp. 235–286.

2

FROM SOCIOTECHNICAL SYSTEMS TO CROSSACTIONSPACES

Things are never what they are. They are always what you make of them.

(J. Anouilh, 1910–1987)

The journey of writing this book started with the motivation to understand learning in the digital networked world. Like many other researchers, I also saw that there is a fundamental difference between learning inside and outside institutions, schools and higher education. Outside educational institutions, we see people that learn what they choose to learn; they use the Internet to solve problems and they are highly motivated; they search for information online; and they share their life, photos and short messages and reply or forward information. Despite challenges such as data privacy and online bullying, humans are engaged with the world around them. Inside education, teaching tries to motivate learners and tries to connect them to the course content; they use collaboration models and many other designs. However, it seems that nothing really closes the gap between learning inside and outside institutions. From this thinking, new questions came to my mind. What if we start with designs for learning at the wrong end? Before we are able to design for learning in schools and universities, we need first a better understanding of our digital networked world and what it really is, how it is socially constructed. When I read Floridi (2007), who argues that we are probably the last generation that distinguishes between off- and online worlds, I was convinced that a new understanding of our networked world could make a huge impact on the designs for learning.

In this chapter, I approach an alternative understanding of the digital networked world that can be named CrossActionSpaces. I provide an alternative view on today's digital networked world and how it can be understood and characterized. I argue that the digital networked world is not one space, nor several systems; it is, rather, the emergence of co-expanded communication spaces. In the following sections, I illustrate the characterizations of such new spaces.

All is communication, and communication does organize itself in "social systems" (Luhmann, 1995). The journey to understand our digital networked world starts with the social system theory by Niklas Luhmann (1995). The main foundation is that the element of a social system is human communication and that communication organizes itself in diverse systems. On the one hand, communication forms diverse sets of patterns, known as expectations and expectations of expectations and so forth, and those patterns are often called roles (Chapter 3). On the other hand, social systems have already formed such patterns. It is a duality of structures (Giddens, 1984) that can be seen as duality of an objective facticity (Berger & Luckmann, 1967/1993): Humans build social systems in online settings when they just act as they act, grounded on implicit or deliberate decisions; but they also see such social systems, patterns of communication and behavior expectations as a fact in front of them that threaten them and limit their possible actions. Chapter 2 is intended to throw light on the hidden mechanisms of social systems, their structures and especially how those systems nowadays are emerging into new forms of CrossActionSpaces. Since teaching and learning is based on communication, the topic of social systems and spaces are of high relevance because they do affect designs for teaching and learning and vice versa.

"Systems theory is . . . a paradox," writes Bailey (2006), because words such as system and social system are well known, accepted, used and distributed; but on the other hand, the system theory is often misunderstood, and many new theories do arise in new forms, for instance, complexity theory and sociotechnical system design. Bailey's work gives an excellent introduction into systems theory in which the key elements are the position of the observer (p. 387) and "boundary recoding" that "is widely neglected, . . . despite its obvious importance" (p. 399). Indicators for recoding boundaries are, for example, when people label themselves as closer to the core of a community or as outsiders.

The phenomenon of social systems and their structures, such as networks of human interactions and patterns of expectations, that lead to roles is not new. Concepts and approaches can be traced back to the beginning of the 20th century. George Herbert Mead (1934/1967) and Ralph Linton (1936) were two representatives of two different approaches. They contributed to an understanding of how society works as it does, how social structures are shaped by human actors, and how these structures and systems shape the thinking and learning of humans. The two perspectives contribute to the question of how social interaction takes place and why they are as they are today.

In the era of the Internet, the same social mechanisms are more or less valid today as in the days of Mead and Linton; but nowadays, we have the expansion of online communication that is not only restricted to a small neighborhood, friends or family members and not limited to writing traditional letters.

Nowadays, the possibilities for communication have changed. Human communication is possible across well-known boundaries to thousands of other humans who are online, in different settings and different contexts. This quotation makes the point: "Twitter is the shortest distance between you and what interests you most." (Karin S-Y, personal communication, January 22, 2014). I call this phenomenon a CrossActionSpace. A person is in one physical place but at the same time in two or several other online spaces. He contributes actively in discussion boards; he shares photos in online networks; or he searches for solutions for how to build or fix a product, such as creating a solar-energy-driven boat at home. And other people do it, too. Human communication is out there, organized in spaces. However, that does not mean that all communication is possible or open. An example of being limited by human interaction is given by the study of the Echo Chamber phenomenon (Wallsten, 2005). The Echo Chamber illustrates that members of online networks experience that their own thinking is constantly echoed back to them, which intensifies their own actions. This phenomenon has two consequences: first, there is little space for new input; second, other or different opinions will not survive.

Web 2.0 is often characterized by informal participation, which means a free cooperation of as many people (and bots) as possible without any restraints from organizations, processes or technical platforms. In contrast to online networks, a formal organization like a company or school consists of rather formal structures, which define what a member is allowed to do, should do and how to fulfill a task by assigning a role. In my study on a sociotechnical on- and offline community called InPUD from 2001 to 2009, which is part of a formal organization of an university department (Jahnke, 2010), the results show that by using interactive, web-enabled technology, the balance between informal and formal structures in institutions is changing; the involved participants always create a specific degree of digital formalization and formalized structures (Jahnke, 2009). The study shows that online groups need such structures for successful sustainability.

Such digital media applications as InPUD transform social groups into sociotechnical systems, where socially and technically supported relationships are highly interwoven. This is also supported by other studies of Internet-based communication. Existing studies show trends that social structures in online communities are evolving; for example, Viegas, Wattenberg, Jesse and van Ham (2007) studied the Wikipedia community and found an increase in coordination activities (especially from 2003 to 2007). Despite the potential for anarchy in Wikipedia, "the Wikipedia community places a strong emphasis on group coordination, policy, and process" (Viegas et al., 2007, p. 1530). Viegas, Wattenberg and Kushel (2004) also show the behavior of Wikipedians in conflict situations; the most activity in Wikipedia is not writing new articles but controlling the quality of written articles, removing vandalism from new articles and acting as mediator for two or more authors (e.g., discussions on spelling). The studies reveal that the social structure of an online group changes over time.

2.1 The Sociotechnical Paradigm—Social and Technical Systems

Collins and Halverson (2009) argue that there is a need to rethink education in the age of technology. By applying the sociotechnical paradigm, new ways of teaching and learning in a networked world might be prepared.

Viewing our current world from the theory of sociotechnical communication systems has its potential in differentiating between different types and different levels of systems, such as technical and social systems that can be observed on micro, meso and macro or grand levels. However, this causes the challenge to identify what social and technical systems are. Does a social system consist of groups of people; is it human behavior or interaction or something else? It is crucial to make clear and to define the elements of a social system because people may assign different things to them. The similarities and differences of the system characterizations are useful in understanding, designing and developing sociotechnical systems. It is especially relevant when we want to understand which elements can be designed and which cannot. Technical systems are developed and externally controlled (maneuverable) from the outside (allopoietic), whereas social systems are self-controlled systems and contingent (autopoietic). This will be explained in detail in the following sections.

The sociotechnical paradigm, introduced by the Tavistock Institute in London, describes "the study of the relationships and interrelationships between the social and technical parts of any systems" (Coakes [2002], referring to Emery & Trist [1960]). The approach of sociotechnical systems (STS) keeps the relevant components together and attempts to improve their relationships. One object of their studies was the British Coal Mine, as a new work system had to be integrated into this organization.

Recently, new forms of sociotechnical phenomena have emerged, such as online communities, Internet-based networks and virtual worlds (e.g., Second Life). People are getting an increasing amount of information through the Internet, e.g., e-mail, web-based discussion boards, instant messaging tools, wikis, blogs, micromessaging tools (e.g., Twitter), and social networking tools (e.g., LinkedIn, Instagram). Social networking applications enable people to contact each other, collaborate, share knowledge and build new relationships. These new forms of sociotechnical structures differ from sociotechnical systems in how people connect: their relationships and ways of communication are technically mediated. Technical and social elements are highly interwoven and affect each other.

O'Reilly (2005) was one of the first who called the evolving Internet-based relationships "Web 2.0." This buzzword emphasizes social software applications and social media platforms that are heavily reliant on human interactions and collaborations. The key feature is their possibility for interactivity. To describe Web 2.0 and newer forms of its applications, it is appropriate to compare Web 1.0

and Web 2.0. For instance, personal websites are disappearing, and blogging is becoming the new favored way of maintaining an online presence. Blogs differ from traditional personal websites in their opportunities to contact other users. Individual publishing is morphing into social tagging. Wikis are expanding pure content management systems. The role of the user is changing from reader to author, from consumer to producer ('pro-sumer'). Web 1.0 is rather 'information download,' whereas Web 2.0 has evolved into 'communication about information' (Jahnke & Kommers, 2009).

Studies on Internet-based communication show how social structures in Web 2.0 emerged. Roberts et al. (2006) analyzed the social presence in web-based systems, and his study shows that online presence has a positive impact on a person's reputation. Forte and Bruckman (2005) as well as Wasko and Faraj (2005) investigated the motivation of Wikipedia users and why they contribute to Wikipedia. One result is that knowledge sharing takes place when people assume their reputation will grow through online participation. Another Wikipedia study by Viegas et al. (2007) shows the increase in coordinating activities from 2003 to 2007. In spite of the potential chaos in Wikipedia, "the Wikipedia community places a strong emphasis on group coordination, policy, and process." Viegas et al. also explored how Wikipedia users feel responsible and how they discuss new entries. The bulk of activity in Wikipedia is not writing new articles but controlling the quality of written articles. Activities include, for example, controlling input and mediating between two or more authors (moderating discussions about spelling or meaning). A new role emerged: Wikipedians created the role of 'vandal hunters' to prevent Wikipedia entries from bad or wrong information generated by visitors intent on writing funny or false entries instead of providing correct data.

The InPUD community (Jahnke, 2010) also reveals such a trend of emerging new social structures and social mechanisms. In our long-term study from 2001 to 2009, we studied the change and emergence of a sociotechnical community and its evolution over time. The learning community was part of the official organization of a European university. The results indicate that a human network evolves from a trust-based community with few formal rules into a community with more formal rules that are socially enforced by its members. At the very beginning of the community, the social mechanisms, and not the software architecture, fostered the community's evolution (Jahnke, 2009, 2012).

When I write about technical systems, I mean forms of web-enabled Information and Technology systems (IT and ICT). In contrast, social systems are built on communication by people, for example, in groups or companies, small groups and large organizations. When we bring people and technology together, what do we have then? As Sommerville (2004) said, it is a sociotechnical system, "a system that includes operational processes that are followed by human operators and that operates within an organization, agencies (rules), procedures and structures."

Typical sociotechnical systems are, for example, groupware systems, knowledge-management systems and applications for social networking. The challenge of such sociotechnical systems is to design the interaction between social and technical parts. Whether this type of system really contributes to learning and knowledge sharing depends on the corporate culture and on the degree to which organizational and technical structures are adjusted to each other and how they are integrated—the technical elements interacts with the social system and vice versa.

In order to explain the interplay of social and technical systems, it is essential to understand the main difference. The constituted element of a social system is contingent communication, while for technical systems it is a deterministic and allopoietic (Luhmann, 1995). According to Eason (1988), Mumford (1995), and Cherns (1987), methods, guidelines and principles are focused to make the integration between social and technical systems a success. Eason emphasized: "a new sociotechnical system must include the in-work roles to co-operate effectively in seeking organizational purposes." According to Coakes' model (2002), the components consist of technical as well as social parts.

The most important question is, what are elements of social systems? Often they are called humans or groups of people. Preece et al. (2004) describe social systems that have some online presence. These groups differ in their size, primary content, lifespan and type of communication, "whether the community exists only virtually, or has a physical presence, or exists primarily through physical connections" (p. 3). My focus, however, lies on the web of communication; in other words, a sociotechnical system is technically mediated human interaction. It is based on and built through verbal or nonverbal communication.

Meeting in an online community platform does not have the same quality as participating in a "bowling team" (Putnam, 1995). Nevertheless, meeting in an online community is better than not meeting at all. Sociotechnical systems such as online groups also have other benefits known as social capital: "Social capital is the sum of the resources, actual or virtual, that accrue to an individual or a group by virtue of possessing a durable network of more or less institutionalized relationships of mutual acquaintance and recognition" (Bourdieu & Wacquant, 1992, p. 119). Members provide immediate support for others and build more social capital than without the technical system. In other words, social capital is access to people, their friends, and support that helps a person to solve her problem, situation or issue. According to Nahapiet and Ghoshal (1998), social capital can be differentiated into a structural dimension that includes "patterns of connections between actors—that is who you reach and how you reach them" (p. 244) and a relational dimension that indicates the "personal relationship people have developed with each other." The more members actively participate in a social network, the more social capital will be created. The building of social capital depends also on the quality of social ties. But, once again, the "development of weak ties is better than not meeting at all" (Preece, 2000, p. 24).

The cultivation of social capital in sociotechnical systems is particularly dependent on trust (Fukuyama, 1995, p. 26). Trust is "the positive expectation a person has for another person, organization, tool, or process that is based on past performance and truthful future guarantees made by a responsible person or organization" (Shneiderman, 2000, p. 58). From this viewpoint, there are three areas for studying evolving structures. These include a structural dimension (what are the structures of a networked world), an activity dimension (how can human action in a networked world characterized), and a cognitive dimension (what kind of knowledge is shared, made, given and learned).

2.2 What Is a System? Differences Between Technical and Social Systems

The book started with the idea to characterize the digital networked world and how it can be sketched with the aim to understand learning in such a new world. So far, I have argued that the digital world consists of social, technical and sociotechnical systems that are evolving into CrossActionSpaces.

This section shows what a system is, and it reveals the interrelationships of technology and human action. Technical systems can be designed; social systems cannot be designed—at least not in the same way.

Technology in general can be understood as "social fact" (Durkheim, 1885/1991). Technology emerged as a product of social processes. The design of technology, its development and use, underlies different forms of social actions (Rammert, 2003). Technology use, development and integration can be understood as a form of social communication processes. Technology is still a mechanical device and machinery, but, behind the product, the conceptual social projection of "technologization" can be seen. This view on technology considers, aside from the technical entities, the social actors who deal with the technology. The social actors create technology as facts that in later generations are seen as an "objective facticity" that we cannot wish away (Berger & Luckmann, 1967/1993), such as TV and radio. It is there; the world never will turn to a world without TV and radio.

From this point of view, neither a structure nor the logic of an individual social actor determine the development of technology. From the first idea to the final product, the technical development runs through various social systems. This complexity limits the control and configurability of new technology (Rammert, 2003, p. 4). For example, many years can pass between the end users of pilots and the engineers who built the airplane in the first place and software engineers and the students who use the learning management systems at universities. The building of those systems is separated from the users. Many years can be between them, from those who had the idea and those who built the product to those who use and adopt the technical products. For example, the NASA Mars robot project starting in the 1970s, and around 20–30 years lay between the idea and finally the arrival on the planet Mars.

In this way, technology development is a social phenomenon. Technology, its use and development occur through social action on the basis of different communication processes and being part of different social systems.

However, conversely, technical systems also affect the social organization. Technology shapes the sequences of social actions in organizations. The way in which the tools can and cannot be used, as well as the functioning or nonfunctioning, affects individuals and social action. The creation of joint book chapters, the admission of new students into the database system and eGovernment processes (e.g., registration of driver's license, ID card, income tax) depend almost entirely on the computer. The production of products is largely controlled by computers.

Computer-mediated communication is limited by the technology itself because it is available to the user only via specific technical functions. For example, a technical e-mail program specifies the form in which text can be entered and creates line breaks; in a web-based electronic calendar, only certain text fields are available to enter text. The user is limited to the specific functions of the programmed technology. The computer shapes both the human-computer interaction and the technology-mediated human-human communication as well. The actions of an actor are adapted and depend on the technical system, and they are more or less formally defined and controlled by the computer. Such a dependency is then most evident when the computer fails—for example, when the technical system is out of order or does not work properly as the user expects. Electronic forms are further examples, such as when the forms do not have enough spaces to add text or they are restricted to a specific quantity of numbers or presentations with electronic slides that have limited available space on the canvases. Prezi.com and SeeMe (Herrmann, 2009) are two examples of different procedures where the canvas has no limits.

To make a brief summary here, on the one hand, information and communication technology (ICT) is influenced and shaped by humans; on the other hand, technology also affects human communication and social actions. "We shape the tools and then the tools shape us" (McLuhan, 1964/2003). With the term 'sociotechnical systems', the perspective is explicitly taken that a complex interdependency of social systems and technology exists. This means that social systems and technical systems are dependent on, and mutually influence, each other. To illustrate the concept of sociotechnical systems in detail, first the concept of system, and subsequently the concept of sociotechnical system, will be introduced.

2.2.1 The General Concept of a System

To explain the approach of system theory and the distinction between social and technical systems, it is useful to consider the term 'system' in general.

The concept of 'system' was first named in the tradition of Socrates, Plato and Aristotle in about 400–300 BCE. The concept of a system comes from a

Greek word and literally means 'composition, structure, construction, a uniform ordered entity.' Its importance became clear in the 19th century, particularly relevant in the works of Karl Marx. Marx (1859/1961) distinguished society no longer as indefinable or a multiplicity of societies. He defined society as a logical and historical category. Society has been considered an organic system. For the first time, the concept of structure in relation to the concept of a system emerged (e.g., economic structures of the social system). Both terms are therefore relatively young: "The totality of these relations of production constitutes the economic structure of society, the real foundation, on which arises a legal and political superstructure, and which particular forms of social consciousness correspond," wrote Marx (1859/1961, pp. 7f, translated).

Around 1948, the concept of a system was first used in a broader theory context. The biologist Ludwig van Bertalanffy (1949) was the first scientist who outlined a draft on a general systems theory (GST). In the 1950s, the concept of a system was used in the sociology of Talcott Parsons. In 1951, he developed the social system theory. The term 'system' was immediately used for the analysis of various structures, e.g., groups, organizations, societies. In 1954, the "Society for General Systems Research" was founded, whose goal was to go beyond the boundaries of individual disciplines and to establish new analytical research methods for studying general systems.

A system is a set of elements: between them there are certain relationships, and they can be distinguished from the environment and other elements. The term 'system' means first that the elements of a system have a relationship and can be distinguished from the environment. The basic properties of a system are first the network of relationships and the structure of the system and second the distinction between system and environment. Key aspects of a general system are the interwoven elements, subsystems and a unit against the environment (Herrmann, 2003).

A system consists of elements that are interrelated (Bertalanffy, 1971). These elements "act" within the framework of the given system and are indivisible units. The elements of a system can be summarized to subsystems. Bertalanffy assumed that the concept of the system is closely related to higher units like the order of an organization. The set of relations forms a unit and differs from the environment and to other systems. All parts of a system, such as elements, subsystems, properties and relations, can be related to each other, i.e., they depend somehow on each other. The unit can have properties that the elements alone do not have. "The whole is more than the sum of its parts" (Aristotle, in Bertalanffy, 1971). Elements and their relations have properties (attributes) that vary. Systems have properties whose expression is empirically graspable. Dynamic systems have different states.

2.2.2 Different Forms of Systems—Structures and Processes

These general considerations apply to all system types: social, technical and sociotechnical systems. In contrast to social networks, systems form a system-environment boundary, which can be distinguished from one environment to nonrelated items. In the case of social systems, a kind of identity and formation can be seen. Networks do not form such identities; they consist of rather loose relationships and microstructures.

Now, it sounds like systems and networks are two different things—in general, they are not different. Looking at a social or sociotechnical phenomenon, one can easily study the system view or the network view. The system view focuses on the outside view and wants to analyze what happens with its established boundaries, what does belong to the system and what does not, and how are the boundaries changing. The network view focuses rather on the inside view and analyzes the connections and nodes and wants to understand its insiders and outsiders, the active core group, the passive users, and the lurkers. These differences in the understandings of systems and networks are explained in detail in the context of communities in Chapter 6.

Dynamic systems such as social systems or interactive systems consist of elements that have a relation to each other (structures) and proceed in processes over time. We can see a phenomenon from a system or structure view and also from a process view. A process view focuses on the activities within the system and how the activities are conducted over time. Inputs and outputs vary; processes can be separated into substeps (Herrmann, 2012, "creative process design").

2.2.3 Technical Systems

Halfmann (1995, p. 211) outlined on the basis of Luhmann's work (1984/1995) a system-theoretical approach to technology. Technology is both a medium of communication and an installation in the environment of social systems— a duality of technology. "Installation" means to take a view on technology as a machine and a process. According to Halfmann, a fundamental problem remains: whether technology is an "enforcement" of the society and to what extent. Most sociological approaches decide that technology is a social phenomenon and should be treated similarly to other social phenomena such as "social norms" or "family." The social systems theory was the first that made a difference and defines technology explicitly as a duality considered as both a social and nonsocial phenomenon at the same time. On the one hand, the use of technology is observed in social systems as a disorder and dysfunction because it is not a social fact. On the other hand, technology is seen as a social product, as a medium and as a machine. Halfmann believes that technology is attributed to the environment of social systems and needs to be analyzed in relation to this system (Halfmann 1995, p 215).

In the last few years, new theories have been developed, such as activity-driven approaches by Engeström (1999), Kaptelinin and Nardi's (2006) "interaction design informed by activity theory," and the Actor-Network-Theory (ANT) by Bruno Latour (2005) that is another approach toward looking at technology as actor, agent and installation. The newest theories focus on relationships and networks that Siemens (2005) called "connectivism." This approach makes it clear that connections between people are central for learning. I agree. However, what the theories ignore is that people cannot connect to each other as they wish. They have to make decisions. These decisions and choices establish boundaries: "the paradox of choices" (Schwartz, 2005). Societies have developed social, technical and sociotechnical boundaries over time and will always create new ones. To make "connectivism" real, we have to understand what the boundaries are and how we as humans rebuild them in our interactions every day. We build visible but also invisible systems—sociotechnical systems that shape our communication and vice versa.

The system theory presented here is grounded in the idea of creating connections within and across such systems. The system theory is a multidimensional approach that is applied to specific parts of the social construction of reality, what I call sociotechnical systems, that underlies a structural coupling of mechanical activities (technology) and human actions (Kunau, 2006). A sociotechnical perspective has the capability to describe and explain how learners, learning networks and communities in and across social systems communicate and learn via technology and how technology shapes and transforms social action. Such a theory must be able to describe how social systems respond to the technical machinery, i.e., how technology as an engineering entity affects the social system and its elements.

According to Luhmann, technology is "a tight coupling of causal elements, regardless of the material basis on which this coupling is based" (Luhmann, 2000, p. 370). This is named as a noncontingent relationship between two or more elements: to a specific cause, X always follows the action Y. This is different to social systems. In technical systems, we expect that the "technical arrangements" work in a causal operation (Luhmann, 2000, p. 372). Software engineers who develop technology and users who use it later have in common that they believe in the causal arrangements. When we set the alarm clock for 8 a.m., we expect that the technology does what we 'tell' it. When we tweet or upload a status on Facebook or LinkedIn, we believe that the technology does what we do in our human-computer interaction when we press some buttons. It would be strange if the alarm clock or Twitter were suddenly to react differently, like a human, and would not do what we programmed. Imagine the clock said "Oh, it's Monday, I am so tired, I will not ring at 8 a.m." or if Twitter answered "I don't like your tweet, please change it."

However, in recent years, the social bots phenomenon tells a different story. Social bots as new forms of intelligent technical systems pretend to be human and follow different purposes. There is a kind of artificial computer machinery that can learn and develop itself. Are they doing what we programmed them to do? Are they a new kind of system between social and technical, such as cyborgs? (Read Section 2.5 on social bots.)

A fundamental difference between social and technical systems is that humans have different expectations toward both types of systems. Technical systems are allopoietic (externally controlled) and generated from the outside. They produce a predictable input-output relation. Technical systems are the result of manufacturing processes, manifested in artifacts; they are reconstructable, and they have a reproducible sequence of desired state changes (Herrmann, 2009). Social systems, however, are autopoietic and self-controlled and have a kind of self-description (Kunau, 2006).

Putting the different pieces together including the perspective of 'communication' and 'social action' and 'human-computer-interaction,' a technical system and its uses can be understood as the communication process of controlling actions, whereas the term 'controlling' refers to tight couplings and predetermined input-output relationships (Herrmann, 2009; Herrmann, Loser & Jahnke, 2007). Thus, technology is twofold: first, technology is an entity that confronts humans as an objective facticity (especially if the people who use it have not created or developed that technology) and is integrated into the environment of social systems. Second, technology is also a technical action of actors (human-computer interaction) where the use of technology becomes part of the social system.

Technology is not technology in itself. There are differences in the quality of various technologies that are relevant for a better understanding. A computer machine implements a completely different concept from other technologies such as pens, traditional phones, hammers, car assembly-line machinery and nuclear power plants, social media or virtual worlds (Luhmann, 2000, p. 366). Technology can be characterized as passive, active, reactive, interactive or transactive and transformative (Rammert, 2003). In this book, I focus on such types of information technology systems, i.e., concepts of technical systems in forms of interactive media, learning technologies or collaborative technology. Information and communication technologies (ICT) embrace interactive and transformative applications.

To make a short summary here, inspired by Fischer and Herrmann (2011), technical systems such as ICT are the result of a construction and production process that we see in artifacts and products; they are controlled from the outside; they are allopoietic; they have predetermined and predictable input-output relations (causal relationships) in which the output is determined through input; and technical systems are reconstructable and reproducible in sequence. First, the elements are developed, and second, they are composed into a bigger system; technical systems are not aware of themselves; they have no self-descriptions, they are not able to describe themselves, they can only be described from outside, and technical systems are transferable into different environments. They are open systems since they are built in an external construction process.

2.2.4 Social Systems—Grounded on Communication

In the abovementioned definitions, a system has been introduced in its general concept. It is useful for various scientific disciplines, such as physics, biology and computer science. If the study subject is a form of social elements, such as human action and social groups, then the unit is referred to as a social system, such as in sociology (Parsons, 1951; Luhmann, 1995). According to Luhmann, there are three types of social systems: 1) interactions, 2) organizations and 3) societies.

Social interactions range from very short forms of systems to a longer period of time. Examples are a meeting at the bus stop where a person asks about the time and a seminar at the university. These forms of systems are characterized by the existence of 'social presence.' In the Internet era, where humans use Internet access to communicate, social systems are characterized by the existence of their communication (e.g., in written forms) and its connectivity to the next communication (e.g., entries on Twitter, Facebook, Instagram).

An organization is another type of social system, which summarizes its communication through the demarcation of membership or nonmembership. Membership is controlled by the roles of the organization.

A society is the larger system, which creates boundaries through its constructed cultures over time. These three levels may need a revision nowadays. There is now the fourth type of social systems: forms of "online groups" and "online communities" (Preece et al., 2004).

Whereas technical systems are allopoietic, i.e., they are generated from the outside, social systems are autopoietic, meaning they reproduce themselves on the basis of their own elements called communication and they create their boundaries toward an environment by taking a self-reference (Luhmann, 1995). What this means in practice is explained in the next sections.

Social systems are based on communication between humans. During communication, something new emerges, and each communication permits or excludes other communication (Luhmann, 1995). This is what Luhmann called connectivity of communication (in German, Anschlussfähigkeit: the ability to connect to a person). A communication and the integrability of the others and their communication becomes a network of capable connections of human communication.

Social systems are both closed and open systems; they are closed systems in their property of self-reproduction, and they are open in terms of reacting to information from the outside. They are not open systems in terms that they limit what can follow on what—the emergence of structures, roles and rules limits the connection of new communication; social systems restrict "what can follow on what" and which communication follows on the next (Luhmann, 1995)—e.g., some entries on social networking sites get 'likes,' comments and replies, while others are not 'connected.' From the position of the observer, there are boundaries in terms of what belongs to the social system and what does not. In that way, they are autopoietic systems: a continuation of self-reproduction through communication and self-description. Social systems consist of self-determined actions; they decide who and what belongs to the system. The unit and the elements develop simultaneously. A 100% control from outside is not possible; it is a nondeterministic, unforeseeable behavior, and only strong effects are possible through a "certainty of expectations," also known as roles (Luhmann, 1995).

2.3 Elements of Social Systems: Communication Leads to Expectations and Roles

The basic element of a social system is communication. That is easy and complex at the same time. Communication creates expectations; expectations create patterns and a framework for behavior. This framework is then an objective facticity for the members of a social system and defines 'good' and 'bad' behavior, 'accepted' and 'nonaccepted' behavior from the perspective of the social system and involved actors. The system also creates a framework on how to treat nonaccepted behavior in 'disciplinary sanctions' and other forms of reprisals. Social systems create patterns for behavior to exclude nonexpected behavior and unwanted behavior in order to reduce the coincidence of human activities. Such patterns can be called social roles—such a pattern implies structures, such as different expectations forming different roles toward the role owner and different actions that go along with a specific role. The relation of the different concepts of behavior, social action and communication as well as the role concept will be illustrated next.

2.3.1 Communication Is Interpretation—The Basic Element of Social Systems: Easy and Complex

Roles arise from communication patterns and social action; they are influenced by communication but also shape communication processes. Therefore, it is helpful to understand what is meant by communication. Before the concept of a role can be explained, the foundation of human communication will be described first.

Social systems consist of communication; each communication permits or excludes other communication. This is called connectivity of communication (Luhmann, 1995), the ability to connect to communication. A social system is, then, a network of capable connections of human communication. A social system is not an open system. There are mechanisms that make it a closed system. The emergence of structures limits communication. Social systems restrict "what can follow on what" and which communication follows on the next (Luhmann, 1995). This is called an autopoietic system; it is the continuing of self-reproduction through its communication.

Simply put, any communication that has the ability to connect to communication, "any social contact," is a social system (Luhmann, 1995), e.g., a conversation at lunch, a seminar, a research group, a department, a university, international business and a company.

This book does not contribute to the theory of communication in detail, yet it is necessary to discuss some important aspects of the communication concept. Since communication is an essential element that constitutes social systems and patterns of roles, some words on communication are relevant. In sociology, communication is seen as a fundamental concept that refers to the exchange of information among humans and, second, to the mediation of meaning between people. Social systems emerge through communication. Communication develops and gives structures to social systems by establishing norms and values solidified over time. A communication structure emerges; it defines who communicates with whom and how. Such communication patterns are stabilized over time through the differentiation of roles.

Human communication is as a process of a triple selection (Luhmann, 1995). Communication "is not simply a communication action that transmits information, but it is an independent autopoietic operation that includes three different selections, namely 'selection of information,' 'selection of message' and 'selection of understanding' linked to an emergent unit which can connect to the other communications" (Luhmann ,1995, p. 267).

Communication is a triple act of interpretation and such a complex phenomenon; therefore, the likelihood is high that it actually fails. Luhmann wrote, therefore, about "the unlikelihood of communication." The process of human communication follows three selections:

- *Selection of what to say.* The first performance from the perspective of a human actor is to select from a range of possible specific information. *You could talk about many things and decide on what you want to say.*
- *Selection of how to say it.* The second performance is to choose between different ways of expression and to communicate the information. The message connects the relationship between the communication partners. *There are many different ways of how to say it and how to express it. Decide how you want to bring the message to the communication partner.*
- *Selection of understanding.* The third performance is to reconstruct the message and to put it into an appropriate context. However, the person in the role of mediating the message cannot determine whether the recipient will understand the message as the mediator has meant. *You cannot be sure that the addressee understands your message in the way as you have meant it. The other person has the choice of an infinite number of different possibilities to make sense of it.*

Communication is always based on these three different forms of interpretations. The traditional understanding of communication, the sender-receiver model (Shannon & Weaver, 1949), understands communication in which a transmitter carries information to a receiver. It is a pure exchange of information; the process is viewed as a factual information transmission from A to B. However, this model reduces human communication to a transfer of information. Human communication is more complex; it follows a 'contingent construction' and a dynamic selection of an interpretive procedure. It also explains why communication can fail.

The concept of communication in the theory of social systems also differs from the understanding of Watzlawick et al. (1969). Watzlawick et al. argue that communication and behavior are very similar. Communication is not only verbal language but also the nonverbal behavior (Watzlawick et al., 1969, p. 23). They go even further and argue that everyone communicates at all times and it is impossible not to do it. Therefore, Watzlawick comes to the statement, "You cannot not communicate" (Watzlawick et al., 1969). When they argue that everything can be viewed as communication, the question is if this is useful for a theory of designing sociotechnical systems. I come to the conclusion that such models are not suitable for the design of teaching and learning. The transmitter-receiver model is too narrow, and the Watzlawick axiom is too wide.

As Ungeheuer (1987) said, a maximal expression of communication leads to minimal understanding. An approach that tries to find a solution for the theory on designing sociotechnical systems can be found in the "context-oriented communication model" by Herrmann and Kienle (2003). In this model, communication is understood as a mediated interaction that refers to a mutual context (Kienle & Herrmann, 2003). In this model, the internal and external context is significant. The approach also uses all three selection processes by Luhmann. However, Herrmann and Kienle use other terms. The three selection processes consist of 1) mediated actions including "idea development," "communication design" and "creating expression," which produce 2) "an expression" itself and 3) the "receiving action" (Kienle & Herrmann, 2003). In addition to the inclusion of the context, another new aspect of the context-oriented communication model is the term 'extracommunicative behavior.' They distinguishes between 1) extra-communicative behavior and 2) communication. 'Extracommunicative' means that actors can act without communicating a message. For example, the yawn of students in a lecture hall is not in principle a communicative message to the faculty that the lecture is boring. It could be that the air is not good due to a lack of oxygen because the air conditioning has failed. Actions, therefore, do not include per se messages. Not every behavior is meant to be communication. However, it depends on the position of the communication partner, if s/he thinks of this yawn as nonverbal behavior intended to communicate something.

The context-oriented communication model by Herrmann & Kienle (2003) represents the "context as a core task of knowledge communication," especially for computer-mediated communication, that can only succeed if the context to which the communications relate is understandable. It means that 'successful' communication is related to a situation; context bound; and needs a specific degree of contextualization, which is a crucial factor for knowledge sharing and learning.

2.3.2 Communication, Behavior, (Inter)Action, Cross-Actions

Communication is a form of symbolic interaction that creates social actions and interactions and can be differentiated into coordinating, cooperating and competing forms of human activities. Besides social interactions, there are also forms of human-computer interactions.

Behavior refers to any activity or response of an organism and also includes instinctive behavior. Forms of thinking, feelings and perceptions are connected and defined as behavior regardless of whether the individual has a subjective meaning, intention, purpose or not. Behavior includes individual behavior and human-computer interaction.

In contrast to behavior, action is, according to Max Weber (1921/1972), "a human activity regardless of whether external or internal act, omission or acquiescence, . . . if and in so far the actors refer with the action a subjective sense." There is a change in the state of the relationship between the actor and the situation.

Weber says action is social interaction when the actions of the past, present or future are based on and oriented toward other human actions (Weber, 1921/1972), such as chats, customers, market participants, Facebook actors, or students in an online course. Humans interact socially when their actions are mutually oriented to each other. In this definition, the social interaction emphasizes the mutual influence of the behavior of individuals or groups. Social action includes cooperation, coordination, and competitive interaction. Social action is intentional toward another person or group of people.

In the digital age, a set of highly dynamic cross-actions have emerged in which traditional social interactions takes place across established boundaries by using interactive media. I characterize the possibility to communicate across established system boundaries as a new form of social action: cross-action.

In addition to human communication, there are forms of human-machine interaction, also known as human-computer interaction or computer-human interaction (HCI, CHI), that also need to be taken into account (Jacko & Sears, 2002). The human-computer interaction is not related to the exchange between people but on how to control and manage as well as use technical systems. As we enter our commands to the computer when using the keyboard, which is described as an individual, nonsocial action, we create an interaction between human and computer. These individual actions can contribute under certain conditions to a social action. For example, typing a text into an e-mail program, Twitter or Facebook is first a human-computer-interaction. Since the person who creates the message already imagines the counterpart who will take the message, it affects his/her typing, choice of words and style of writing. Writing an e-mail to a specific person seems to be easier when the other person who gets the message is well known. Knowledge about the other and his or her level of knowledge makes it easier to create a message. Twitter and Facebook are different. Who are our 'others' that will read our message? For whom do we write? Imagine a massive open online course (MOOC) where thousands of learners want to learn; what is the level of knowledge toward a specific topic and what kind of context and information must be contextualized that the others understand themselves? Independently from the others, the act of writing is a kind of social interaction. When composing an e-mail, it is a social act. This is more obvious when the message has been sent and first reactions on Facbeook occur. When sending the e-mail to the other person, the ability to connect to this communication is initiated—under the condition that the e-mail reaches the other person.

2.3.3 Characteristics of Social Systems

Social systems consist of elements that are nothing more than events of very short duration, such as communications, payments, decisions, etc., that can be distinguished from an environment of unrelated communication (Luhmann, 1995). When actors select from a range of possible options of communication to enter into communication with others, then this constitutes a social system. The selection first leads to a system-environment distinction that generates a social system as a result.

Social systems are contingent in two ways. This means that it is not 100% predictable how Ego (Person A) will respond to Alter (Person B) and vice versa. It is only a suggestion as to how one might react to the other. In order to reduce this suggestion, social systems generate a kind of a 'certainty of expectations,' constituted as person-linked, persona-linked or role-based expectations that narrow the range of possible reactions (Luhmann, 1995). Transfer Luhmann's thinking onto teaching: in a school classroom and university course situation, we expect what good teachers and good students do—and usually it is within the range of possible actions and we are right in our assumptions. When the behavior and interactions are not within such a range, there will be negative consequences for the role actor.

In this book, I do not want to focus on the entire system theory by Luhmann. The main features of social systems are illustrated below. Educational institutions are social systems and have the features of a social system, and they affect designs for teaching and learning.

A social system watches and thematizes itself. It can refer to itself and follow a self-reflection. This also means that it perceives a difference to its environmental systems and to other systems (Luhmann, 1995). Social systems are autopoietic and self-referential. Autopoiesis refers to the self-reproduction of a social system. The term refers to the operation of a system by which all the elements are generated by the selective connection of the elements themselves. By selected communication, new communication is possible. This is called connectivity of communication (Luhmann, 1995).

Social systems are both closed and open systems (Luhmann 1995, p. 63). They are open for inputs from outside and deliver outputs to their environment. But in their deep structure, social systems are closed in their self-reference—and in their ability to produce themselves again and again. This is called operational closure of the deep structure. This is a difference from the new systems theory of Luhmann (over his older approaches). Self-referential systems appear as closed systems. In contrast to the system-theoretical postulate of the fundamental openness of complex systems, social systems are closed in their mode of operation and in their internal control pattern. Only communication can connect to communication—nothing else. To explain the openness of social systems, Luhmann has chosen the concept of information by Bateson (1972), who writes: "a bit of information is definable as a difference which makes a difference" (Bateson, 1972, p. 315). The difference between system and environment begins as soon as data are selected and interpreted as information. Social systems are not open to all information because they already have a view; they have already made a selection earlier and have contextualized some data to information. The operational closure is an informational unity.

The system-environment difference leads to an identity of a social system, "in difference to other" and a separation from others (Luhmann, 1995).

Social systems appear, according to Luhmann, as three distinct types of systems (Luhmann, 1995, p. 16). Social systems can be briefly volatile types of communications, which are often seen as nonpermanent social interactions. Such simple social systems are first of all interaction systems (micro level); for example, seminars at a university limit their communication through a physical presence. But what happens now when all students and teachers use web-enabled technology? Suddenly, the established walls are vanishing. New forms of sociotechnical systems appear. The second type is an organization (meso level) where communication is bounded through the memberships and derived roles. The most complex social system (macro level) is a society. Characteristics like communicative accessibility and belonging to a culture are crucial—the affiliation to a specific society is evident in cultural patterns and social practices. In a networked world, we must add a fourth type: forms of online groups (Preece et al., 2004). In contrast to Luhmann, we live in the age of transformative technology where a society is differentiated into more social systems, such as online communities and online networks. Their communication draws new boundaries. These types of social systems reveal a journey where social systems have emerged into sociotechnical systems.

Organizations and formal groups occur in small and large sizes. Organizations draw communication boundaries through the demarcation of membership and nonmembership. The university is a special type of organization. Its boundaries are generated through the enrollment of students and employees by contract. Unlike the other types of systems, an organization is operating in the communications of "decisions" (Luhmann, 2000). Luhmann does not mean that a decision takes place in the mind of an individual; it is carried out as a communicative social appearance (Luhmann, 2000) in which a decision is to select an option of existing alternatives. A crucial feature of organizations and formal groups is the distinction and forming of membership roles that regulate the admission and access for participation. Such organizational systems have gained, as formal organizations, a specific meaning in modern societies that primarily regulate their communication, themes and boundaries, based on membership roles (Luhmann, 1995, p. 268). The membership role also recalls the positioning of a role owner toward other roles within the system with the purpose of also remembering to what department it belongs (Luhmann, 2000, p. 113). With the term "membership roles," Luhmann stresses all those formal roles that exist in organizations and neglects the fact that there are also roles in society as well as informal roles that affect communication and learning.

Our world is full of systems; some stay on the level of system, but others are changing into CrossActionSpaces.

One question that the reader might ask herself is why this knowledge of system theory is important and where the relevance is for designing for teaching and learning.

One answer is because it shows that we do not live in an open world, nor do we have open education. The system theory shows the hidden social constructions in our everyday life without questioning the social mechanisms of inclusion and exclusion, the coding and recoding of mainly social driven boundaries. Educational institutions such as schools and universities are social systems on different levels (classrooms, school, and policy levels) that become formal organizations. To prepare teaching that enables both surface and deeper learning in educational institutions, teachers, students and decision makers need to understand the underlying restrictions of such formal organizations; they also need to understand how to design for learning in CrossActionSpaces. Understanding of the boundary mechanisms comes first, then we can proceed with developing designs for learning.

This world that was separated in offline and online worlds is changing. The system boundaries have dissolved into diverse sets of different communication spaces. Some people call them open spaces. However, there is a fallacy. These new forms of communication spaces are not only open; they also have similar characterizations, as the social systems approach told us. Communication spaces provide a better opportunity to collaborate and share information, but the recoding of boundaries that limits other communication has already started.

2.3.4 System Theory for Designing Teaching and Learning?

Our empirical studies of media tablets in schools and higher education illustrate how innovative teachers design sociotechnical-pedagogical processes for enabling student learning (Jahnke et al., 2014; Jahnke & Kumar, 2014a, 2014b). It became clear that the majority of the new designs created by the teachers included mobile technology, especially with the aim to reach the full potential of web-enabled technology, such as creating communication possibilities with the world outside the classroom, collaborative learning and reflective learning processes.

However, we also saw patterns of designs that do not foster learning; some classrooms looked like chaos to the point that the students could not see the way to learn, and some designs even limited the opportunity for students to learn at all. The question is, can we explain the weaknesses of the not-so-innovative patterns of Digital Didactical Design, especially the problems of such designs?

I use the example of student distraction in classrooms to show the potential of the system theory and how this view helps for designing teaching and learning. Student distraction includes those activities or practices in which students do all kinds of things except following the class; for example, they play, they write on small pieces of paper, they chat online and so forth.

View 1 takes a psychological view and explains student distraction as the result that students are not engaged and not motivated. They have the individual as the starting point to explain the social situation. Some argue that the students deliberately exclude themselves. Those studies show how to motive students and how to create more student engagement.

View 2 takes the system theory. It argues that the situation when students play games, instead of following the class, is just the outcome of having no connectivity to communication in the classroom. From the systems theory view, the ability of connectivity means that the communication is not connected. Students might be motivated and engaged, but they are not able to connect to the classroom or teaching instructions. Students started to play because the ability to connect to existing communication during class is not available for them. And because there is no connectivity for them, they become demotivated and less engaged. These students do not exclude themselves explicitly; rather, the design for teaching and learning is not designed in such a way that the students are able to connect to the communication. This view shows that demotivation and less engagement are the outcomes and not the independent variables. In other words, the student motivation and engagement is dependent on the quality of connectivity to communication within classrooms.

The system theory helps to understand the social phenomena of designing for learning from a different angle. It shows that not only the individual learner matters but also the design for connectivity to communication and the ability to connect to teaching and learning, which is embedded into the didactical design. This gives a new view on the design for teaching and learning.

The (non)ability of connectivity to communication has many reasons. For example, the pace of the learning is too fast, students do not understand what the teachers want from them, or students do not understand the words in their deeper meanings. Here, empirical studies are required that clarify the many different reasons for the breaking points of the communication connectivity. It does not lie in the person of the students alone; rather the problems lie in the communication that is embedded into the digital didactical design.

Teachers design sociotechnical-pedagogical processes that should help students to connect to learning. When the students do other things, it is an indicator for changing the design. So, instead of asking only how to motivate and engage students, the system theory view includes the analysis of the didactical design, such as: in what parts of the process design is the likelihood high that students might be disconnected to learning, and what can educational actors such as school leaders and teachers do to change this into a higher degree of connectivity?

2.3.5 Structures of Social Communication Systems: Made of Expectations While Making Connections

The advantage of the system theory is that it makes visible the external and internal structures of social phenomena in the context of their environment.

Social systems are created on the basis of reducing complexity through meaning-making—i.e., out of the abundance of the possible, only one meaning is selected (Luhmann, 1995, p. 384). Meaning here refers to the connection of linking different possibilities and options. Social systems are also called meaning-processing systems, in contrast to technical systems that cannot respond to surprises from the environment—at least not today (perhaps in the future?).

Technical systems can only respond to those conditions for which they have been programmed, and this dictates their internal structure. This probably will change in the future. There will be technical systems out there, which are interactive and transformative, and might act similar like humans. There will be robots out there that might help learners during learning processes—some are just interactive, but others are robotive learners. For example, there is currently an experiment about a robot called HitchBot that travels through the world, and it learns while traveling. Although this is a funny story and the robot cannot walk without the help by humans, the sobriety lies in the future potential of what technology might be and is able to do. In the future, we will probably have different kinds of technology and program them based on what they should 'not' do—although they technically could do it. There will be different robots for different purposes.

The internal structures of social systems are expectations. Expectations allow that social systems select certain options from the abundance of possibilities (Luhmann, 1995, p. 392). Since social systems are double contingent, there are more than just simple expectations. A social system consists of expectations of expectations. Such expectations, and expectations of expectations, help a social system to select communication. Social systems exist permanently when they are able to stabilize their structures against deviations. To achieve this, the expectations must be normalized. This means that social systems institutionalize their expectations into formal structures and establish roles.

Due to the complexity of modern societies, the mode of institutionalization of expectations has changed (Luhmann, 1995, pp. 85ff). Expectations are standardized at the level of individuals and roles but also go further—a society generates expectations into programs and values (Luhmann, 1995, p. 429) and even through digital media. Behavioral expectations may refer to a specific person, a specific role or a specific program (such as research programs, study programs, societal projects and European agendas) or to specific values (key competences, professional teaching competence, pedagogical competences) (Luhmann, 1995, p. 85). In a networked world, we can see an increase of decoupling mechanisms of expectations toward persons, roles, programs, norms, online worlds—it climbs a ladder of abstraction.

Expectational structures depicted in roles, programs or norms and values occur toward the actors almost as an objective facticity (Berger & Luckmann, 1967/1993) and are quasi-objectified. Roles have a duality: they are, on the one hand, negotiated in interactive communication by human actors, but at the same time roles are also available as a disturbing object in a system—an "annoying fact" (Dahrendorf, 1958). Roles give the individual a profile and certainty, but they also lift the individual out into a general and foreign situation. The person is separated from his own perception (Dahrendorf, 1958, p. 26).

One message here is that behavioral expectations on the one hand are placed on specific individuals where the expectations are personalized and bound to a person (person-based expectation); on the other, expectations refer to roles (role-based expectation) (Luhmann, 1995, pp. 85, 87). The increasing separation of expectations within a social system, i.e., the interchangeability of persons due to role-based expectations, is accompanied by a simultaneous increase in structural complexity.

Expectations addressed to roles are distinguished from personal expectations. Role-based expectations systematically hide personal or private aspects of the participants. The connection of expectations to roles is a crucial prerequisite for formal institutions (companies, administrations, universities, groups) because it allows independent and permanent existence and functioning as a social system. Roles have the function of setting expectations independently from the actors, i.e., when actors change, the institution still exists. Every new actor has to learn to take existing expectations to a certain degree. Roles can be distinguished from the individual person as their more abstract aspects of the identification of the context of expectation (Luhmann, 1995, p. 430). Luhmann defines roles as certain patterns of communication. From recurrent patterns of communication, finally roles are produced: "Roles are an expected bundle. . . . By a role, expectations are transferable from person to person" (Luhmann, 1995, p. 86; read chapter 3 in detail).

In a digital media world, every connection we humans make is at the same time the drawing and creation of a new boundary made through expectations toward others and the self; a 'like,' a reply, and making Facebook or Instagram friends show such a boundary; in doing so, we choose (and decide) who is part of the social system and who is not (a made choice). In a digital media world, there is a new level of tension between technical openness and social limitations.

2.4 Sociotechnical Systems Turn Into CrossActionSpaces

Information and communication technology (ICT) in educational institutions is used to support communication, such as e-mail, discussion forums, chat rooms and technical platforms such as content-management platforms. The communication is computer supported, computer mediated and technology enhanced. From this angle, technical systems have a significant impact on the educational organization, and they affect the involved roles and knowledge-sharing processes. The use of computers shapes the social system. "The fact that they thereby change the ways of communication, decision-making and power is obvious," wrote Luhmann (2000, p. 365). Because of the interconnection of communication offline, computer mediated across established boundaries, a new social action and communication space has emerged.

In this book, I do not follow those authors who identify the new communication space as "virtual reality" or as "special worlds technically generated." As Floridi (2007) argues, we are probably the last generation to make a clear distinction between offline and online worlds. I follow Floridi and argue that technically generated social systems have become the norm and may not be seen as communication disorder. Without technologies, communication cannot happen, or at least only very redundantly and without any progress. Every social system depends on technologies—it is just a matter of the degree—from very simple structures where ICT just supports e-mails or exchanges of files (server system) to purely online virtual worlds like Second Life. As examples, the online auction site eBay, Wikipedia.de and the Linux community can be mentioned here, as well as evaluation and quality management systems in universities and schools or content or groupware management systems such as Moodle.

Interactive technology constitutes new technology-mediated communication and generates a new quality of sociotechnical systems. Almost every organization has a website, e-mails are taken for granted, and online discussion forums or WIKI formats are often offered that allow the users to actively participate in the exchange of knowledge. There are plenty of different forms of web-based collaboration platforms. Are there any organizations out there that do not support their communication processes by means of ICT? It is essential to understand these new forms of communication processes—it is the foundation for knowledge sharing and learning—to understand their structures from a sociotechnical perspective in order to inform a design and development for teaching and learning.

A sociotechnical system is, simply formulated, a network of social elements such as communication and social structures such as pattern of communications, known as roles and technical systems. The elements from originally two systems are interlinked and influence each other. It is therefore a combination of social, organizational, technical and cultural structures and interactions (Herrmann, 2003, p. 60). Originally, the concept of a sociotechnical system was created in

1950 at the London Tavistock Institute to study the interdependencies between technical and social systems. This was illustrated by empirical studies in the English coal-mining industry and the Indian textile industry. Mumford (1987) developed the concept and transformed it to computer systems. The sociotechnical approach emphasizes in particular the interdependence and mutual character between a social system and technical components. ICT is used, but the technology also shapes the social system. The social process of use, adoption and appropriation of technology needs to be investigated.

2.4.1 What Is a Sociotechnical System? (A Definition)

A sociotechnical system (STS) is a mutually dependent interwoven network of human communication and controlling actions (human-computer interaction) that can be distinguished from the environment of nonrelated communications (Fischer & Herrmann, 2011)—an STS depends on the position of the observer. Different people in different roles 'see' the system differently; the elements belonging to the system vary.

A feature is that communication is partly or in total computer mediated, i.e., communication is performed by controlling operations. A sociotechnical activity consists of both human communications and human-computer interaction. Communication is the primary element. It is available in two different forms: 'human-to-human communication,' which is based on social interaction and cross-actions, and 'human-computer communication,' which occurs when a person interacts with technical systems, i.e., in a very simple way, she acts in a special way with a computer to enter commands into the technical system. Soon, this kind of human-computer interaction will be voice controlled, and wearable technologies will support this development.

Social and technical systems build an interwoven and merged network of human communications and controlling actions, partly technology mediated, toward sociotechnical systems with the following characterizations: the technical system is operated by the social system; there might be a change of the technical system through the social system. It is technology-mediated communication in which human communication goes through the technical system. The social system talks about the technical system; it is on the agenda and becomes part of the communication. Social (sub)systems interact and use the technical system for this; the communication is influenced and limited by the rules of the technical system. Without the technical system, the social system would be different and would not exist in the same form, quality or structure.

In short, it is the interplay of communicative human interaction (the social), human-computer interaction and interaction between the technical elements (the technical) (Herrmann, 2009).

The integration of the social and the technical is a matter of design (Herrmann, 2009; Herrmann, Hoffmann, Kunau & Loser, 2004). Those three criteria are necessary in the sense of indispensability, and all of the three components have interdependencies. Herrmann (2012) makes it even clearer when he writes "rules can be designed, but conventions evolve." Such a system view sets the framework for designing human interaction; human actions are not totally random but also not predefined or deterministic (Herrmann, 2009).

Grudin (1988) illustrated why a sociotechnical system tends to fail. It is difficult 1) to know all the requirements that such a system needs; 2) different learners and groups have different ideas, interests and aims that could be contradictory and are not clear or intuitive to software programmers; and 3) it is a dynamic system and the boundaries change over time.

2.4.2 From Sociotechnical Systems to Co-expanding Communication Spaces

The digital networked world is not just a network of social, technical and sociotechnical systems. Through the emergence of web-enabled technology, CrossActionSpaces are evolving that have very much the same features and elements as sociotechnical systems; however, they are more open and flexible but also create a new tension between openness and social closeness. The elements are human communication and partly technology-mediated communicative interaction. They differ in terms of openness and closeness. While a system appears to be rather closed, a communication space appears to be rather open; while both of them are open and closed, there is a shift in the tension of what appears as more open and more closed. The tension of appearing as open and closed acquires a new quality.

The 'space' also differs from the 'system' depending on how we look at the phenomenon: from a system, process, or spatial view (Dourish, 2006). The system view supports a more static view and has the purpose of inquiring about how the elements, relations of the elements (structures) and the boundaries are established and rebuilt or dissolve over time, whereas the CrossActionSpace view focuses more on the idea that a sociotechnical system becomes a more dynamic phenomenon and that agents in such dynamic sociotechnical systems are able to connect to each other across established systems and networks, but they do build new system boundaries over time (recoding of system boundaries). The purpose of a process view is to make visible the actions and activities over time, the resources they need and the different roles that emerge or are rebuilt over time across different systems and in creating new system boundaries.

Our digital networked world is changing from social and sociotechnical systems toward co-expanding communication spaces. CrossActionSpaces are dynamic, overlayered, expanded spaces, both physical and online places, that connect existing systems, networks and communities in which knowledge-sharing and interactions based on communication as social practice takes place in and across those spheres using web-enabled technology. It is the expansion

TABLE 2.1 Toward a sociotechnical society (adopted from Jahnke, 2009)

First phase	Second phase	Third phase	Next generation
a) Mainly trust-based virtual communities, very informal rules (architecture of free participation)—"living lab of freedom"	b) Clear rules (conventions, boundaries, etc.) that are mainly socially enforced—lab of policies	c) Clear rules, also technically determined (but for most people obscure)	Basis for emergence of new sociotechnical spaces → first phase begins again but on a higher technical level
e.g., Wikipedia's level of development in 2005	e.g., Wikipedia in 2010	e.g., Google page ranking algorithm strategy	Next loop begins
	→ Evolving toward CrossActionSpaces →		

of communication beyond the physical walls and stresses the dynamic processes across established boundaries in a digital media world.

I choose the term CrossActionSpace because the term 'space' stresses the dynamic processes across established boundaries in a digital media world. Cross ActionSpaces are flexible dynamic forms of networks of technology-enhanced human communication processes across different spheres (offline, online, clouds), but they also do build new boundaries such as structures and roles over time; their communication, expectations and assumptions by humans decide what follows what, and this limits the appearance of openness.

Despite the perception of Web 2.0 "as living lab of freedom" (as Wolfgang Prinz labeled it on the conference called E-CSCW 2007), it will turn into a living lab of roles, structures, conventions and policies. Where humans are involved, they create conventions, roles, and policies due to different reasons, e.g., to sustain a status quo (Table 2.1).

The study of InPUD (Jahnke, 2009) illustrates evidence of the transition from undefined to defined regulations, from loose to formal structures. Social system boundaries—socially and technically mediated—are emerging in different forms. Online communication and relationships are at first mainly trust based, socially enforced, and later also technically determined. As a result, a continuous process of dissolving and remodeling of the boundaries within and across spaces is taking place.

2.4.3 Educational Institutions: From Systems to CrossActionSpaces

Luhmann's system theory is based on the assumption that the complexity and unmanageability of the world causes the formation of different social systems. The result of differentiation and reduction of complexity is the diversity of social systems. Social systems enable individuals to operate and act—only under the condition of selectivity (Luhmann, 1995, p. 16). Educational institutions such as schools and universities develop a particular type of communication system that reproduces itself. The internal operation is grounded on the communication of decisions (Luhmann, 2000, p. 123) and choices the system makes. A decision is a rational choice for existing alternatives; and thus the result of a communicating occurrence also communicates what has not been chosen. In order to achieve the organizational goals, the organization creates tasks and solves problems.

One such decision in educational institutions is how to design teaching and learning activities, what are appropriate process-based feedback and feedforward mechanisms, how to evaluate study programs and so forth. What we can learn from Luhmann's theory is that educational systems and structures are made by communications, and, although it seems difficult to change them, they can be changed. It is one vision of this book to make such social constructions visible. 'Seeing' the hidden mechanisms is one step toward preparing designs for teaching and learning.

One of the hidden social constructions is the feature of emerged roles (e.g., membership roles in organizations). Luhmann emphasizes the importance of roles in formal organizations because they control the boundaries and access for participation (see Luhmann, 1995, p. 268). The membership roles also point to the positions related to other positions within a system, i.e., to which department the role belongs (cf. Luhmann, 2000, p. 113). Roles are the structures of both social and sociotechnical systems. They are formed on the basis of repeated behavior expectations. Through a solidification of expectations and patterns of expectations, they receive names and become roles. The educational institutions depend on people—but we do not see the individuals; all we see from outside are the roles, the teachers, the students, the administrators. We have the ideal role in our minds that defines what makes a good teacher. However, the ideal role and the person who performs the role differ. Social systems generate expectations into a bundle of expectations of roles which, in turn, affect the social system. The roles that humans have taken are central because they decide which communication belongs to the space and which does not—which communication is able to connect and which is not. People communicate those issues that belong to their roles; it differs if a person is in a situation at home in a father or mother role or at the university in a teacher or student role. The taken role gives the corridor for the person's communication (Chapter 3).

Besides formal organizations, business companies, and educational institutions, which can be characterized as sociotechnical systems, new forms of communication spaces emerge that are more flexible, dynamic, multi-existing and co-expanding. Educational institutions will also notice such a shift in communication. Within those institutions, learners are in the physical classroom but also use the Internet to discuss, share or connect to further issues with experts online. Those situations take place in spaces of five minutes or one hour, for example, or they continue for weeks and months.

This does not mean that all intuitions and formally organized social systems turn into dynamic spaces. It rather means that within those formally organized structures, more flexible spaces have occurred and are emerging—due to the fact that we have web-enabled interactive media at hand, in our pockets and handbags.

The formal communication in such systems is still relevant to meet the goals and tasks of an organization from the viewpoint of the institution. The term 'formal' refers to such communication that contributes primarily to the task of processing and achieving the goals of the organization. For example, the examination office has the main task of organizing the examination of applications for students and to check who has logged out early or who has failed due to, for example, illness. In addition, the scores of the tests are administered in the office. Goals also underlie communicative occurrences; they are not just 'there' or objective. They are made by communication acts from roles performed by human actors. But goals can become an objective facticity in which other communication perceives the goals as given, without scrutinizing them. For example, we do not question the goal of schools or universities in general. The goals are educating students so that they are able to become members of society to prepare them for life and to help them to progress in their intellectual development. Schools and universities also have many functions, such as cultural innovations, values, socialization and integration. However, in the years from W. von Humboldt's idea to today, the goals have changed, and other subsystems in society have discussed the aim of schools and universities. Nowadays, the aim of the university is also to prepare students for their work in, for example, the corporate sector.

Informal communication can be observed in informal cooperation, for instance, when employees across offices and departments discuss unsolved problems on the phone. This is straightforward, and it usually helps to solve the problem quickly and easily. If the person from the examination office changes, the access to such informal communication is gone, and it cannot be accessed. Then, official and formal requests to the examination office are needed, which is a time-extensive process. The example shows that informal communication has a huge impact on knowledge sharing. In addition to the formal communication, the informal communication is a relevant part as well, for example, in forms of social networks and across those networks and communities. Sometimes, informal communication has more power than formal communication; then, this kind of decision-making is not visible, it is hidden in the informal parts. Both formal and informal structures exist, but the relation between them may differ.

2.5 Social Bots as New Forms of Sociotechnical Agents? Antisocial Media

We cannot see but we communicate with them—the 'Social Bots' phenomenon.

Recent studies (Boshmaf et al., 2011; Wagner et al., 2012) on social bots in online networks illustrate intelligent software codes that almost successfully pretend to be human. Are these only software programs, or are they new forms of socio-technical systems, such as cyborgs? The studies show the potential of such bots for coming closer to passing the Turing Test (Levy, 2011) of intelligent machinery. In the 'wild life' outside laboratories, when does a person accept a social bot knowingly or unknowingly as if the person is communicating with another human?

Social bots such as Twitter and Facebook bots are software programs that pretend to be human and imitate human behavior in order to accomplish specific tasks or purposes. They are never neutral; different people assign to them good or bad objectives depending on different factors and depending on the people who are affected to a greater or lesser extent. The "Bot Traffic Report" from 2013 argues that 61% of all networked communication is initiated by such robots in short bots. The purposes of bots include different forms of data collection. This includes the gathering of user profiles and e-mail addresses, the distribution of spam, buying fake followers, spying on the online behavior of humans, and using data to start political propaganda or initiate wide-range advertising, which attracts the attention of humans. For human users, it is difficult to differentiate whether the agents are human or computer software programs.

According to Alexis C. Madrigal, senior editor of the *Atlantic*, he flooded the short message service Twitter with thousands of automatically generated 'auto tweets' and caused 100,000 visits to a single web page, in a way that no one noticed that they were made from the same Internet address. The basics of hunting for fake traffic through the Web are simple, concluded Madrigal.

Facebook bots are another example of such automated software programs, programmed to control a fake Facebook account and generate a profile by collecting and distributing images and information from other sources. They grow by friending other Facebook users. Boshmaf et al. (2011) infiltrated Facebook with different automated social bots (Social Bot network, SbN) that went on for eight weeks, "friending thousands of users and harvesting their personal information." After the first six weeks, the bots sent out 3,517 friend requests to human Facebook users; 2,079 (59%) were accepted on average. After eight weeks, this increased up to 80% for some of the bots. The experiment illustrates that human users followed the social bot and its fake profile. It was successful in creating tweets and messages—at least with such a quality that the users did find it interesting (i.e., either they liked it or they were attracted to follow the social bot) without knowing that it was a social bot.

Another example is Twitter, which has attracted a large number of social bots. They generate "a large amount of benign tweets delivering news and updating feeds, while malicious bots spread spam or malicious contents" (Chu et al., 2010). Their study exposes three types: social bots, humans and cyborgs. Cyborgs are "in the middle between human and bot, . . . either bot-assisted human or human-assisted bot." The researchers collected 500,000 Twitter accounts and studied the difference between the three types with regard to tweeting behavior, tweet content, and account properties. Their system classifies Twitter as follows:

48.7% of the users as human, 37.5% as cyborg, and 13.8% as bot. The "population proportion of human, cyborg and bot category roughly as 5:4:1 on Twitter." To summarize the studies, 60% of Facebook users have accepted social bots as a friend, and around 50% of Twitter accounts are nonhuman accounts, without users knowing that these are fake profiles.

Bots and the Turing Test (The Imitation Game)

Alan Turing's (1950) great effort was the creation of the Turing Test known as Imitation Game. He assumed that computers in the future would be intelligent enough to appear as human. He defined a computer as intelligent when humans cannot tell the difference between it and a human. In the Turing Test, a person (interrogator) receives the task of questioning two subjects in order to find out which subject is the machine ("imitation game"). The software program tries to fool the interrogator, and the human also tries to convince him that she is the human. "If the interrogator cannot distinguish the computer from the person, the computer is judged to be intelligent" (French, 2012).

I do not want to question the Turing Test itself. I just observed that some researchers apply the idea of Alan Turing in some contexts that need more explication. Especially, I argue that there exist some false assumptions when applying the test outside laboratories.

Three False Assumptions About Identifying Intelligent Robots

First of all, in the 'wild life' of social media, humans do not question with whom they communicate in general. Jackson argues that social bots did not pass the Turing Test because the "human Facebook users never really questioned them" (Jackson, 2011). This is exactly the point! In the Turing Test, the interrogator is given the explicit task of questioning the behavior of the subjects to find out who is human and which is a software program. Humans do not act like this in the world of daily-life online communication and computer-mediated, human-human interaction. If humans do not know that there are automated intelligent software programs that act like humans, then the majority of humans will never find out whether it is a social bot or a human user with whom they are interacting (read study by Wagner et al., 2012). In other words, there are already computers and bots out there that passed the Turing Test.

Second, the design of the Turing Test needs a differentiation—in addition to the traditional laboratory test, a wild-life test in a networked world might be useful. According to the Turing Test, later illustrated by Weizenbaum's ELIZA (1966), the requirement for the test is that the person knows that she has to find the possible nonhuman agent. The interrogator has to question the behavior of human and computer agents, and this is the design of the Imitation Game. This concept is valid for designing an experiment inside a laboratory useful for simulation, but it is not totally valid for the world outside laboratories. In reality, humans do not have the task of scrutinizing everything around them. Our world does not work like this. Social life is more complex. If humans were to question every piece of online communication on Twitter, Facebook, LinkedIn, etc., then Web 2.0 and social media would not be possible. It would not exist as we know it. To find out whether a computer is intelligent or not, the Turing Test needs a differentiation. An enhanced Turing Test puts the computer into the social life of humans, and researchers find out whether the humans are skeptical about the behavior of humans and nonhumans; and if yes, to what extent.

Third, specific social bots such as Twitter/Facebook bots illustrate that the Turing Test is too generally designed—the test is designed for all kinds of human communication; it is not differentiated enough for social media applications like Twitter, where communication and online interaction are restricted to specific forms of online communication. Twitter and Facebook are good examples of human communication being partly restricted: Twitter allows 140 characters, while Facebook is intended for writing small stories, finding friends, engaging in small talk, 'liking' or other small messages. Having those kinds of restrictions, software developers and social bots might have an easier task of successfully pretending to be human. Twitter messages, even from humans, are sometimes very cryptic and hard to understand. It is not a coincidence that even humans sometimes assign other human followers on Twitter a social bot function. It is also not a coincidence that a chat with a social bot can seem like chatting with a good friend. Our social world is upside down.

A Set of Questions Informs New Criteria for Studies

These new insights lead to the argument in favor of creating a new set of questions that are useful when studying online networks that consist of both human and nonhuman communication:

- In life outside the lab, how many steps of communication are required until a human user finds out that he is talking to a nonhuman (without giving him the search order)? Are five steps a crucial number, or is 100 a better number; what period of time is acceptable, one year or five years? The longer it takes, the more the bot can collect data and can try to manipulate the human. What is the number of communication steps *before* the human knows that the bot is nonhuman and *after* the human knows?
- In the world outside laboratories, when does the human user accept the non-human agents as equal communication partners *as if* the nonhuman were human? In what situations?
- Is there a benefit level in which the human user accepts the nonhuman user as an equal partner? What is the level of benefit/profit for the human user to accept the nonhuman as equal or human-adequate? What kinds of benefits?

- Does the human user assign to another human user a bot function without knowing she is human? Are there any situations where the nonhuman user is a better communication partner than a human? There are good and bad human communication partners as well. How do trust and mistrust change over time in a network of humans and nonhumans? Do humans assign bots a human role, and is the bot becoming a new 'social role'?
- Are there any social or technical mechanisms that press the human users to accept the nonhuman agents as equal communicators against their own values (restrictive systems)?

There are two issues to which researchers and educators can contribute toward making the bot phenomenon visible and studying the consequences for learning. First, there is a need to educate human users, teachers and students who use Facebook, Twitter and others about the bot networks and their different intentions. The aim of educating Homo Interneticus is that humans can decide for themselves if they want to be part of such an online network or not—but they have to get access to knowledge about such hidden sociotechnical mechanisms. Second, there is a need to make the network of humans-bots-cyborgs visible and to call it what it is—it is not social media; it is 'asocial' or antisocial-in-social-media of nonhumans and humans.

2.6 Summary

This chapter introduced the term 'system' from a communication perspective and discussed the constraints and how they affect human activities in the digital age. In detail, the chapter shows that the digital networked world is turning from sociotechnical systems into CrossActionSpaces as a new complementary form for communication. The chapter also shows that we do not live in a solely open world. Such systems and new spaces are open in the sense that one can easily access them, and more people are able to share their ideas over the world. However, they are closed due to decisions that humans make on a daily basis regarding what space to enter and what not to enter; this includes and excludes communication. Although interactive media helps to expand the social and sociotechnical boundaries, our human-made CrossActionSpaces are closed systems in terms of the 'echo chamber' because the expectations and actions lead to new structures that restrict the totality of openness. Every connection creates new boundaries in terms of what belongs to the system and what does not. It is technically open but socially closed due to coding and recoding of boundaries (Bailey, 2006). It is a new quality of the tension between openness and closeness.

The network communicates increasingly with itself—not always with the best intentions, as the social bot phenomenon shows. Once established, the human and nonhuman communication within such systems builds new expectation structures and affects new boundaries. The phenomenon of the 'shitstorms' ('flame war' with hundreds/thousands of not nice emails or posts in a thread on social networking sites) is one example of how such social mechanisms work. This example also shows the power of the networked humans in the digital interactive media world. Thousands and millions of people show their interests in online petitions and hashtags and are capable of creating a huge influence on companies. Information today is faster and circulates around the world more easily than centuries ago. The networked world affects the dynamics of information, conditions and situations, which are more volatile, uncertain, complex and ambiguous (VUCA model) than in the nondigital era.

Over time, social systems have turned into sociotechnical systems, and those are emerging into CrossActionSpaces in which human and nonhuman communication work in context and in relations. In the digital age, the newly developed technology-enhanced communication spaces by human actions have shifted from traditional role development into multiple cross-actions (Chapter 3), and learning is then the critical-constructive reflective 'doing' of such MultiCross Actions in Relations (Chapter 4).

2.7 CrossActionSpaces Linking Systems, Networks and Communities

> *Don't believe everything you think.*
>
> (Street slogan seen in Berlin, March 2014)

In the sections above, I made clear the concept of a system that is created based on communication patterns and how the digital world is turning into multi-existing spaces made by communication.

The system theory is not the only attempt to characterize society and groups of learners. Another approach is called Communities of Practice, which was a much-hyped expression in the 1990s and had its peak when Etienne Wenger et al. (2002) published their book titled *Cultivating Communities of Practice.* In following years, the various lines from different disciplines and topics such as organizational learning (Argyris & Schön, 1978), communities of learning (Lave & Wenger, 1991), knowledge management (Herrmann, Loser & Jahnke, 2007), collaborative learning and group cognition (Stahl 2006) were brought together.

According to Wenger (1998), the question is not whether communities exist in institutions and organizations. They exist in a variety of different forms often not visible within the formal structures. Informal communities are like an invisible web within the formal institutions. Informal communities are informal ways of communication. They offer just-in-time communication and just-in-time learning (Jahnke, 2010). Several studies show that such communities are an expansion of the formal structures and lead to more effective ways of knowledge sharing and learning. For example, in one of my studies of InPUD (Chapter 6), the findings illustrate that the learners obtained better, more flexible access to information. The InPUD community helped the learners to go beyond role-constrained learning. The InPUD study shows the importance of such communities for learning, especially how to cultivate them in schools and higher education. As Wenger said, such communities always exist, partly in hidden structures, and the question is how to make them visible for all actors. This creates access for all to such a learning resource.

Communities are self-organized and cannot be controlled from the outside. They are not manageable without losing their characteristics as informal communities (Reischmann, 1986). The ideal of a self-controlled community is a 'wildflower.' Communications of the actors in such an informal wildflower community can therefore not be forced or directed; they can only be supported in their joint development toward a 'cultivated plant.'

Cultivation refers to activities and supports the stages of life of communities and their building in the beginning, maturing, development, sustainability, further development and transformation. In contrast to knowledge management, which emphasizes the formal organization of learning and knowledge, a cultivation is rather a bundle of support tools that especially take into account informal communication.

Learning expeditions need a design that includes the formal structures and processes for teaching and learning and is combined with informal open spaces for learners in a community of reflecting peers so as to explore the learning content. This all happens in CrossActionSpaces where roles develop over time.

Communities and Networks

The analysis of social communities began with Tönnies' (1887) "community and society." Communities are, according to Tönnies, characterized by traditional patterns of behavior that have three types of community: 1) the communion of the blood-kinship, 2) the community of the place—neighborhood, and 3) the community of the spirit—friendship. Max Weber used this distinction in early 1920 and expanded it to the extent that a variety of social forms of relationships exist that occur as a form of socialization and communitization. According to Weber (1921/1972), a social relation is then a form of socialization when it is based on values, a purposive-rational balancing of interests that triggers social action. However, it is a form of communitization when it relies on subjectively perceived emotion or tradition and a shared identity, which provides a feeling of belonging together (Weber, 1921/1972).

The main difference between the concept of communities and institutions is that communication and actors within a community are rather loosely coupled and nonformally bound. The relationship is not made from a formal contract. Communities offer the opportunity for their members to support and help each other due to their emotional ties, whereas in an institution the members are coupled by a formal contract. The personal connections in communities are significantly higher than in other groups and organizations. When actors face problems or have a lack of knowledge, the other members help with their knowledge to find a solution to the problem.

Lave and Wenger (1991, p. 98) understand learning as a form of "communities of practice" that emphasize the informal ways of communication in formal organizations. They explore how beginners and freshmen learn to become recognized equivalent members of this 'practitioner' community. This resulted in a new learning theory of learning trajectories in which the learners want to move from the peripheries of a network to the core of a community (Lave & Wenger, 1991; Wellman, 1997; Brown & Duguid, 1991; Lesser & Prusak, 1999).

Lave & Wenger stress the different degrees of networks of relationship within communities. "A community of practice is a set of relations among persons, activity, and world, over time" (Lave & Wenger, 1991, p. 98) and, supplemented later, "who share a concern, a set of problems, or a passion about a topic, and who deepen their knowledge and expertise in this area by interacting on an ongoing basis" (Wenger et al., 2002, p. 4). The work by Wenger (1998) shows that there are three characteristics for such informal relationships of networks.

- *Action* is one of the most important aspects of a community's joint cooperation (collaboration) of the members (Boland & Tenkasi, 1995). This means that the members are connected through common activities and content-shared values (shared repertoire, Wenger, 1998) and develop a common process of social learning and knowledge-sharing culture. The actors can then combine knowledge resources and social capital. At the center of such a community is the exchange of ideas and knowledge as well as mutual aid and support toward a common topic.
- *System.* A community is characterized by the networking of interested actors ("mutual engagement," Wenger, 1998) that develops a shared identity.
- *Structure.* Communities can be seen as the opposite to formally structured organizations. Organizations (like schools and universities) have a more formalized social structure and have a division of labor as well as differentiated roles and organizational goals. Communities, in contrast, have a rather weak social structure and do not follow a system-specific goal. The individual interests are at the center. "Communities are defined as collections of individuals bound by informal relationships that share similar work roles and a common context" (Snyder, in Lesser & Prusak, 1999).

Communities of practice cannot be described—following Wenger (1998)—through the existence of common goals identified by the stakeholders. A community is a sociotechnical system, which consists of informal communication and relationships. It is how the actors learn and participate in the community: "It crucially involves participation as a way of learning . . . the culture of practice" (Lave & Wenger, 1991, p. 95).

In contrast to communities of practice, there are communities of interests (Fischer, 2011). The difference between (1) communities of practice, online and learning communities and (2) communities of interest is that the first are established by participation and not by the same interests. Wenger (1998) assumes that actors within a community connect to a similar culture, a shared practice. It is not the interests of the actors that make this a community but rather the common enterprise to work on a joint topic. This discussion shows that there exist different forms such as sociotechnical communities, online communities, knowledge communities, communities of interests, communities of practice or learning communities. They all say that learning takes place in groups, but the focus of their context may differ. Some designs for learning in communities start by sharing the same interests; others start by sharing the same cultural practice and so forth.

For this book, with the goal to share and discuss new technology-enhanced designs for teaching and learning in a networked world, it is relevant that there is a difference between informal and formal ties. A community shares a common characteristic of trust built on informal relationships, rather than being formally bound by work contracts. The members of a community feel emotionally bound. The research on 'learning communities' also illustrates the link between formal educational institutions such as universities and their learning conditions; while they are structured more by formal roles, the learning needs more space for informal roles. The question remains: how do we design for such informal communities in formal educational institutions? How can we bring informal settings and formal conditions together; how can we design for them?

In every institution (firms, schools, universities, etc.), there are formal structures, which are visible in the organizational charts, but there are also informal networks, for example, private conversations with colleagues or contacts in the kitchen with staff from other departments. The gossip in the coffee room and the emergence of rumors in organizations are some examples of informal social relations. Nahapiet and Ghoshal (1998, p. 243) show that the exchange of knowledge, i.e., the ability of groups to work together to create and share knowledge, depends on both the network of actors and trust. These networks play an important role for all in the explication of knowledge and in the communication of information and learning processes.

Networks

In contrast to the theory of social systems, there are newer theories such as the Actor-Network Theory (ANT; the founder of this theory is Latour, 2005). He argues that there is no such thing as 'units of systems' in the world. The building of such units would not explain the dynamics of organizations nowadays. Ciborra therefore suggests a theory of "Information Infrastructure," i.e., sociotechnical networks instead of sociotechnical systems (Ciborra, 2000, pp. 74–75, 77). Individual elements do not form a unified system but consist of different elements such as technical and nontechnical infrastructures (IT components, people and their skills), which is understood as a network. This network includes elements, such as technical elements and social processes; however, they do not build a closed unit or system because it cannot be defined what belongs to the network—everyone can get in touch with everyone. Because there are no boundaries, the world does not consist of systems, only networks. For example, anyone can participate in an open Internet discussion forum on mathematics or on other social online sites.

But this view on open infrastructures neglects the fact that not everybody can join every online network, institution or organization. There are boundaries and units that have barriers, and such boundaries control participation. The term 'network' implies that the world has no limitations; this might have been true for some online communities such as Wikipedia in their early stages, when more or less everyone could participate. But even Wikipedia, due to its size and social dynamics, has created roles, formal ones, over time (see the studies by Viegas et al., 2007), and there are indications that these roles restrict behavior and boundaries have been drawn; these new roles take the form of organizing roles, spam-checking roles, discussant roles, and valid-information-checking roles.

The point is that a system boundary is drawn and constituted by the communication of the actors, by their decisions they make, and by the communicative behavior itself. Once an actor decides to enter into the communication, they form a social system, online forum or sociotechnical system under the condition that the communication is capable of allowing connectivity where others can make themselves understood and interact. The expectations of the actors regulate the structure of a system. The concept of the 'system' and its unit is therefore not made up of static or fixed boundaries. Rather, a social and sociotechnical system has open system boundaries that change dynamically, even though they are closed in their operations. The self-reference of communication is closed because only communication that can connect to the system communication can be understood from the perspective of the system. The basis for communication in Wikipedia is to write articles as in an encyclopedia—all other communication such as selling things, uploading class lessons and making commercials is not in line with the Wikipedia 'connectivity,' and the products of such activities would probably be deleted. So, there are boundaries in CrossActionSpaces and they are not open; it is only under specific conditions that they appear as open.

The Potential of Communities and Networks—Easy Access to Social Capital

A community emerges when a system's inherent interest converts into a personal interest; for example, students learn in the course of the first semester that study planning needs more attention and start to collect information from experienced students or academic study advisors so as to understand the process better than before. Then it is no longer a factual-instrumental goal (study organization and study conduct) that is at the center of interest but rather the exchange with others who have already overcome such similar problems. Motivation may be activated from such socio-emotional experiences, and active participation, mutual support and shared learning of persons are more strongly encouraged than without such personal considerations (Koch, 2002), for example, through feedback processes, annotations, ideas, answers to questions, review and support for collaborative reflections. This is called the activation of social capital (Putnam, 1995; Fischer et al., 2004). Through community building, social capital allows individuals to do their jobs and learning assignments better than without social capital: I'm doing this for you, even if I do not receive direct reward, because you or someone else will eventually help me later when I need support (Putnam, 1995). A community supports the building of social capital because the actors perceive themselves as a joint enterprise (Wenger, 1998) and act even then with confidence, although they would otherwise not behave in that way. A study by Wellman et al. (2001) shows that members that increase their access to social capital are better in their own task performance and more successful than with less social capital (read also Huysman & Wulf, 2004).

Systems, Communities and Networks—It Does Matter How We Look at It

What we can learn from the discussion of system, communities and network theories is that all of them exist. To understand how the world works, and what kind of didactical conditions do exist in educational institutions (and why), it is necessary to see the world with the eyes of all—systems, communities and networks in sociotechnical forms.

Every sociotechnical phenomenon consists of a relation of both—informal network and formal structures of a system regulated through the connectivity of communication that regulates who participates and who does not. It is a mix of degrees from informal to formal processes and structures. Online communities such as Wikipedia have a stronger emphasis on the informal, while traditional universities place stronger emphasis on the formal. Wikipedia started as an informal open network and developed more social structures over time and more formal roles and structures. So, after some time, organizations drift from the informal to the formal to handle the complexity of workload while creating routines and standards.

A Characteristic for Networks—Absence of Communication

A major difference of viewing systems and networks is the way in which their elements are related to each other. A social system view is an interweaving of communication, which implies a communicative presence. A sociotechnical system is also based on a communicative presence expanded through technology-enhanced and computer-mediated possibilities.

In contrast, the view of social networks is useful to uncover the informal, indirect and unmanageable relationships of microstructures, which are mainly characterized by the absence of communication. Communication absence means that knowledge of the participating social relations exist, but a network is primarily the awareness of people and the capital of relationships, i.e., a network of mutual awareness, which a person has in her mind. A network consists of the knowledge that there is the One or the Other that can be useful sometimes. "It's not what you know, it's who you know" (Cross & Prusak 2002, p. 105).

Systems Follow System Goals—Networks Follow Individual Interests

Another differentiating view is the aim and objective. A system does not exist for itself but follows one or more specific goals, which do not necessarily coincide with the personal objectives of all its role holders.

In contrast, a network is understood as a social phenomenon when several actors are in a more indirect social relationship, which does not follow higher goals. A network has temporal interactions, mainly from the knowledge of each other in which the individual interests of actors are at the center. The function of a network lies especially in the access and opportunities in the form of social capital (Huysman & Wulf, 2004), which is accessed by the network actors when there is the need at irregular time intervals.

Learning Expeditions in Spaces Across Networks, Communities and Systems

I am aware that I have complicated things. Why should we discuss the characteristics of networks, communities and systems? Because they provide different conditions for learning in and across social and sociotechnical systems, and they provide different spaces for reflective cross-actions.

While the systems view shows how communication and learning is restricted due to roles and role-based actions in educational institutions, the community view illustrates the more informal side of group learning without clear rules, and the network view informs about the web of access to social capital with strong and weak ties.

Learning takes place under such conditions and cannot be seen nor understood in an external space isolated from these social forms.

When I argue that learning in a networked world is reflective of MultiCross Actions, I mean that learning today takes place in all of these contexts and even across systems, communities and networks, more or less at the same time. I call this phenomenon the 'relations': MultiCrossActions in Relations (McAiR). From a learner's point of view, she has to learn to handle her roles in different situations in the different contexts. The complexity of social contexts has emerged over the last years, and, due to new technology, it will become even more complex in the coming years.

This kind of increased complexity for learners and teachers is not mirrored in our educational institutions and curricula today. Educational institutions do not prepare either the students or the teachers. There is still a teacher-student loneliness where the teacher has no clear organizational support, such as a coteacher or colleagues, to reflect the teaching practices within a teacher's community-of-practice. There are some examples of good practice, e.g., the Scholarship of Teaching and Learning (SoTL) from England and the Tomas Cochrane initiative in New Zealand (Cochrane & Narayan, 2011). There is a need for schools and universities to understand the design of teaching processes as a collaborative learning effort by teachers.

Teaching and learning is then the reflective making of cross-actions in different co-located off- and online communication spaces that become a complementary process in an Internet-driven networked and digital media world.

2.8 References

Argyris, C. & Schön, D. A. (1978). *Organizational Learning: A Theory of Action Perspective.* Reading, MA: Addison-Wesley.

Bailey, K. (2006). Systems theory. In: J. Turner (Ed.): *Handbook of Sociological Theory.* New York: Springer, pp. 379–404.

Bateson, G. (1972). *Steps to an Ecology of Mind.* New York: Ballantine Books.

Berger, P. & Luckmann, T. (1993). *The Social Construction of Reality.* Frankfurt: Fischer. (Original work published 1967)

Bertalanffy, von, L. (1949). General system theory. *Biologia Generalis,* 195, pp. 114–129.

Bertalanffy, von, L. (1971). *General System Theory. Foundations. Development. Applications.* London: Penguin Press.

Boland, R. & Tenkasi, R. (1995). Perspective making and perspective taking in communities of knowing. *Organization Science,* 6(4), pp. 350–372.

Boshmaf, Y., Muslukhov, I., Beznosov, K. & Ripeanu, M. (2011, December). The social-bot network: when bots socialize for fame and money. In *Proceedings of the 27th Annual Computer Security Applications Conference (ACSAC '11).* Technical report: http://lersse-dl.ece.ubc.ca/record/272

Bourdieu, P. & Wacquant, L. (1992): *An Invitation to Reflexive Sociology.* Chicago, IL: University of Chicago Press.

Brown, J.S. & Duguid, P. (1991). Organizational learning and communities-of-practice: toward a unified view of working, learning, and innovation [Special Issue: Organizational Learning: Papers in Honor of (and by) James G. March]. *Organization Science,* 2(1), pp. 40–57.

Cherns, A. (1987). Principles of socio-technical design revisited. *Human Relations,* 40(3), pp. 153–162.

Chu, Z., Gianvecchio, S., Wang, H. & Jajodia, S. (2010). Who is tweeting on Twitter: human, bot, or cyborg? In *Conference ACSAC '10,* December 6–10, Austin, TX.

Ciborra, C. (2000). *From Control to Drift. The Dynamics of Corporate Information Infrastructures.* New York: University Press.

Coakes, E. (2002). Knowledge management: A socio-technical perspective. In: E. Coakes, D. Willis & S. Clarke (Eds.): *Knowledge Management in the Socio-technical World*. London: Springer. pp. 4–14.

Cochrane, T. & Narayan, V. (2011). DeFrosting professional development: reconceptualising teaching using social learning technologies. In *ALT-C 2011 Conference Proceedings*, pp. 158ff.

Collins, A. & Halverson, R. (2009). *Rethinking Education in the Age of Technology: The Digital Revolution and Schooling in America*. New York: Teachers College Press.

Cross, R. & Prusak, L. (2002, June). The people who make organizations go or stop. *Harvard Business Review*, pp. 105–112.

Dahrendorf, R. (1958). *Homo Sociologicus*. Opladen, Germany: Westdeutscher Verlag.

Dourish, P. (2006, November). Re-space-ing place: "place" and "space" ten years on. In: *CSCW 2006 Conference*, Banff, Alberta, Canada.

Durkheim, E. (1991). *Die Regeln der soziologischen Methode* [*The Rules of Sociological Method*]. Frankfurt: Suhrkamp. (Original work published 1885)

Eason, K. (1988). *Information Technology and Organisational Change*. London: Taylor & Francis.

Emery, F. E. & Trist, E. L. (1960). Socio-technical systems. In: C. W. Churchman (Ed.): *Management Sciences, Models and Techniques*. London: Pergamon.

Engeström, Y. (1999). Activity theory and individual and social transformation. In: Y. Engeström, R. Miettinen & R. Punamäki (Eds.): *Perspectives on Activity Theory*. Cambridge: Cambridge University Press, pp. 19–38.

Fischer, G. (2011, May–June). Understanding, fostering, and supporting cultures of participation,. In: *Communications of ACM Interactions*, 18(3), pp. 42–53.

Fischer, G. & Herrmann, Th. (2011). Socio-technical systems: a meta-design perspective. *International Journal of Sociotechnology and Knowledge Development*, 3(1), 1–33.

Fischer, G., Scharff, E. & Ye, Y. (2004). Fostering social creativity by increasing social capital. In M. Huysman & V. Wulf (Eds.): *Social Capital and Information Technology*. Cambridge, MA: MIT Press, pp. 355–399.

Floridi, L. (2007). A look into the future impact of ICT on our lives. *The Information Society: An International Journal*, 23(1), pp. 59–64.

Forte, A. & Bruckman, A. (2005). Why do people write for Wikipedia? Incentives to contribute to open-content publishing. In *Proceedings of GROUP 2005*.

French, R. M. (2012). Moving Beyond the Turing Test. *Communications of the ACM*, 55(12), 74–77. doi:10.1145/2380656.2380674. http://cacm.acm.org/magazines/2012/12/157871-moving-beyond-the-turing-test/fulltext

Fukuyama, F. (1995). *Trust. The Social Virtues and the Creation of Prosperity*. New York: Free Press.

Giddens, A. (1984). *The Constitution of Society*. Cambridge: Polity Press.

Grudin, J. (1988): Why CSCW applications fail: Problems in the design and evaluation of organizational interfaces. In *Proceedings of the Conf. on Computer-Supported Cooperative Work (CSCW)*, ACM Press, pp. 85–93.

Halfmann, J. (1995). Kausale Simplifikationen, Grundlagenprobleme einer Soziologie der Technik. In: J. Halfmann, G. Bechmann, & W. Rammert (Eds.): *Technik und Gesellschaft, Jahrbuch 8: Theoriebausteine der Techniksoziologie*. Frankfurt: Campus Verlag, pp. 211–226.

Herrmann, Th. (2003). Learning and teaching in socio-technical environments In: T. J. van Weert & R. K. Munro (Eds.), *Informatics and the Digital Society: Social, Ethical and Cognitive Issues*, SECIII 2002 -Social, Ethical and Cognitive Issues of Informatics and ICT. Boston, MA: Kluwer Academic, pp. 59–72.

Herrmann, Th. (2009). Systems design with the socio-technical walkthrough. In B. Whitworth & A. de Moore (Eds.): *Handbook of Research on Socio-Technical Design and Social Networking Systems.* Hershey, PA: Idea Group, pp. 336–351.

Herrmann, Th. (2012). *Kreatives Prozessdesign (Creative Process Design).* Heidelberg: Springer.

Herrmann, Th. & Kienle, A. (2003). Kolumbus: context-oriented communication support in a collaborative learning environment. In: T. J. van Weert & R. K. Munro (Eds.): *Informatics and the Digital Society. Social, Ethical and Cognitive Issues,* SECIII 2002-Social, Ethical and Cognitive Issues of Informatics and ICT. Boston, MA: Kluwer, pp. 251–260.

Herrmann, Th., Hoffmann, M., Kunau, G. & Loser, K.-U. (2004, March–April): A modeling method for the development of groupware applications as socio-technical systems. *Behavior & Information Technology,* 23(2), pp. 119–135.

Herrmann, Th., Loser, K.-U. & Jahnke, I. (2007). Socio-technical walkthrough (STWT): a means for knowledge integration. *International Journal of Learning Organisation,* 14(5), pp. 450–464.

Huysman, M. & Wulf, V. (2004). *Social Capital and Information Technology,* Cambridge, MA: MIT Press, pp. 355–399.

Jacko, J. A. & Sears, A. (2002): *The Human-Computer Interaction Handbook.* Mahwah, NJ: LEA.

Jackson, W. (2011). How smart are Social Bots? http://gcn.com/articles/2011/12/05/cybereye-how-smart-are-social-bots.aspx

Jahnke, I. (2009). Socio-technical communities: from informal to formal? In B. Whitworth & A. de Moor (Eds.): *Handbook of Research on Socio-Technical Design and Social Networking Systems.* Hershey, PA: Information Science Reference, IGI Global, pp. 763–778.

Jahnke, I. (2010). A way out of the information jungle—a longitudinal study about a socio-technical community and informal learning in higher education. *International Journal of Socio-technology and Knowledge Development,* 4, pp. 18–38. doi:10.4018/jskd.2010100102

Jahnke, I. (2012). Technology-embraced informal-*in*-formal learning. In A. Ravencroft, S. Lindstaedt, C. Delgado Kloos & D. Hernandez-Leo (Eds.): *21st Century Learning for 21st Century Skills.* 7th European Conference on Technology Enhanced Learning. Berlin: Springer, pp. 395–400.

Jahnke, I. & Kommers, P. (2009). Introduction. Web 2.0 goes academia. *International Journal of Web Based Communities,* 5(4).

Jahnke, I. & Kumar, S. (2014a): iPad-didactics—didactical designs for iPad-classrooms: experiences from Danish schools and a Swedish university. In: Ch. Miller & A. Doering (Eds.): *The New Landscape of Mobile Learning: Redesigning Education in an App-based World.* New York: Routledge.

Jahnke, I. & Kumar, S. (2014b). Digital didactical designs: teachers' integration of iPads for learning-centered processes. *Journal of Digital Learning in Teacher Education,* 30(3), pp. 81–88. doi:10.1080/21532974.2014.891876

Jahnke, I., Norqvist, L. & Olsson, A. (2014, September 16–19). Digital Didactical Designs of Learning Expeditions. In: C. Rensing et al. (Eds.): *Open Learning and Teaching in Educational Communities.* The 9th European Conference on Technology Enhanced Learning, EC-TEL 2014, Graz, Austria, LNCS Vol. 8719, pp. 165–178.

Kaptelinin, V. & Nardi, B. A. (2006). *Acting with Technology: Activity Theory and Interaction Design.* Cambridge, MA: MIT Press.

Kienle, A. & Herrmann, Th. (2003): Integration of communication, coordination and learning material—a guide for the functionality of collaborative learning environments. In *Proceedings of HICSS, 36th Hawaii International Conference on System Sciences.*

Koch, M. (2002): Interoperable community platforms and identity management in the university domain. *International Journal on Media Management*, 4(1), pp. 21–30.

Kunau, G. (2006). *Socio-technical self-description, framework for supporting the integration of software-engineering and organizational change in CSCW-projects* (Dissertation, TU Dortmund University, Germany).

Latour, B. (2005). *Reassembling the Social—An Introduction to Actor-Network-Theory.* Oxford: Oxford University Press.

Lave, J., & Wenger, E. (1991). *Situated Learning: Legitimate Peripheral Participation.* New York: Cambridge University Press.

Lesser, E. & Prusak, L. (1999). Communities of practice, social capital and organizational knowledge. *Information Systems Review*, 1(1), 3–9.

Levy, S. (2011). Twitter bots will pass the Turing test. http://www.wired.co.uk/magazine/archive/2011/09/ideas-bank/steve-levy

Linton, R. (1936): *The Study of Man.* New York: Appleton-Century-Crofts.

Luhmann, N. (1995). *Social Systems.* Stanford, CA: Stanford University Press. (Original work published 1984)

Luhmann, N. (2000). *Organisation und Entscheidung [Organization and Decision].* Wiesbaden: VS Verlag für Sozialwissenschaften.

Marx, K. (1859/1961). *Zur Kritik der politischen Ökonomie [The Criticism of the Political Economy].* MWE Bd. 13. (Original work published 1859)

McLuhan, H. M. (2003). *Understanding Media. The Extension of Man.* Critical edition. Berkeley, CA: Gingko Press. (Original work published 1964)

Mead, G. H. (1967). *Mind, Self and Society.* London: University of Chicago Press (Original work published 1934)

Mumford, E. (1987). Sociotechnical systems design. Evolving theory and practice. In: G. Bjerknes, P. Ehn & M. Kyng (Eds.): *Computers and Democracy: A Scandinavian Challenge.* Aldershot: Avebury, pp. 59–77.

Mumford, E. (1995). *Effective Systems Design and Requirements Analysis: The ETHICS Approach.* London: Macmillan Press.

Nahapiet, J. & Ghoshal, S. (1998). Social capital, intellectual capital and the organizational advantage. *Academy of Management Review*, 23(2), S242–266.

O'Reilly, T. (2005). What Is Web 2.0? Design Patterns and Business Models for the Next Generation of Software. Retrieved July 25, 2007, from http://tim.oreilly.com/

Parsons, T. (1951): *The Social System.* London: Routledge & Paul.

Preece, J. (2000). *Online Communities: Designing Usability, Supporting Sociability.* Chichester: John Wiley & Sons.

Preece, J., Abras, Ch. & Maloney-Krichmar, D. (2004). Designing and evaluating online communities: Research speaks to emerging practice. *International Journal of Web Based Communities*, 1, 2–18.

Putnam, R. D. (1995). Bowling alone: America's declining social capital. *Journal of Democracy* 6(1), S65–78.

Rammert, W. (2003). *Technik in Aktion*: Verteiltes Handeln in soziotechnischen Konstellationen. [Technology in action—distributed action in socio-technical constellations]. TUTS Working Paper 2–2003, TU Berlin University, Technology Studies.

Reischmann, J. (1986, October). Learning *en passant*: the forgotten dimension. In *Proceedings of the Conference of Adult and Continuing Education*.

Roberts, T., Lowry, P. & Sweeny, P. (2006). An evaluation of the impact of social presence through group size and the use of collaborative software on group member "voice" in face-to-face and computer-mediated task groups. *IEEE Transactions on Professional Communication*, 49, 28–43.

Schwartz, B. (2005). *The Paradox of Choices. Why More Is Less*. New York: Harper Perennial.

Shannon, C. E. & Weaver, W. (1949). *The Mathematical Theory of Communication*. Urbana: University of Illinois.

Shneiderman, B. (2000). Designing trust into online experiences. *Communication of ACM*, 43(12), 57–59.

Siemens, G. (2005). Connectivism: a learning theory for the digital age. *International Journal of Instructional Technology & Distance Learning*. Retrieved March 24, 2014, from http://www.itdl.org/Journal/Jan_05/article01.htm

Sommerville, I. (2004) *Software Engineering* (7th ed.). Amsterdam: Addison-Wesley Longman.

Stahl, G. (2006). *Group Cognition: Computer Support for Building Collaborative Knowledge*. Cambridge, MA: MIT Press.

Tönnies, F. (1887). *Gemeinschaft und Gesellschaft [Community and Society]*. Berlin: Carl Curtius.

Turing, A. M. (1950). Computing machinery and intelligence. *Mind*, 59(236), 433–460.

Ungeheuer, G. (1987): Vor-Urteile über Sprechen, Mitteilen, Verstehen [Prejudice about speaking, communicating, understanding]. In: G. Ungeheuer & J. Juchem (Eds.): Kommunikationstheoretische Schriften 1. Aachen: Alano, Rader, pp. 229–338.

Viegas, F., Wattenberg, M. & Kushel, D. (2004). Studying cooperation and conflict between authors with history flow visualizations. In: E. Dykstra-Erickson & M. Tscheligi (Eds.): *Proceedings of the 2004 Conference on Human Factors in Computing Systems*. Los Alamitos, CA: IEEE Society, pp. 575–582.

Viegas, F., Wattenberg, M., Jesse, K. & van Ham, F. (2007). Talk before you type: coordination in Wikipedia. *Proceedings of Hawaiian International Conference on System Sciences (HICCS 2007)*.

Wagner, C., Mitter, S., Körner, C. & Strohmaier, M. (2012). When Social Bots attack: modeling susceptibility of users in online social networks. In *Proceedings of the WWW*, Vol. 12.

Wallsten, K. (2005). Political Blogs: Is the Political Blogosphere an Echo Chamber? *American Political Science Association's Annual Meeting*. Washington, DC: Department of Political Science, University of California, Berkeley.

Wasko, M., & Faraj, S. (2005). Why should I share? Examining social capital and knowledge contribution in electronic communities of practice. *Management Information Systems*, 29(1), 35–57.

Watzlawick, P., Beavin, J. H. & Jackson, D. D. (1969). *Pragmatics of Human Communication*. New York: Norton.

Weber, M. (1972). *Economy and Society (an Outline of Interpretive Sociology)* (Vol 5, rev. ed.). Berkeley: University of California Press. (Original work published 1921)

Weizenbaum, J. (1966, January). ELIZA—a computer program for the study of natural language communication between man and machine. *Communications of the ACM* 9(1), 36–45.

Wellman, B. (1997). An electronic group is virtually a social network. In: S. B. Kiesler (Ed.): *Cultures of the Internet*. Hillsdale, NJ: Lawrence Erlbaum, pp. 179–205.

Wellman, B., Hasse, A., Witte, J. & Hampton, K. (2001). Does the Internet increase, decrease or supplement social capital? *American Behavioral Scientist*, 3(45), pp. 437–456.

Wenger, E. (1998). Communities of practice. Learning as a social system. *Systems Thinker*, 6.

Wenger, E., McDermott, R., & Snyder, W. M. (2002). *Cultivating Communities of Practice: A Guide to Managing Knowledge*. Boston, MA: Harvard Business School Press.

3

DYNAMICS OF ROLES IN CROSSACTIONSPACES

Enabler and Hinderer

Don't just wish for a great new year. Make it so!

(J.-L. Picard, *Star Trek*)

In Chapter 2, I introduced a thought experiment about our digital networked world that is full of emerging CrossActionSpaces, which I characterize as multi-existing co-expanded communication spaces. Such spaces evolve from communication. Our digital networked world is made of such a set of diverse and dynamic variety of spaces, which are not totally open. They are in a tension between openness and closeness by coding and recoding boundaries through social action. When our world is such a variety of spaces, then the next question is, what is and how can human action be defined and characterized in such spaces? What constitute those spaces?

In this chapter, I argue that human action in such CrossActionSpaces does not rely on *inter*actions but rather can be understood as several cross-actions within and across such spaces. These cross-actions are evolving from interaction and communication and happen within a context. That means that the characterization of cross-actions can be best understood when starting with existing concepts of human behavior, interaction and communication. Every communication organizes itself (consciously or implicitly) in and around such spaces, social systems, communities and networks. Patterns of behavior expectation occur, well known as the emergence of social roles.

Wherever humans are, they create expectations and assumptions about the Others. We meet new people, and we create stereotypes based on their looks, based on their behavior, based on what they say and how they say it, and we put them in some of our mind boxes. We expect at the next meeting a similar kind of behavior based on how we judge them. This is a social phenomenon that I illustrate in detail in this chapter. We all create conscious or implicit expectations that guide us and them, which enables communication and learning, but also can hinder and restrict us and them in our learning. Reflections about those patterns of behavior expectations (roles) are relevant to break through established learning barriers and to become an active agent of a reflective maker.

This chapter illustrates the development of a networked world toward multiple cross-actions that are heavily relying on the basic elements of communication and patterns of expectations, known as roles. The roles that humans take and play are a kind of paradox; they enable but also limit learning as communication.

In a networked world, I argue, there is need for a complementary teaching and learning theory that describes teachers' applied designs-in-practice and the learners' interaction in constructing learning from the approach of CrossAction Spaces. Before I describe new models of designing for learning in co-expanded communication spaces in Chapters 4 and 5, I focus on human activities in such spaces and propose to call it MultiCrossActions in Relations (McAiR)—in short, CrossAction.

The role theory is one key element in understanding the relationships among different systems on different micro, meso and macro levels in society (Turner, 2006).

The book journey started with social systems and the structure of such systems in Chapter 2 to describe the characteristics of CrossActionSpaces. In those spaces, expectation and expectations of expectations occur that people create when they are part of such spaces. In other words, such spaces open up more possibilities for communication but also restrict communication. It is the coding and recoding of what belongs to the space, what is accepted to belong to the space, and what is not.

The foundation of this view is social role theory, which has a strong traditional background and has been included further into the social system theory by Luhmann (1995; Chapter 2). However, we have almost forgotten about the role theory, or people argue that it focuses too much on a 'structuralism' perspective—but roles are both: they are made bottom-up in communication and they are also influenced by this communication top-down. There exists a duality of roles.

One reason why educational research and educational institutions avoid taking an explicit step toward a 'social role approach' might be that the handling of social roles within a group, an organization and in societies usually takes place implicitly. This means that during social interaction, roles will be developed, assigned, or taken over but usually without a conscious, explicit decision. In general, actors do not talk about *roles* and *role development*; they talk about *people and competence development*. There are some exceptions, such as team-building processes, which assign roles explicitly to people, for example, Person A becomes the role of the moderator in Meeting A.

However, because we neglect an explicit discussion about the "dynamics of roles" (Jahnke, 2006), this makes it much harder to understand why teachers, students, instructors, educational developers, study program leaders, etc. act as they do. When we talk about teachers and teaching practices in schools and higher education and neglect the 'role', it often sounds like we judge a person instead of judging the role. The role is important because it has a duality: first, the role delivers a framework for what is allowed for the person when s/he is in a role and doing the role action—a negotiation space; and second, roles can be changed by human interaction regardless of what it would take to change the role definition (e.g., the role of a teacher or student). Roles affect persons in their roles. When persons change their expected role behavior, it can lead to irritation, and then the role image and role actions develop into something new—a new role or a new understanding of a role.

The earlier section on social and sociotechnical systems in Chapter 2 illustrated the key feature of organizations such as schools and higher education. The key component is communication in interaction and the developed structures of expectations over time. The summary of all these multiple structures of expectation and patterns of communication can be called social roles. A role is more than just expectations or expectations of expectations. Over the last few years, a new understanding of roles has been developed that includes positioning within a group and network, functions and purposes of roles assigned to the position, multiple implicit and explicit expectations and role-playing within and across established boundaries. This characterization is a first indicator that there is more than just a role. It might be useful not to call it 'roles' because we are trapped in traditions and old-fashioned understandings of roles; instead, a new term is useful to make visible how human action is evolving from traditional role-based interaction toward cross-actions.

This chapter aims to make visible the old role concepts with the purpose to illustrate the development of human action in a digital world toward cross-actions. There are many different role concepts: from social sciences, in software development and in computer sciences. A role is useful as a concept that helps to understand the gap between individuals, groups and society. Why is it that people and groups such as educational actors, teachers and learners behave in certain ways, although they could behave in totally different ways in theory? Roles are patterns that are not just there or exist, and humans do not just adopt them. Roles underlie certain social mechanisms. Roles are taken by people, roles are assigned to others, roles dynamically change and new roles arise over time. There are different role types, formal and informal types of roles. Altogether, this complexity might be called MultiCrossActions in Relations and will be illustrated in detail in the next sections.

MANY DIFFERENT CONTEXTS

Often, the concept of a role is in competition with other concepts, such as the concept of a job taken by an individual. This is because the term 'role' is used in different discourses. For example, it is used in everyday life (roles of mother, father, gender), roles in theater and film, roles of leaders in business and in the context of games (role-play). The role concept is also used in different knowledge disciplines, for instance, in sociology and organizational psychology or in software development, e.g., in programming and administration of technical groupware systems. The similarities and differences between such role concepts are often unclear.

HISTORY

The term 'role' has a long tradition. First discussions toward a role approach began in 1930, especially in American sociology. George H. Mead (1934) and Ralph Linton (1936) dealt with the subject from different points of view. The two paradigms of "symbolic interaction" (Blumer, 1969) and the "functionalistic perspective" try to explain the relationship between the individual and society, between a person and the system.

Mead looked at roles more from an interactionist perspective and Linton from a structural-functionalist perspective. Mead assumed that society is composed of interactions. These interactions develop into role structures. The symbolic interaction approach emphasizes that roles are formed on the subjective will of the actors. In contrast, the functionalistic perspective (e.g., Parsons, 1951; Dahrendorf, 1958) is characterized by the idea that society determines roles, which are defined by a set of normative expectations and sanctions. The functionalistic approach suggests the existence of objective structures, which determine the individuals' behavior.

Today, we know that both paradigms influence each other (Herrmann, Jahnke & Loser, 2004; Jahnke, Ritterskamp & Herrmann, 2005; Jahnke, 2010). Social roles always refer to social interaction. In social interactions, the individual (ego) and the counterpart (alter ego) perceive themselves in different roles. *Ego* expects a specific behavior of *alter* and vice versa. *Ego* tries to anticipate how *alter ego* might behave and vice versa.

The role theory was criticized, especially in the 1950s to 1970s, as not being fully able to explain the complexity of social systems. In the late 1950s, Dahrendorf (1958) developed a perspective on the role theory. His work *Homo Sociologicus* is an essential contribution to the American discourse. An overview of sociological and social-psychological role approaches can be found in Biddle and Thomas (1966). Bales (1950) studied small group interactions and realized that a role is then a perceivable interaction pattern created through the repetition of social interaction.

In the beginning of the 1970s, the role concept was picked up again, and it was expanded and developed through a highly critical attitude by Frigga Haug (1972/1994). It also was criticized by Krappmann (1977). He argued that the role approaches do not focus enough on the individual actor; the actor is regarded as too passive from this role-theoretical point of view. This raised the new question of whether and how the individual contributes to an active role adoption. Terms such as self-management in roles emphasize this approach (Sievers & Beuer, 2006).

That older role approach has the great capacity to make social structures transparent. In the critical discourse, it became clear that the concept of the role alone cannot explain the complexity of societies; social system; and, nowadays, the new forms of sociotechnical systems, networks and interconnectivities. The older role concept was not enough adapted to social behavior in order to explain social regularities.

With Giddens' term (1984), the role was expanded to include temporal processes and became part of social structures that form the basis of a duality. On the one hand, a role is created by those who interact; on the other hand, there are simultaneously inherited rules, resources, regulations, values, norms and social relationships that are produced and reproduced during human interactions.

Thus, the approach itself was no longer considered as a stand-alone sociological theory. The term 'role' has been integrated as a basic term in contemporary social science. Contemporary social systems theory, especially Luhmann's theory, included 'role' as a basic term (read also other studies on 'role transitions' and social phenomena, e.g., Ashforth [2001] and Montgomery [1998]). In particular, the discipline of the sociology of organizations have used the role concept for the explanation of organizational structures and processes. In addition, computer sciences use the concept of roles for artificial intelligence research to create technical roles and human-technological roles, for instance, cyborgs, which consist of humans and technology and social bots, that had been discussed at the symposium of "interdisciplinary roles" in Arlington, Virginia (Jahnke, Ritterskamp & Herrmann, 2005).

3.1 Roles—The Interactionism Point of View

The role approach had its beginning in the research work by George Herbert Mead. He started from the assumption that a society consists of interaction and that through these interactions, role structures emerge. Mead himself did not publish much, but his remarks were published after his death by Blumer (1969). Blumer developed the theory of symbolic interactionism. This theory is based on the following three premises: 1) people act toward things based on the meanings that these things have for them; 2) the meaning of these things arises from social interaction with others or is caused by them, and 3) these meanings emerge in an interpretive process in dealing with the things.

Later, Erving Goffman (1972) developed this approach further. He understands social interaction as a process of mutual perception, role taking and role assignments, constantly negotiated between individuals. He put the role approach into an activity approach called role action or role-playing. The tradition of interactionistic approaches is supported by Krappmann (1977). In the process of role negotiation, the dimension of the individual gained a stronger meaning.

Krappmann postulated that interaction partners also take the role of the Other. Conversely, *Alter* (Person A) must also take into account the position of *Ego* (Person B) in order to grasp his intention. The interaction patterns must be able to respond to different needs of the counterpart in order to ensure the progress of the interaction (Krappmann, 1977, p. 315). Krappmann refers to works by Nadel (1957/1969) and Uta Gerhardt (1971, p. 37). Nadel describes social structure as "the web of interacting" (p. 63). In the era of technology, this quotation gains a new light, and roles are only useful in connection with the concept of social action—technology-mediated interaction or offline. The common ground for the analysis of social phenomena considers roles as in activities, action and communication. Table 3.1 shows the mentioned scientists.

Interactionist's views do not primarily assume that the institutional environment significantly affects the system. They stress, moreover, the relationships of individuals and the emergence of roles over time, i.e., how individuals in their roles influence social structures.

The role approach bridges the individual and the larger sociotechnical systems and provides one of several approaches to explain how individuals and institutions related to each other through the role and how it has been developed bottom-up over time:

Individuals → situated in roles → 'organize,' develop social structures in organizations and co-expanded spaces

The Interactionism theory understands society as a collection of individuals who negotiate the everyday things in social interaction and provides a bottom-up approach. Systems derived from human interaction. The social interaction is from this point of view a process of multiple continuous activities in which the individuals develop their patterns of behavior in different situations and

TABLE 3.1 The interactionism perspective

Sociologists	Description
George H. Mead, 1934 (1863–1931)	Society consists of interactions. Interactions form roles and role structures.
Herbert Blumer, 1969 (1900–1987)	Three premises of symbolic interactionism; negotiation of the meanings of things in social interaction as interpretive process.
Erving Goffman, 1972 (1922–1982)	Social interaction is seen as a process of mutual perception, role taking and role assignments. It can be summarized in the concept of role action.
Lothar Krappmann, 1977 (German representative)	Krappmann stresses the dimension of individuality; a stronger meaning of individual actions within the process of negotiation.

in different relations. In a process of interaction, they need to coordinate their developing actions to each other. For example, Person A shows Person B what to do, and Person B interprets the action indicated by Person A. In order to have a connection to its ongoing human communication over time, humans are dependent on their counterparts' meanings. When they are able to adopt their counterparts' points of view to understand the attributed meanings, communication happens. Without understanding the context, it is difficult to succeed in communication (Herrmann & Kienle, 2003).

3.2 Roles—Structural-Functionalism Perspective

In contrast to the interactionist approach, the normative role concept has been developed. This is often called the classic role theory and conventional role concept. In the structural-functionalist perspective, it does not focus on individuals and how they make social structures work. It rather illustrates the social structures that shape human actions by means of roles and control (Balog, 1989). Representatives are Linton (1936), Merton (1949), Parsons (1951) and Dahrendorf (1958), who argue that roles are defined on the basis of normative expectations (a set of role norms). Social action is therefore a standard behavior within a social system.

The first scientific studies on the role-compliant action were performed by Linton, published in *The Study of Man* (1936). He sees a role as the totality of cultural patterns (attitudes, values, behavior) that are associated with a certain social status. Linton understood the expression 'status' as a social position within the society. Human behavior is a dynamic aspect and the dynamic part of the role. According to this approach, a role is considered as the sum of all behavioral expectations associated with a particular social task coming from the society.

The functional perspective assumes that roles are addressed to the members of a society. The role holder is in a certain social situation, and the role guides expected behavioral settings, which meet each role holder in about the same manner. The role refers to a regularly occurring behavior that is expected in certain situations. An example is the role of the teacher. Each role holder (teacher) has the same task, which is to teach—regardless of how unclear this responsibility might be. The reference group, such as school leaders and parents, has the ability to punish the role holder, for example, to tell her what kind of textbook she has to use. Those expectations regarding the role of a teacher are socially and culturally dependent and therefore can change over time and in different cultures. The same is valid for the student's role. The reference group (parents and teachers) has the power to tell the students how to behave within a range of behavioral settings, and society also has an ideal imagination about what makes a good student and a good teacher. From this angle, a role is a bundle of the normative behavior expectations of one or more persons related to the owner of a certain social position. It can be expressed in a top-down direction where the organization influences existing or creates new roles that affects individuals in their behavior, interaction and communication:

> Individuals ← a framework of roles ← sociotechnical structures, organizations and co-expanded spaces

The term 'normative' means that a role exists of generalized, unified and standardized behavior expectations and the reference group has a certain power to make sure that the standardized behavior and values will be conducted. The reference group is the sum of all people who relate to the role in different ways. For example, the father and mother roles refer to the child role and the student role refers to the teacher role; in companies and institutions, the different roles are seen in the organigram that is a model of the job position hierarchies. The reference group combines all possible counterpart roles (alter roles) that refer to the ego role. The group has different sanctions for punishment if the role owner does not behave as expected, and they also have options for rewarding a special role behavior so as to enforce behavioral expectations or to enable new behavior. The roles of a social system ensure that different people, in the same roles, perform more or less a similar behavior. From this view, deviation from the normality is seen as a threat.

There is a problem with this approach. The role holder is absolutely dependent on the reference group and has no other alternatives than what the reference group intends to do. It seems that the role definition of the structural-functionalist perspective is often one-sided: it gives a certain perspective and stresses the reference group but does not include the vision of the role holder and neglects the creativity of role owners—of course, there are deviations of standardized behavior, otherwise no progress in society would be possible. The question of how innovation or even evolution is possible remains unresolved from the functionalist perspective. Another criticism is that the role is defined with terms which in turn involve larger concepts but remain undefined. For example, the term 'social position' (introduced by Linton) and the place of an individual at a particular time in a particular place is not well enough connected to the role-play by humans.

Institutional Conditions

In 1951, T. Parsons developed the theory of social systems. He assumed that the structure of social systems affects the actions of social systems significantly. From this perspective, the institutional conditions became the center of the societal analysis. It was the aim to improve the structure, not the role actions or the relationship of individuals to each other, as understood by the interactionists. Parsons examined the structures of social systems, whether and to what extent they contribute to the stability of the system or not. He described four identified elements, named AGIL. AGIL is the abbreviation for Adaptation of the system to the structures (A), reaching the Goals of the societal system (G), Integration (I) and Latent pattern maintenance (L). According to Parsons, the stability of a social system is a necessary basic condition. The connection between the social system, its AGIL structures, and the behavior of individuals is the role. The role guides different expectations and shows the role holder what an appropriate role behavior is. The role defines an alleged correct behavior. Table 3.2 gives an overview of the structural-functionalist role concepts.

The structural-functional view was much criticized. Humans themselves are not only victims of the societal will; they are also willing and able to fit into a chosen role. How is it possible that the annoying fact called 'society' is bearable for an individual? (Dahrendorf, 1958)

Both perspectives are required to see the bigger picture. Although the understandings of the two approaches from interactionists and structural-functionalists do differ, they are still both relevant for the understanding of the role concept as a whole. There is a recurrent influence on each other:

Individuals ↔ situated in roles / roles as a defined corridor for behavior and communication ↔ organizations and co-expanded spaces

Roles are created due to complex social interactions that are not static but dynamic, changeable social phenomena, as will be explained in the interpretive, interactionistic paradigm. Roles are made of social actions, and the role mechanisms are not always visible.

The normative, structural-functionalistic perspective is useful since it explains a role-compliant and standard behavior that is filled with a function and tasks and requires a fulfillment and processing of role holders in relation to the role ideal. The role holders are faced with the sanctioning power of the reference groups within a system. The institutional conditions affect individuals, but the structures also give a framework for performing and filling a function.

TABLE 3.2 Structural-functional perspectives on role concepts

Sociologists	Description
Ralph Linton, 1936	Separation of status and role: both exist independent of an individual.
Talcott Parsons, 1951	Theory of structure: the structure of society influences the social systems, therefore the institutional conditions are in the focus of analysis to examine whether or not, and to what extent, they contribute to the development of social systems.
Ralf Dahrendorf, 1958	Social action means behaving in a range of norm-compliant role action in a society where sanctions (power) exist to maintain the standards (difference of Can, Should and Must expectations).

Today, where we live in a time of multiple offline and online possibilities, the dynamics offers a wider range to make a significant contribution toward existing and new roles. Because of today's dynamic groups, organizations and institutional frameworks, the interactions among role holders are faster, and there exist many more interactions and cross-actions than in previous ages. It is an acceleration of the role dynamics.

3.3 Roles in Technology and Software Development (Roles in CSCW)

In software development and in the research and development domains of computer-supported cooperative work (CSCW) and computer-supported collaborative learning (CSCL), there exists another term of 'role' that is used usually to design access rights on data management in technical systems. Software developers use the role concepts to determine which users have which permissions to access which documents in which form (Sandhu et al., 1996, role-based administration). The role concept is reduced to access control mechanisms; it is simplistic and is equated with the concept of formal authority (job) and thus implies a high degree of formalization and low individual flexibility, with little informality (Jahnke, Ritterskamp & Herrmann, 2005).

However, as seen in the sections earlier described, a role involves more than just the allocation of tasks, responsibilities and rights. The dynamics of roles and role structures, the change of role expectations and the creation of new roles characterize knowledge sharing and learning processes. When a role is too rigid and too formalized, then it prevents students from learning.

In computer science, the notion of role-based access control (RBAC) refers to a well-known approach to designing the role mechanisms. In the broader context, in information and communication technology (ICT), an access control mechanism is a method of restricting or allowing users to have access to a system, functionalities or data. From a software program perspective and technical system viewpoint, it is important to the concept of RBAC that users do not have discretionary access to the functions or data provided by a system (Ferraiolo et al., 1995). Instead, roles are used as a mediating construct, each one of them offering a specific set of access permissions. RBAC uses the term 'role' in a narrowed sense, being almost solely described in terms of its position, associated functions and tasks. For instance, take the following definition created by Sandhu et al. (1996): "A role is a job function or job title within the organization with some associated semantics regarding the authority and responsibility conferred on a member of the role." Here, roles are characterized as entities referring to a position within an organization, describing the functions and tasks that are linked to this position.

Roles in the context of an ICT system have the purpose to manage access control. The technical role concept goes along with the notion of 'privileges'

(Nyanchama & Osborn, 1999). A role, then, is a named set of privileges to which users can be assigned (Nyanchama & Osborn, 1999). Privileges can only refer to tasks and functionalities that can be formalized within an ICT system. Consequently, there is no possibility of expressing the properties of a role that exceed the boundaries of the technical system, e.g., expectations on how a person is considered to conduct a role and whether she meets these expectations or not.

These considerations of RBAC exemplify that the conceptualizations of a sociological role within an organization and a role in RBAC are not the same. Roles in a technical sense serve as a rather static concept for describing jobs, functions and tasks in such a way that they are defined independently of persons filling this position. From the perspective of RBAC, people are assigned to a set of usually predefined roles depending on their duties and responsibilities—they do not redefine existing roles, nor do they create new ones—there is no support for the dynamic development of roles as it is common to social systems. Jahnke, Ritterskamp and Herrmann (2005) provide an overview of the different concepts of roles of RBAC and social roles.

Although there are some extensions to the core concept of RBAC, e.g., dealing with the implementation of separation of concerns, conflicts of interest and hierarchical ordering of roles (Simon & Zurko, 1997; Gavrila & Barkley, 1998), the dynamic nature of roles is insufficiently considered. The RBAC understanding is highly formalized and offers less individual flexibility.

As we have pointed out in Jahnke, Ritterskamp and Herrmann (2005), an extended conceptualization of roles in ICT that additionally accounts for aspects of roles derived from sociology and organizational management may foster knowledge sharing and learning in computer-supported collaborative settings. The basic idea is that by trying to preserve the diversity of the sociological conceptualization of roles when applying them to computer-supported collaboration, we can build up an environment that helps to reduce the amount of disadvantageous ambiguity present in collaboration and trim down frictional loss accordingly.

3.4 What Makes Human Behavior Into a Role? Multiple Dimensions

Learning is usually analyzed from the perspective of 1) knowledge sharing and competence development, 2) traceability (e.g., awareness, structuring of information, incentives, motivation), and 3) technology support. The relevance of the interplay between formal and informal role structures and multiple role structures as cross-actions has not been sufficiently taken into account. We have almost forgotten the knowledge of roles and the importance they have for the interplay between teachers, learners and the system of the educational institutions.

Multiple Sociotechnical Actions Condensed in Roles

From a sociological point of view, individuals and actors act on the foundation of roles. A role helps them to perceive that they belong to one or more social systems. With the help of the role concept, it is possible to study a more comprehensive phenomenon, to make the social relationships between individuals and educational systems visible more than the terms 'social action' and 'communication' could do alone. The role analysis enables us to capture the social context in a more differentiated way than without the role approach (Balog, 1989, p. 123).

The term 'role' embraces the invisible social activities of multilevel actions (Balog, 1989) and multiple sociotechnical actions. How can individuals know what behavior is appropriate when they are in the context of a family or in a seminar at a university? This is done, according to Balog (1989, p. 109), by clusters of communications, interactions and attitudes and is repeated in roles. "A family is realized as a social system when it acts in role patterns, it is then visible as a social phenomenon. The role as repeating interaction patterns makes a family as family visible, people who belong to the family are identifiable and can be recognized, and gives proof on the existence of families in a society" (Balog, 1989, p. 13). The same is valid for teachers and students in schools and higher education. There are established patterns and routines that remind us every day what 'appropriate' behavior means in this system.

Certain human actions and repeated actions become clusters, and moreover patterns, that form roles and role structures. Following the social system theory, certain recurring communication patterns (re)produce roles (Luhmann, 1995). The structures of social systems are therefore structures of expectations that are personal bound or role bound. "Roles are a bundle of expectations. . . . By the identity of a role, expectations are transferable from person to person" (Luhmann, 1995, p. 86).

Roles always depend on the context (Balog, 1989, p. 141), and thus they are relative within a system. This means that, first, roles can only be identified within a system and context as Role X or Y, and, second, not all repeated patterns of interaction create a role.

With the concept of roles, social activities can be illustrated within social systems. For example, the variety of roles in an organization, a university or a small group such as a seminar show their diversity of actions and their structural complexity of formal and informal activities.

Roles Are Relative—Toward MultiCrossActions in Relations

A social role is often defined as a set of activities performed by individuals (Goffman, 1959). "A role is a set of prescriptions defining what the behavior of a position member should be" (Biddle & Thomas, 1966, p. 29). This is not enough to understand comprehensive role behavior. A role also defines the range of expected behavior within a group. For instance, a person who teaches has special behavior patterns such as 'giving some instructions to the group,' 'beginning when the class starts,' 'supporting students' learning' or 'standing in front of the class.' Consequently, the reference group labels a person who behaves in accordance with these patterns as a 'teacher' (this is a type of role assignment). If the person in the teacher's role undertakes *totally* different activities than expected, parents, students, institutional leaders or other teachers would probably intervene. They would give correcting feedback. If interaction and discussion did not lead to a change of behavior (no impact on the role), probably the school leader would try to apply negative sanctions until the teacher rectified his behavior. To conclude, a role and its role-playing depend on the preexisting values and norms of a group, community, social system or society and the possibility or power to restrict alleged incorrect behavior. Therefore, a role, good or bad role-playing, is always relative to its cultural setting (e.g., in Society Z, the didactical expected behavior is different to the Society X).

A role is more than the sum of all behavioral expectations of a social system of the role holder. It also includes the role actor who is in a certain position linked to a purpose and function that underlies explicit and implicit interactive negotiation processes. In a networked world, a role also includes the controlling actions of human-computer interaction. Such a complexity of the role phenomenon can be named as multi-cross-actions in a networked world.

Following the approach of interactionism and structural-functional views, and developing it further to apply it to a networked society in the digital age, role-based action is infected by different dimensions.

Roles are strongly influenced by four dimensions, such as the relative position within a system or space, the purpose or function and assigned tasks, the informal and formal expectations, and the role-playing by the role holder and counterparts.

From the symbolic interactionism to the functionalistic paradigm, four dimensions of roles illustrate a comprehensive role concept in a networked world (Table 3.3):

TABLE 3.3 Four dimensions of roles that constitute MultiCrossActions in Relations

Dimension	Description
Position	A relative **position** within an organization, institution or community, which the member of the group gets assigned and takes (e.g., organizational chart; network position).
Purpose/ function	A **purpose/function** and intended set of activities/tasks of the role, performed in accordance with the position (e.g., tasks associated with the position such as the job description of a teacher, moderator or student—some positions are more explicitly described than other positions, which are rather implicitly taken or developed).

(Continued)

TABLE 3.3 (Continued)

Dimension	Description
Expectations	**Expectations** from others that are placed to the position owner; expectations are explicitly (e.g., in documents, descriptions) and implicitly available (e.g., oral feedback; often we do not know all the expectations but expect that we will know them; we develop them over time during socialization and internalization; Nonaka & Takeuchi, 1995); rights, duties and obligations, Can-Should-Must expectations, including mutual trust; negative consequences, punishments or positive rewards from the others in the reference group ensure and limit the range of assumed behavior clusters.
Role doing	Interactive **doing in a process is** role-playing performed by the position holder that does not take place in a totally free space but is context-bound; there exists a negotiation space in which the role holder might act. Each role is filled slightly differently. Role doing also stresses that roles are not just there; the role actor creates the role actively. To some extent, she can say whether she wants to take the role or not.

These four dimensions together constitute role actions and role structures. It represents the dynamics of roles, and forms of behavior clusters in a networked society interwoven by digital media. It constitutes cross-actions.

a) Position

A role refers to a position within a system in which the position is linked to a purpose, function and tasks. In the older role approaches, the term 'position' referred to a social status in a society or to the hierarchy level in a business enterprise (e.g., organizational chart). Here, I propose, the position indicates the relation to other roles. Positions have relations to other positions in a social system and represent the structure. The position shows the relation to other positions and stresses the structure aspect (Linton, 1936). This is also valid for informal or new, emerging roles. For example, the teacher's position relates to the students in a different relation than to the school leader or to the parents and the IT administrator etc. The sum of all positions in a system mirrors the structure of the social system.

The position can be a formal one, such as student, teacher, study management advisor or moderator, assigned by work contract or membership. It can also be an informal position such as opinion leader, conclusion maker or promoter of the procedure. The term 'position' has no relation to a physical location.

Ilgen and Hollenbeck (1991) discuss the relationship between role and job in organizational systems. For this purpose, it must be mentioned that the term 'job,' especially in the sociology of organizations, is similar to the concept of position. According to Ilgen and Hollenbeck (1991), the relationship between position and role is such that the position is more related to the fixed and immutable part, i.e., the position is relatively rigid and varies only slightly. In contrast, the role is more flexible and depends on which actors have held the role and how the actors are 'doing' the role. A position is initially independent of people. A position then becomes a role if one or more people fulfill the position and the associated purpose, function and tasks. The name of the position often shows what the purpose is (e.g., a teacher teaches; a goal keeper tries to keep the ball; a student learns).

b) Purpose/Function

The position implies a special purpose including functions and tasks, usually in the form of explicit and documented expectations, rights and obligations, which are addressed to the role owner by the members of the social system (e.g., job descriptions, work contracts and task assignments). The aspect of 'tasks' focuses on what an organizational or community member in a specific position does or what the person is expected to do from the viewpoint of the system and what the different primary activities are, for example, teaching, consulting, moderating and/or contributing. Tasks and activities are close to the position held by a person.

An example illustrates the relationship of a position and functions to a role. Usually, in each department of a university, there is an office of advisors that has the purpose and task of supporting students when they have questions or problems in their studies. In a department where I worked from 2001 to 2005, there were six research assistants who had taken the role of study advisors. Each filled the same spot slightly differently: one responded to e-mails regularly and offered a telephone consultation; the other scheduled appointments for face-to-face meetings and consultations; the third tried to do as little as possible; and the fourth was very active, coordinated and tried to develop a team. Although the position holder took the same position within the organization, the tasks associated with the position were to be filled and conducted slightly differently—but not totally differently! As long as the position holder can expect no negative consequences or positive reinforcement, there is no need to change their role performance and role refinement.

Both dimensions A (the position) and B (the purpose/function) share the structural part of a role. As we know from the different approaches of interactionism and structural functionalism, this is not enough if we are to understand a comprehensive role behavior. A role is a more complex phenomenon than a task or job since it develops in a web of social expectations and the possibilities of positive or negative consequences and sanctions. "Roles exist in the minds of people" because "expectations are beliefs or cognitions held by individuals" (Ilgen & Hollenbeck, 1991), where:

- Positions "are viewed as a set of established task elements" that are objective, bureaucratic and quasi-static, but
- Roles embrace more than a position. They also include informal and implicit expectations grounded on interactive processes.

c) Behavioral Expectations

The role concept covers more than the formal position or job description. There are also expectations that are not necessarily explicit. This includes informal notions and agreements (Harrison, 1972). For example, contributors to an online discussion forum often share certain conventions, e.g., how to contribute without annoying someone, what is off-topic and does not belong to the forum, how to formulate politely, how to use emoticons, etc. Violating the conventions can causes negative sanctions, leading even to exclusion from the community.

Here the term 'expectation' refers to what people expect that a role holder, depending on a specific position performed by an individual, can, should, must and should not do. In formal organizations such as educational institutions, expectations are often linked with the job description. The expectations are rather illustrated explicitly. However, expectations can also be communicated nonverbally and implicitly; it is not illustrated anywhere. It includes informal notions, commitments and agreements. Those expectations can be seen when nonroutine actions happen, such as what to do when X takes place.

d) Role Doing in a Process Over Time (Role-Playing)

Within the boundaries of a social system, the role holder has the chance to shape the role she has taken. This shaping process is dependent upon interaction with other participants in the social system and follows the restricted means of communication. Roles are the results of an often unseen negotiation between the role actor and those with whom he interacts, either face-to-face, computer mediated or both. The role owner *transforms* the role expectations into specific behaviors: he gives life to the role during 'doing' it (role making). It is an interpretive process, and, thus, each role actor fills the same role differently. To a specific extent, roles are therefore modifiable.

A role underlies different, partially contradictory expectations; positive or negative consequences are implied. This means that the role doing by an actor can be judged by different people in other roles who have the power to develop positive or negative consequences when the role owner deviates from expectations, which might cause inter- and intra-role conflicts.

People have expectations about what a role owner should and should not do, but a role is a dynamic phenomenon and therefore is also changeable by individuals. Within certain limits and within the corridor of negotiation, the role actor can actively shape a role she has taken. The role actor *transforms* the role expectations into concrete behavior, and, thus, the same role might be played (slightly) differently. However, such changes depend on 1) the anticipation of people's power that could restrict nonconformist behavior and 2) different role mechanisms (read later the different role mechanisms).

With these four dimensions, it becomes clear how complex the roles of teachers and students and other roles in educational institutions are; but there is also the advantage that with such a concept, we get the opportunity to study the dynamics of roles. Now, we are able to empirically observe role actions and role structures in teaching and learning within the broader context of educational institutions. *Position* and *purposes* characterize the *structural dimension* within groups, i.e., how people relate to each other. Expectations and role doing mainly focus on the *action dimension*, i.e., how a person performs the position and plays the role.

3.5 Summary—Roles Enable and Hinder MultiCrossActions in Relations

Roles are expected communication patterns in relations, socially framed, that repeat over time; they are made through human communication that is technology-mediated or face-to-face communication; they are influenced by the role owners and reference groups that have an ideal role pattern in mind.

If we were to ask the role owner and the reference group members about a role such as mother or father, professor or student, we would get a common ground and partly shared understanding of this role. In reality, we have many different people, developing different identities, who fill the same role slightly differently. That is why we observe different actions in the role of professors, though they are all in a corridor of behavior possibilities. If they behaved outside this frame, e.g., by skipping class and going to a football game instead, there would be negative consequences.

Not only the formal, explicit expectations of the role holders but also the informal, rather hidden and sometimes not-obvious expectations affect roles, role structures and role doing, which is negotiated in a process of interaction and might change dynamically over time. Such a negotiation is not a conscious process of people who interact. It is not that two people sit together and discuss how to act based on their role. Social interaction is more a complex phenomenon that takes place on many different levels and is often not 'seen' in the daily life of humans; it is rather grounded in the minds, in self-expectations as well as in conceptions, assumptions and perceptions constructed by different role holders.

A role emerges in conjunction with the variety of expectations and the specific patterns of consequences (positive and negative powers) that are attached to the role position and described in the 'right' way for the role actor. On the one hand, the options for actions are limited by the role definitions from all other system members. The role defines and constrains access to related resources and information. On the other hand, the role holders have access to certain alternatives. For example, persons in the position of an educational didactical developer access different information from the central examination office, the dean or the leaders at the university. This makes clear why organizations create roles. Roles coordinate role actors in certain positions, guiding them in their behavior and routines. Routines are everyday activities and tasks meant to reduce the complexity within a system. Roles then ensure a regular and predictable behavior that is the basis for continuous predictable interaction, thus satisfying a general social orientation (Turner, 1956).

A sociotechnical system like a university or a school is based on both explicit formal roles and informal, emerging roles, or implicitly developed roles. Both formal and informal roles underlie an interactive role development.

Problems arise, however, when functions and duties associated with the position change, when actors not only have one role but several, when they change the roles, and when the role expectations of the system members point to different behavior and lead to conflicts. Furthermore, roles change over time, and new roles emerge. This means that the requirements and expectations for a certain role emerge and develop over time. Depending on the actor and his understanding of the design of his role, the same role is played a little differently. Roles are not static; they are linked to ongoing learning activities, and they are negotiated and defined in processes by role holders, the system members and other reference groups.

Roles in a world of CrossActionSpaces have two functions. They first enable communication and define what can follow on what; second, roles also do hinder or limit communication, and the expectations give a frame for human action and what people do not do or which space they enter. Only in theory, people could enter all the millions of communication spaces. In practice, boundaries emerge due to decisions people made based on time limits, cognitive load restrictions or other resources.

Here is an interesting example. In January 2015, a girl in Germany used Twitter to express what she learned in school but also to emphasize what she did not learn. Roughly translated into English, she wrote, "I'm almost 18 and have no idea of taxes, rent or insurance—but I can write poem analysis in 4 languages" (Jan. 10, 2015, @nainablabla). She got 5,500 new followers in the first day, with more than 12,000 Twitter users marking it as favorite, and 6,000 retweets; traditional media also wrote her story. Later, she added in a newspaper interview that she thinks that she learned important things in school but emphasized again that this does not prepare her for real life. She was so overwhelmed by the reactions of the crowd that she even closed her Twitter account. She performed a multi-cross-action as I described in Chapters 1 and 2. By using Twitter, she communicated not only to her friends or her school; she also shared her view across established systems, with thousands of others, and got thousands of replies. This is one example of millions of things that people do act in multi-cross-actions. Besides the positive effect of her tweet that society started to think about the role of schools, interesting also is that she could use the same interactive media channels to find answers to her question for which she blamed the school. Perhaps she even did that and discussed the variety of different answers in school—if so, it is then an example of a reflective crossaction. She could easily ask 'how to do taxes, rent or insurances' on many other online networks. She could easily search for answers online. There are thousands of answers in the Internet. What hindered her? Why did she not do this?

One explanation is that roles do restrict such thinking. She has expectations of schools and teachers as well as expectations toward her own role as student. From the Twitter tweet, we can assume that she expects the school to tell her all the right answers. The problem is there is not a single right answer but very many possible useful answers available. This example makes the point how important it is for schools to discuss expectations. It shows how important it is for schools and universities to create conditions and designs for learning that support reflective multi-cross-actions and explicitly integrate designs for reflections on roles.

In summary, roles:

- Are not static, but highly dynamic phenomena;
- Underlie a continuous learning process of negotiation;
- Are more than implicit and explicit expectations, commitments and perceptions;
- Underlie a relative position to other roles, follow an agenda of functions and purposes;
- Exist as formal and informal roles, biological, cultural and assigned and taken roles;
- Are behavior and communication patterns—a person has several roles at the same and different times, places and situations;
- Are made in sociotechnical construction in interactive role doing;
- Follow a trajectory of role mechanisms like role assignment and role taking;
- Are an objective facticity—although made by humans over time, the next generation perceives the developed role as a strong socially manifested fact that affects communication and the behavior of individuals;
- Can be changed, and new roles can be developed; and
- Roles also create boundaries (coding and recoding of boundaries).

The different forms of role mechanisms are described in the section below. It is not possible to freely decide every type of role taking; for instance, taking biological roles (such as daughter and son, father or mother) can be considered as set—the decision to become a mother or father is open, but when the child is born, such biological roles cannot be changed (think about exceptions e.g., transforming gender roles; female, male and a third gender role offered in Sweden and Germany).

3.6 Teaching, Learning, Roles—Problems in Teachers' Roles and Students' Roles

The research field of computer-supported collaborative learning (CSCL) was a driving force in the discussion about the shift from considering "teaching as transfer of objective knowledge" to an understanding of learning as cocreation and "collaborative knowledge construction" (Stahl, 2006, 2013).

With this shift, new forms of social interaction lead to an extended variety of roles and role-playing in the context of teaching and learning. Studies of computer-supported collaborative learning in schools and higher education revealed that learners and teachers fulfill different formal and informal roles (Strijbos, Martens & Jochems, 2003). These roles characterize the sharing of various tasks during the learning process and lead to many different subroles. The students carry out typical sets of tasks in order to organize their collaboration (e.g., facilitation, documentation, triggering metareflection, etc.) or play the role of various experts with different levels of experience. The role of the teacher is also split up into more differentiated subroles. From a sociotechnical design perspective, the question is whether the roles can be formally 'implemented' or assigned to the learners by technical and organizational means, whether they mainly develop spontaneously (within the learning community), or whether a combination of both is the most common way for roles to evolve.

Teachers' Roles and Students' Roles

Imagine a school many years ago in the 1950s or even at the beginning of the 20th century, where the role of the teacher and the role of the student were clear to everyone. It was clear what the teacher's job was, and it was clear what to expect from her. The teacher was the expert, and her role was to give this knowledge to the students. The teacher's role was more or less balanced. The position, the purpose, the expectations and the role-play of teachers were in a balance—without judging the quality of the teacher's role. Some readers might say that the understanding of this former role of the teacher was quite bad, but that is not the topic in this paper. There was a balance, and the role was simple to be played; it was not complex at all. The teacher had the authority. School leaders, parents, politicians, and society all more or less agreed on the teacher's role; the ideal role of a teacher was not in question.

Then, many years later, Web 2.0 and social media were invented. Social structures have changed—at least, they have been affected by new technology (Jahnke, 2009). Suddenly, the students have access to information and are able to create new knowledge more easily than before. The students nowadays may download information to which the teacher also has access, and the students also have access to information that even the teacher does not. It is obvious that the innovation of technology such as Web 2.0 has affected student behavior. Students 'google' and search for information online during class to reflect what the teacher has said and use their own devices for performing different activities, for example, Internet surfing, playing, and communicating via social networking services. The students can easily solve a problem because of the easy access to information. Here, I want to stress that the students are able to solve a problem quickly nowadays, *independently* from the formal structures of the teacher's role and the school environment. Only 10 years ago, before Web 1.0 was launched, students had to go to the library to search for an answer; nowadays, people carry the knowledge with them on their mobile devices in their pockets.

So far, this is nothing new. Researchers and teachers know this situation. It is not new that a social media world affects teaching and learning as well as the understanding of the teacher's role. There are many demands to the teacher coming from outside the class, from parents, researchers and policy makers. The main problem nowadays is that these different demands are sometimes contradictory.

It is not new that the teacher's role suffers for various reasons. Why is there trouble with the teacher's role? The answer is simple: because different people have different expectations. What makes a good teacher? Different people in different positions would answer differently. The main point here is that the different expectations of the teacher's role do not match. Even if the teacher develops skills and competences to play many different informal subroles such as mentor, planner, assessor, supporter, or coach (Jahnke, 2010), the formal job description does not match. There is a huge discrepancy of the role description coming from different institutions outside and inside schools and higher education institutions; the role purpose and the different role expectations toward the role owner and how the actor plays the role of a teacher differ.

The effort, I argue here, is to illustrate—from a broader societal perspective— why the teacher's role still suffers by applying the advanced theory of social roles. Then, I make a proposal as to how the problem can be solved; in particular, I address how to enhance the development of the teacher's role from the perspective of Digital Didactics. One possible development is to understand teachers as "collaborative learners at the workplace" (Goggins, Jahnke & Wulf, 2013). Table 3.4 illustrates the situation.

The stability of the established educational institutions is based on explicit, formal roles and less on informal, emerging, implicitly developing roles. The role development for these roles is not as dynamic as roles in online communities such as Wikis. Communities have few formal roles but many dynamically developing

TABLE 3.4 A fictional example of teacher and student roles 100 years ago—*exaggerated*

Elements	The role of the teacher (50 years ago)	The role of the student (50 years ago)
Position	Hierarchical position, teacher is on the higher level than the student	Hierarchical position, student is on a lower level than the teacher
Purpose (function)	Teacher 'delivers' knowledge to the students	Student receives knowledge
Expectations	Society expects that the teacher does her/his job and educates the children in how to behave correctly in society	Student expects boring classes
Role doing	Teacher acts like a strong expert	Student sits and waits to receive the teacher's knowledge

informal roles. Perhaps the roles at educational institutions need greater flexibility and more explicit discussions about the 'roles' of teachers and students (such as the different expectations, purposes, role doing)?

The Teacher's Role and Why It Suffers

This advanced role theory is a plea for looking at roles, which makes clear how humans socially construct their reality. Social roles are in human minds, but they *become* a *reality* when humans act on their role expectations and inscribe the construction in the actions ("the social construction of reality" by Berger & Luckmann, 1993). This view on social behavior and society from the role perspective is useful when exploring patterns of group interactions within social systems such as organizations and institutions—the actors, the group and the system are parts of that role theory. The role theory explains the co-construction of knowledge by social actors situated in roles contextualized in social systems; the role serves as a mediator between the social actor and the social system:

Individual person ↔ situated in roles (teacher /student) ↔ school/university

A role is not a static phenomenon; it is rather a more-or-less ongoing, socially constructed formal and informal negotiation of actors and systems influencing each other. Roles are not suddenly *there* and do not suddenly exist or *appear*; roles always have a history, and this history forms the current understanding of a specific role, such as that of a teacher or student. To understand how roles developed over time, it might be useful to make the history visible; this is what I call the 'dynamics of social roles.' The dynamics of social roles also include the different role mechanisms such as role taking, role definition, and role assignment. From this theoretical perspective of social roles, it becomes clear why the teacher role suffers.

Table 3.5 wants to make clear that the teacher role today is not balanced. By 'balance' I mean that the four elements that constitute a role do not match; the elements are contradictory to each other, and the result is that a person in this role feels a strong conflict with regard to how to do the job correctly. The formal job description that describes the position of a teacher role does not match the different expectations, which the various other role owners (school and university leaders, parents, students and society in general) have; this does not fit into the role-play by the actors in the role of a teacher.

The other role owners 'see' a diffuse role-playing, and the actors in the teacher roles 'perceive' a diffuse feedback by the other actors. What makes a good teacher is not simple anymore; the ideal of a teacher varies. There is a second problem: the different stakeholders expect an ideal role and act as if there is an optimal teacher role. A closer look shows that there is no such single ideal image in a complex society; different images of a good teacher role exist. There are so many

TABLE 3.5 Why the teacher role suffers (with the example of history and future)

Elements	50 years ago	Today	50 years in the future?
Position	0	0	2
Purpose (tasks)	0	0	2
Expectations	0	1	2
Interactions based on role-playing	0	1–2	2
All the 4 elements, which constitute the role of the teacher . . .	Were in balance. The expectations more or less were fulfilled by the actors.	Are not balanced. A diverse picture; the formal job description (position, purpose) **does not match** the different expectations and **does not fit** the role-play by the actors. What is a good teacher today? Diverse and different answers available.	Will be developed and then balanced again. New names for the teacher role: learner-companion, process mentor, process designer. New names for student role: discussant, moderator, problem solver; → diversity of roles.

0 = how it was in earlier years; 1 = something changed over time; 2 = something new emerges

expectations, some of them contradictory. The teacher has to deal with these complex situations; different solutions such as competence development have been offered to them, but many of these solutions focus only on the *person* and neglect to develop the *role*.

What Can We Do?

What all stakeholders in educational institutions and teacher education programs have missed so far is that the schools, leaders and decision makers need to react by developing the position, purpose and expectations so that the *role* once again attains a balance. It is not enough merely to address the teacher's personal level—this is only one piece of the puzzle. In a broader perspective, there is an urgent need for multi-cross-actions in a didactics development (see Figure 1.2); in particular, 1) academic staff development, 2) curriculum development and 3) institutional development (including examinations) in schools and universities must support the changing needs of teachers' and students' roles.

A role-based analysis of teaching and learning in education is helpful to make the "multi-level actions" (Balog, 1989) visible. Knowledge sharing, learning and work processes (teachers are learners at the workplace), IT-structures and the behavior expectations of group members in networks and organizations are not separate from each other. Teaching and learning require an overall review in the context of dynamics of social negotiation within a space of negotiation.

The dynamics becomes particularly clear when the role holder performs differently than usually expected by the others. When the groups see a gap between expectations and the performance of a role holder, then social mechanisms such as negative sanctions come into play, which try to steer the role holder in the 'right' way—that is, as the reference group expects the right way to be—although there is, in fact, no 'right' way because there is always a range of different opportunities for action.

The design of the role doing is dependent on values and norms that exist within a group, community, network or organization. As illustrated in Giddens (1984), the role doing always refers to temporal and historical processes that have a duality: first, there is the role-playing (negotiation of the expected behavior) of members who interact; at the same time, there are already existing past rules, regulations, resources and values—a constructed but given reality—that are produced and reproduced, which limit the degree of freedom for role-playing.

Roles and Learning in a Networked World, Web 2.0

With regard to digital media, the challenge is designing such sociotechnical systems in teaching and learning that enable and encourage role doing and do not prevent active participation. This is not as easy as it seems because sociotechnical systems are often characterized by formal regulations for particular sociotechnical systems as part of an official organization. It depends on the right balance. Thus, the members of the schools and university are dependent on job conditions, and social synergies of a community can be lost, according to Whitworth (2009), when some members "steal" something from the other, such as time (waste of time), money (cheat), credibility (lies) and reputation (bad gossip). The interactive effect of knowledge sharing in communities can generate a huge benefit. However, the synergy for 'me' and 'the other' is only one possible type. Table 3.6 shows other forms.

Roles are of vital importance for cooperation and collaborative learning. They help to describe how cooperating actors are expected to behave, depending on their functions and tasks. Being closely related to social interactions and

TABLE 3.6 Effects in a networked world (from Whitworth, 2009, p. 17)

Outcome/Consequences for		The others		
		Benefit	Low effects	Loss
Me	Benefit	**Synergy**	Chance	Antisocial
	Low effects	Service	Nothing	Malicious
	Loss	Victim	Suicidal	**Clash**

expectations, roles provide a rich context, which may provide scaffolding for collaboration. This is especially important in technology-enhanced teaching and learning that requires building a common ground for social online presence.

3.7 Role Mechanisms—Assigned and Taken Roles

Roles in the context of learning can, on the one hand, be described by specific labels such as teacher, student, advisor, facilitator, examiner, examinee, freshman, mentor, tutor, etc. On the other hand, it can be defined in a conceptual way: a role comprises a set of patterns of behavior that include rights and duties, which are temporarily assigned to various role holders, but the role holder also has taken the role; she agreed to the role. For example, in different settings, a person will be seen as a child when the person is visiting his parents; the same person can also be a student when she is at university, and in discussions she takes the role of a facilitator to push the group forward—the role that one has taken is dependent on the context of the social setting and differs within societies. Accordingly, not a single dimension but rather a set of expectations, obligations and rights are addressed and communicated to the person who has taken the role. A role gives a name to a pattern of behavior conceptualized by humans in a social situation. The role actor behaves as he does because of the anticipation of possible rewards and punishments.

If the person does not behave as expected, there are diverse means through which the reference groups intervene to bring the person back to what the groups think is an appropriate way. We humans have a range of ways of behaving and ideas of what constitutes good behavior; when the behavior is outside of the circle, a society needs to develop new rules and roles. Sometimes, when this happens, a new understanding of roles and new roles emerge (role mechanisms).

The question is how expectations and behavior evolve into roles. Some researchers (cf. Herrmann, Jahnke & Loser, 2004) point out that expectations are a result of the position within an organization (school and university) that is presented by *role doing* (e.g., being a teacher, being a student—behaving like one), or what is called formal roles. Second, roles also develop informally through communicative interactions within an organization or a community (e.g., facilitator, opinion maker). Therefore, a differentiation between formal and informal roles is needed. The relevance of informal roles increases with the emergence of noninstitutionalized settings of learning (e.g., online communities).

Roles are both *facts* as well as *products* of social interaction:

Structure: Roles are *facts* that deliver the foundation for social interaction; roles exist as objective facticity (Berger & Luckmann, 1993). They become the structure in which people perceive roles as existing facts and external social 'installation.' The term 'installation' stresses the popular perception of a role such as father or mother, a manager at a bank or a teacher at school within a society. People have cognitive concepts about a popular role behavior in mind. The society or community itself 'defines' what 'popular' is. This is a complex social process in complex social structures (see Giddens, 1984). Roles are gradually developed to support the stability of organizations by repetition of social interaction patterns of expectations. The development of roles is accompanied by the shaping of interaction patterns for role taking and role making, etc. These patterns can metaphorically be described as role mechanisms (Herrmann et al., 2004).

Process: Roles are *products* of social interaction; roles are developed dynamically in social systems by repetitively perceiving social interaction patterns and expectations (e.g., the moderator, the decision maker, the informal leader, the opinion leader). Roles emerge in role doing within a process over time. The shaping of (new) roles depends on the characteristics of the persons who assume a role and on how they play it (role making) as well as on those who assign a role to others. However, these simply circumscribed dynamics are embedded in complex social structures within an organization, community or society. The most relevant patterns of role dynamics are role assignment, role taking, and role making, which are defined in the following sections.

Role Assignment and Role Taking (Role Distance, Role Change)

There are various types of role assignments. One or more persons assign a role to a person; the person can decide to take the role or not. A person assigns a specific role to another person by either urging her to take it, or the person takes a role voluntarily. This may happen by applying means of social sanctions and threats of negative consequences (a range of weak to strong consequences such as a serious talk or exclusion from the community). A person decides independently if she takes a role and other people (within the social system) will agree more or less.

A person takes a role, and she becomes a teacher, a student, a learner. She can decide to take the role, and the reference groups are able to decide about the role taking. Role taking indicates that a person acts due to the expectations of a specific role. These expectations can potentially be enforced by positive sanctions (rewards) or threats being imposed to the role holder. An individual role holder develops an individual attitude regarding the expectations of a role—even if she has already taken it—and she is able to reflect on her role. It is a mental distance to the role and means looking at one's own way of acting in the role (role doing). Role distance includes a competent, critical, evaluative attitude toward the expectations, which influence a role and vice versa. "Role taking . . . is a process of looking at or anticipating another's behavior by viewing it in the context of a role imputed to that other" (Turner, 1956, p. 316).

A person usually takes several roles or switches between them (e.g., a person can take the role of student, learner and informal conflict moderator in a class;

a person often is not a teacher *and* a student, but a person in a student's role could also take the role of a tutor, that is, a student who teaches other students in classes).

In principle, a person holds various different roles at the same time or in sequence (a role set, Merton, 1949) and individuals also change their roles. A role change means taking on a new role while giving up another: for example, one can be a scaffolder in a community, structuring a discussion, but also a regular contributor.

There is another aspect to consider: in computer science, there is the distinction between a *class*—a concept of a role, which may be taken by various persons—and an *instance*—a role being taken by a concrete person (role owner) (Jahnke, Ritterskamp, & Herrmann, 2005). In communities, the existence of a 'facilitator role' can generally be accepted at the level of the class. Nevertheless, not every person is allowed to take this role, e.g., groups prevent newcomers, newbies, and new members from being in powerful roles.

Development of Role Doing (Role Making, Role Conflicts, Role Definition)

Role making characterizes how a person acts in a role and how she transforms the expectations into behavior. Role making is embedded into interactive processes; it takes place in a process of social interaction, where people negotiate the expectations that are significant for a role (Goffman, 1959). A negotiation is not two people sitting together and discussing the role—it is a process that takes place during interaction and often proceeds implicitly and is not reflected on by the actors. And this is actually one problem in schools and universities; if communication about roles and role making took place, it would be useful in developing the teachers' and students' roles.

The driving force of role making is the difference between the role taker's individual attitude toward the role and the expectations that are assigned to the role by its social context, expectations assigned by the society, community, group or school/university organization.

The problem (from an organization's point of view) is that the role actor has a certain attitude to the role (role distance) and this attitude can differ from the original expectations (Goffman, 1972)—this causes an intra-role conflict.

If a person in an organization and community takes more than one role at the same time or switches frequently, a conflict between these roles can occur, which has effects for the person that holds the two conflicting roles (Merton, 1949). It results from the different demands of different roles, and the role holder needs to juggle these separate roles. For example, a person takes two roles, such as moderator and participant at the same time in a seminar. In the first situation, she structures the participants' discussion and therefore should take a neutral position; in the second role, she provides her own input and argues for her own opinion, and a conflict arises between the person's competing interests.

The Development of New Roles

Existing roles are dynamic and not static, such as the position. Roles can be changed, and new types of roles can emerge. A role gives a framework for humans as to behave and which tasks to perform. This framework varies over time. New tasks are added; some tasks are modified or the reference groups expect a changed behavior. Sometimes, the new expectations and social requirements produce new roles, or the role holder redefines the role (see Table 3.7).

Table 3.8 illustrates the differences of role mechanisms in social systems and technical systems. There is a gap between the social dynamics of role doing and the restriction in a technical system. For a networked world, where teachers and learners use an online or blended learning system, this means that technical systems often limit the social interactions and the evolution of new roles; that is, technical systems are required that allow the members to create metareflections and discussions on their roles.

When we follow the theory of didaktik (Chapter 5), which focuses on teaching as the creation of conditions for social relations to support learning, every teaching practice and every course and classroom needs to reflect explicitly on the teachers' and students' roles. A design for learning explicitly needs reflections of roles.

TABLE 3.7 From modifications and changes of human behavior to the emergence of roles

Type	Description	Examples
A modification of behavior	Person A lives the role A slightly differently than five years ago—an individual development without role development	Teacher A fosters more self-organizational parts in learning than five years ago
A modification of a role	Role X has been developed to Role Xi	The role of a teacher at a traditional university has developed to a teacher in a distance teaching university
Role changing	Person A in Role X changes to Role Y	Person A changes from learner role to teacher role
Development of new roles within a social institution (e.g., school, university)	Role Z is new in system A	A university needs social media administrators and roles that are responsible for data ethics
New roles in the world	Roles Q, R, S, are developing	New roles emerge, e.g., officer for data privacy, whistleblowers

TABLE 3.8 Support and nature of role mechanisms in social and technical systems (from Jahnke, Ritterskamp & Herrmann, 2005)

In social systems	*In technical systems*
Role Taking	
Although roles are often assigned by others to a certain person, this person has freedom to decide whether she takes the role or not. It depends on the role taker as to how far he or she accepts the rights and duties associated with a role.	A person can log into a system as a certain user to whom certain roles (which typically are conceptualized to be a named set of privileges) are assigned. A well-defined set of roles usually is taken with the login procedure. Although role changes within a single session are supported by some systems, this is not common: usually, a set of roles is strictly assigned to the session context.
Role Assignment	
Roles are assigned by others to a person (e.g., by a contract). That means that the person is allowed to take the role or is urged to take it under certain conditions. It may also be the case that someone assigns a role to themselves. Whether the assignment of a role takes place or is successful is often a matter of negotiation.	The assignment, as well as the withdrawal of roles, is handled very formally in technical systems and can best be described as a left-total relation between user accounts and roles, usually defined by an administrator. Therefore, assigning and withdrawing a role can be realized much more easily than in social processes.
	Assigning a role to someone is arranged by giving someone the right to use the system with a certain user identification. Therefore, assigning a role and withdrawing the assignment can be handled very formally and is far easier to enact than in social processes.
Role Change	
Giving up one role and taking another can be a very fluid transition, which is not always visible to others because it depends very much on the decision of the role taker. Role change can be realized in a tentative way, while checking how the social environment reacts—e.g., if someone moves from the role of a boss to a mentor.	Role changes within systems are very definite. They take place in one step and are highly visible. It is clearly defined whether someone can keep old roles when taking a new one or not.

Role Making

A role-owner can fulfill the role in their own way with respect to the expectations and can give new aspects of possible behavior while interacting in the role with others. Role making includes the possibility of being inventive in the way rights and duties are handled.

The privileges assigned to a role are highly determined and formally controlled by the system. There is no degree of freedom for the user to adapt the rights, for instance, with respect to learning processes.

Inter-Role Conflict

The different rights and duties of different roles being assigned to a person can lead to conflicts, especially in the case of frequent changes. A certain duty of Role A can be opposed to a duty of Role B. This might lead to conflicts that also have emotional impact for the role owner.

Inter-role conflicts are not and cannot be handled by the owner of the conflicting role. They are mostly of logical but not emotional character. However, the administrators or the system's managers have to decide how to reconfigure the system to avoid or diminish conflict.

Role Definition

Social interactions cause change to existing roles or create new roles. The potential owners of new roles are often integrated in the social process creating this role.

Role definition is more or less a technical process conducted by technically oriented administrators, often based on formal descriptions of an organizational structure. The role owner is not necessarily involved and details of how a role is defined are often hidden in the system's logical constraints.

3.8 Different Types of Roles—Informal, Implicit and Formal, Explicit

Following the previous sections, the question arises of how to capture roles and how to observe or measure them empirically. Is the CEO (chief executive officer) a role name? Is 'scaffolding' in learning a role? Is 'active participant' in a workshop a separate role? Is a friend or colleague a role? Are diverse learners perceived as different roles? Is acting as a role model a role? These questions make the overall question visible of when a communicative behavior, an expectation and a set of expectations, an activity and properties become a role and a role title. In clarifying this, the various types of formal and informal roles are relevant.

Linton (1936, p. 115) differentiates roles into "achieved and "ascribed" roles. Ascribed roles are those roles due to biological characteristics (age, gender) or attributed on the basis of their nationality. Examples of such roles are Swedish man, British mother, boy from the lower class, girl from the upper class ('It girl') etc. In contrast, achieved roles are such roles that an individual has taken himself, we have more or less chosen, and are relatively easy to set aside; for example, the roles of a teacher and a student.

Banton (1968, p. 33) supports this distinction; he called them "basic roles" that depend on the age and sex of a person, and "general roles," which are independent roles that are independent of the biological properties, or "recreational roles." Uta Gerhardt (1971, pp. 226ff) added to the independent roles the distinction between "situational, position and status roles." Dahrendorf (1958) distinguishes professional and recreational roles (both are assigned roles); he distinguishes between acquired and assigned roles.

The set of roles by Merton (1949) refers to the combination of role relationships; the role holder is in a network of related roles. Such a set includes partially different or contradictory expectations. The role holder must learn to deal with these conflicts and what she can do to resolve them. Gross et al. (1958/1966) show that roles are linked together in varying degrees. They assume that the structures of the role sets affect the role actors. Therefore, the institutional conditions need to be considered, analyzed and developed as well. And we have learned from the interactionists (read the sections above) that role actors can influence and change the structural institutional processes and conditions.

A role set describes the different roles an individual holds and also describes what different reference groups belong to it. For example, Ms. X is 24 years old (biological acquired role), is Swedish (ascribed role) and a student of mathematics (achieved role). Further assigned/taken roles are: she is a representative member of the student council, she is a friend of Catherine, she engages in sports in the karate club and she is a trainer for children aged 8–13 years. She is a daughter (biological role). To these roles, complementary roles also exist: for example, mother and father are the reference roles to the daughter role. The reference roles

TABLE 3.9 Descriptive categories of roles

Sociologists	Descriptive categories of roles
Linton, 1936	Distinction between ascribed and achieved roles
Merton, 1949	Role set, the complexity of the role doing
Dahrendorf, 1958	Difference between work and leisure roles Difference between assigned and acquired roles
Gross et al., 1958/1966	Roles are connected to different degrees and extents
Banton, 1968	Basic roles, general and independent roles
Gerhardt, 1971	Independent roles are situation roles and status roles

TABLE 3.10 Types of sociocultural roles with examples (Roles Type 1)

Roles Type 1	Description
Biosocial roles (come natural to somebody)	• Biological sex (male, female) • Roles by age (child, youths, adults) • Mother, father, daughter, son → These roles cannot be set aside.
Sociocultural roles	• Social milieu (person of lower, middle, higher class) • Nationality (e.g., German, British, Turk) • Gender: socially, culturally and socially learned gender roles of women and men → These roles are rather hard to change.

to the student role are, for example, colleagues, students, professor, faculty, and student council. Table 3.9 captures the descriptive aspects of a role set.

Linton, Dahrendorf and Banton differentiate roles in biological, ascribed and acquired roles (cf. Dahrendorf, 1958, p. 55). Table 3.10 lists the biological and ascribed roles.

A study by Bales (1950) indicates that in contrast to formal roles, roles are useful in helping the actors in groups to capture the communication structure. Bales investigated empirically small groups and could derive 12 patterns of behavior: "interaction patterns" (Bales, 1950, p. 9). These patterns show a dynamic group interaction of informal roles. Such informal roles, identified by Bales, were long neglected in sociological theories. To understand the whole picture and interplay of actors and to inform designs for teaching and learning, it is relevant to include informal roles to the discourse. I draw a difference between 1) assigned formal roles that are created by contract or through order and 2) assigned informal roles that develop more spontaneously in flexible interaction events. Table 3.11 shows these types of roles with examples.

TABLE 3.11 Types of assigned and taken roles; formal/informal roles (Roles Type 2)

Roles Type 2	Description
Assigned and taken **formal** roles (by formal contract/ job position, order)	• Professional roles / institutionalized roles (academic staff, students, examination offices at universities, cab driver, professional coach) • RBAC access roles, workflow roles (technical rights to access documents in technical systems; reader, member, coordinator) • Leader roles (manager, professor) • Activity roles (business roles), situation roles, functional roles (tutor, mentor, presenter, examinee, teacher, guest)
Assigned and taken **informal** roles (without formal contract, rather spontaneously, flexible, group dynamics)	• Communication roles, conversation roles (speaker, listener) • Mental roles (the dominant, the insulted person, the opinion maker) • Group dynamic roles (passive, active participants) • Leisure roles (card player, football fan) • Activity roles (business roles), situational roles and functional roles (knowledge brokers, knowledge takers, structuring agents, content providers, lurkers, car drivers)

Time Dimension

The development and emergence of informal and formal roles can be arranged on a time dimension to understand them better. This scale ranges from a rather short-term, quick role change to such roles that exist over a longer period (lasting role taking). The communication roles change relatively quickly depending on the community and institution. Two persons who are in a conversation change very frequently between the speaker and listener roles. This is different than a lecture at a university; the lecturer is about 90 minutes in the speaker role, if they do not allow any intermediate questions. In contrast, a professional business role usually is several hours a day.

A Set of Roles per Person

The role types show that a person never takes only a single role. A person has always taken biological-social, acquired and assigned roles at the same time. Depending on the situation, a person always has a formal and an informal role. The diversity of roles makes the analysis of roles and their impact on learning even more complex. The variety of role types is not clearly separated from each other. An institutionalized role can be a status role simultaneously. The variety is only an image of different contexts, for which different role terms are used, although the same role pattern is hidden behind it. Depending on in what roles the role of holder is, roles are perceived differently. For example, the role of a student advisor is from the perspective of students a status role, but from the perspective of senior researchers it is not perceived as such (Jahnke, 2006).

Role Complexity Within an Educational Institution

In addition to the variety of role types and sets that shows what roles a person has taken, a role complexity is the number of roles in relation to the people in an institution, i.e., it is composed of the number of roles that are in proportion to the number of role holders. A minor role complexity is present when there are just a few roles in relation to the number of role holders, for example, one role for 600 role holders (student beginners at the department of educational science) or three roles for 30 role holders (professors, academic employees). A high role complexity exists when many different roles exist, for example, 30 roles for 30 individuals, 100 roles for 1,000 actors.

A Role Name Depends

We also have to consider that a role name depends on the context, perspective and the role classification scheme (Role Type 2). The role of a moderator (facilitator) can be taken formally, in which a person who wants to supervise a workshop is formally determined or negotiated. The role also can be taken informally and spontaneously by another person during a session where the person takes scaffolding activities—due to different reasons, for example, the host is not prepared.

When Do Behavior or Properties Get a Role Name?

There is the need to clarify how a behavior or a property becomes a role. This requires a differentiation between formally (explicitly) and informally (implicitly) assigned roles.

Formal roles emerge when a social system performs new functions and tasks; it classifies and describes such new functions as one or more new positions. When the institution then finds a person who fills this position, a new role is born (e.g., officer for data privacy, evaluator for study programs, teacher supporter). Roles also occur in a system when within a system and its communication, new expectations are created that aim to ensure a certain expected behavior in the future. For example, a facilitating activity can become a role for coordinating activities developed into a formal coordinator role (e.g., chair of a meeting).

A social phenomenon, for example, a behavior or a property of a person, becomes a role when the person's behavior is assigned to a function within the institution, when the reference groups perceive the person's behavior as a pattern and start to 'normalize' the behavior. It becomes a new 'standard' that this new behavior is potentially enforceable and can be sanctioned positively or negatively.

An activity of a person also becomes a new formal role if she has signed or completes a contract. This is different to informal roles, where no contract exists.

New Formal Roles

An elderly woman and an elderly man are, due to the property 'old,' included in the council of elders and receive the role of experts. The reference group 'council of elders' decides that the two can have this role because they are 'old' and, in addition to their biological age, they have a lot of knowledge: they are assigned as 'wise.' Through a formal admission to the council, they are included in the membership of the institution. In general, such memberships are fixed in organizations with a membership contract.

A father, who is actively working for the school his daughter attends, gets the formal role of the parent-school speaker because he was formally elected by the reference group (other parents and teachers).

A person is a student when s/he has enrolled in a university. The role of student is a formally acquired role. A student formally receives the role of an examinee and master candidate if s/he has enough credit points and has applied at the examination office.

New Informal Roles

The development of behaviors and individual characteristics into informal roles depends on the following three criteria: 1) there is an observable behavior pattern or repetition of properties; 2) there is an expression of social relations, including the awareness that the person exists, the degree of her/his competence, and the degree of assertiveness; and 3) there emerges an idealized metaimagination of this new phenomenon, and the new role receives a name.

The development of informal roles is further explained below, under which a group no longer speaks at a group meeting only of structure-giving activities of a person but assigns the person the new role of 'coordinator,' 'scaffolder' or 'chair.'

1. Properties or behavior patterns develop into a role when the reference group is able to generate a bundle of expectations that can be assigned to the person that repeats this behavior expectation. This requires a reference group that observes such repeated operations several times.

2. Behavioral repetitions depend both on the duration of the behavioral observations and on the other group members of the reference group, i.e., to what extent the person is perceived (awareness) and her level of competence. It is necessary to distinguish whether it is a first-time meeting and whether the person is less well known or if the person is assessed as serious, technically competent or authoritarian. Another crucial factor is the enforcement ability (assertiveness) of the person who wants to take a new role and the enforcement ability of the other people within the reference group, i.e., whether other powerful people ensure that the repeated activities will be seen as a newly established role and attributed to the potential role holder or if no one takes the

step of supporting the person to get the new role. A role doing is always a dual-structured activity—the person who wants to take a role and the person of the reference group who allows or denies it; it is the interdependence of role taking and role assignment.

The reference group considers the aforementioned criteria and accepts the repeated behavior as a new role, for example, the new role of a coteacher. This decision usually does not start in an explicit discourse: 'We now sit together at the table and decide whether the repeated observed activities are to become a new role.' No. It is rather a more implicit happening in a group-dynamic process of interactive, implicit negotiation.

It does not have to be like this. A reference group can also assign roles and role acceptance to a person explicitly and a new role can be explicitly implemented. 'This will take too long, so we will be sitting here again tomorrow. I take this in my hands and decide what to do.' When a boss makes this statement at a team meeting, he will probably get this role. A person who is less well known as a facilitator may not get far with this behavior.

3. In addition to the criterion of repeated action, the criterion of the idealized meta-imagination toward a new role is crucial. The role of a meta-image means to have a picture of a designated ideal role in mind and how the role should be filled—an ideal role imagination includes a range of good and not-so-good role behavior from the position of the role holders and other role holders and the reference groups. Objectively, a 'good' role does not exist; it is socially constructed. A meta-image of a good and bad role behavior follows a socially constructed reality that is grounded on social negotiation processes and depends on different cultures and societies. The image of a 'good teacher' and 'good student' is shown *as if* it is an objective fact, *as if* it is the truth. In contrast to the idealized meta-image of a role, there are the images of a role self-perception taken by a person, i.e., how a person perceives the role. And there are the 'foreign-images,' i.e., as the reference group conceptualizes the creation of an allegedly 'good' role that is filled by a person. The reference group finally considers whether the person fits these meta-images, if he is a "good coteacher" or not.

With newly acquired roles, however, it is not certain that the person automatically acts according to the expected role behaviors. Role doing is based on role taking, role making and role performance and is an informal learning process. It is an active negotiation between the role holder and the reference groups. Behavioral and communication patterns do not per se emerge to a new role. The creation of a new role depends on the system; it is therefore relative. Therefore, one cannot speak per se of whether a person who has a certain property, e.g., stutters, is also in the role of 'stutterer' or if this is a property. It depends on the role holder, the reference group and the three criteria mentioned above.

3.9 Summary: Human Interaction Is Evolving Toward Multi-Cross-Action—Roles as Paradox, They Enable and Limit Cross-Action

Roles and role development depends on the position of the observer, the role holder and the reference groups such as other persons in other roles. Roles are not just there; it is a name for a developmental process of behavior clusters and communication patterns as social practice in a networked world.

The sections above illustrated that roles are useful for guiding and supporting individuals within an institution, but roles do also restrict actions and activities and limit a range of possibilities due to their own role expectation and due to different reference groups, which have different expectations. The reference groups are those that have the power for positive reward or negative threats to the role holder. The reference group is not a homogenous unit; it is a bundle of other diverse role holders with diverse interests.

This perspective shows that roles, built on complex interaction and communication processes over time, follow a duality (Giddens, 1984, duality of structure). Roles have two consequences for their actors. First, the roles restrict the opportunities for action and guide which information is at one's disposal and which is not available for a specific role but is available for another role. Second, some actions get rewards, while others entail costs.

To make a short summary here, in a digital networked world, roles give a frame for MultiCrossActions in relations that are condensed patterns of social interactions based on position, function, expectations and role doing. Roles are not static but a highly dynamic phenomenon changing over time and involving a continuous learning process of negotiation. They are more than implicit and explicit expectations, commitments and perceptions. They are in a relative position to other roles, which follow an agenda of partly hidden interests and exist as formal and informal roles, biological and assigned roles. A person holds and creates several roles at the same and different times, places and situations. Roles are made in and through sociotechnical constructions in interactive role doings. They follow a trajectory of role mechanisms such as role assignment, role taking and role development and build an objective facticity—although created by humans, the next generation perceives the developed role as a strong socially manifested fact that affects communication and the behavior of individuals. Seeing multi-cross-actions from this perspective of roles, they can be changed and new roles can be developed, but it often comes with a cost or conflict since different interests lead to a clash.

Roles are like a house—built by the parents as an ongoing project but manifested as an objective facticity for their children, who strongly believe they cannot put the house away; when the children are older, they build new apartments and houses.

Roles have a relevant impact on knowledge-sharing processes and learning. Roles limit multi-cross-actions and make it more difficult to learn. A design for teaching and learning is required that takes role-based learning into consideration and goes further; a new design is needed that makes the complex role structure and role actions visible; it is time for a digital didactical design that integrates the design for social relations and multiple roles in actions.

The impact of roles on learning is studied by March and Olsen (1975). They investigated that the action of an actor arises primarily from its role perception and not from the analysis of the situation. This problem is called role-dependent learning and "role-constrained learning"; it is a role-typical behavior. According to the studies by March and Olsen, a major barrier to knowledge sharing and deeper learning is the dependence of roles and the limitation of learners through their roles and the roles of the counterparts and reference groups. This means that learning by individual actors takes place from the perspective of their adopted roles. Learning processes are selected from the perspective of the role and thus significantly affect the progress of learning. Learners decide on the basis of their taken and assigned roles which knowledge is relevant and which does not appear as relevant. The role decides what information will be constructed, how and what kind of meaning will be derived and what actions are possible. The selection of knowledge is not 100% controlled by the role, but it is very strongly affected by the role that strongly affects the role holder. The role that has been assigned to a learner affects the selection of knowledge and the learning process.

When developed roles affect ways of teaching and learning, we need to learn to reflect on them and also to set our roles aside and develop new ones if needed.

In a nutshell, society often reduces actors and roles without seeing that an individual can take several informal and formal roles. For example, in educational institutions, it is often neglected that the person in a student and learner role is also a knowledge giver or the expert of something, and teachers are not only in the teachers' role; they are also educational designers and even learners at the workplace, for example, when they develop new ways for teaching and learning.

In a networked world that is understood as CrossActionSpaces in which offline and online are merging together metaphorically (Chapter 2), human interaction is based on communication patterns, oral and written, verbal and nonverbal communication, and it is 'organized' around expectations patterns, known as roles. Such diverse sets of informal and formal roles give a frame and corridor for Multi-Cross-Actions in Relations. Roles enable but also restrict or limit communication possibilities.

Multi-: Instead of using the traditional term of *interactions*, I have chosen the term multi- and multiple actions in order to stress that human action is more diverse and flexible than before the Internet era. Multiple interactions are possible at the same time in different settings using mobile technologies and interactive media applications. A person is able to act in a set of different online spaces, sometimes even at the same time—not with his or her physical body but with the capability to communicate in written forms and nonverbal and verbal forms.

Cross-Actions: Instead of using interactions, I have chosen *cross-actions* to stress that human action in the networked world is distributed 'across' traditional boundaries that take place in usual or unexpected spaces in different online and offline contexts, settings and situations. Interactive web-enabled media affects the expansion; dissolves and re-defines; and codes and recodes new and existing boundaries of social, sociotechnical system and co-expanded spaces (Jahnke, 2010).

in relations: I have added the term 'relations,' which refers to the mechanism of recoding boundaries, in order to emphasize that human interaction is evolving into multi-cross-actions but this happens in 'context' and creates new boundaries through its self-referential mechanism. Such spaces are context related. Every kind of human action is role based, and each role-based action builds new structures and boundaries. These structures are affected by already existing structures, rules and informal or formal roles, which develop and emerge over time.

In a summary, I define cross-actions as a highly dynamic type of human interaction and communication as a social practice happening through written, verbal, and nonverbal expressions. Cross-actions constitute CrossActionSpaces. There exist many different such spaces, and while conducting cross-actions new spaces emerge (co-expanded spaces), some exist over a longer period of time, others live shorter; multi-cross-action bridges existing technical and social systems but also happens across traditional and established system boundaries (e.g., communities, networks, sociotechnical systems). The space and its cross-actions are affected by existing and new roles and role behavior that enable and hinder the possibility of connectivity toward further communication in those spaces.

Learning is a form of reflective multi-cross-action but is limited due to existing roles. This is known as "role-constrained learning" (March & Olsen, 1975). Humans are born into a world where roles already exist as "objective facticity," but, of course, they can be changed regardless of what it would take to change them. Knowing that taken roles and assigned roles and the underlying rights, obligations and expectations affect us humans in our roles of students, teachers, leaders and decision makers, the question arises as to what kind of designs for teaching and learning we need in a networked world so as to support learning, and what kind of learning should be supported (Chapter 4).

3.10 References

Ashforth, B. E. (2001). *Role Transitions in Organizational Life, an Identity-Based Perspective.* Mahwah, NJ: Lawrence Erlbaum Associates.

Bales, R. F. (1950). *Interaction Process Analysis. A Method for the Study of a Small Group.* Chicago, IL: University of Chicago Press.

Balog, A. (1989). *Rekonstruktion von Handlungen.* Opladen, Germany: Westdeutscher Verlag.

Banton, M. (1968). *Roles. An Introduction to the Study of Social Relations.* London: Tavistock.

Berger, P. & Luckmann, T. (1993). *The Social Construction of Reality.* Frankfurt: Fischer. (Original work published 1967)

Biddle, B. J. & Thomas, E. J. (1966). *Role Theory: Concepts and Research*. New York: John Wiley.

Blumer, H. (1969). *Symbolic Interactionism: Perspective and Method*. Upper Saddle River, NJ: Prentice-Hall.

Dahrendorf, R. (1958): *Homo Sociologicus*. Opladen, Germany: Westdeutscher Verlag.

Ferraiolo, D., Cugini, J. & Kuhn, R. (1995). Role-based access control (RBAC): features and motivations. In: *Proceedings of 11th Annual Computer Security Applications*.

Gavrila, S. & Barkley, J. (1998). Formal Specification for role based access control user/role and role/role relationship management. In: *Proceedings of the 3rd ACM Workshop on Role-Based Access Control*. New York: ACM Press, pp. 81–90.

Gerhardt, U. (1971). *Rollenanalyse als kritische Soziologie [Role Analysis as Interpretive Sociology]*. Berlin: Hermann Luchterhand Verlag.

Giddens, A. (1984). *The Constitution of Society*. Cambridge: Polity Press.

Goffman, E. (1959). *The Presentation of Self in Everyday Life*. Garden City, NY: Doubleday.

Goffman, E. (1972). *Encounters: Two Studies in the Sociology of Interaction*. London: Allen Lane, pp. 85–132.

Goggins, S., Jahnke, I. & Wulf, V. (2013). *CSCL@work, Computer-Supported Collaborative Learning at the Workplace*. New York: Springer.

Gross, N., McEachern, A. & Mason, W. (1966). Role conflict and its resolution. In: B. J. Biddle & E. J. Thomas (Eds.): *Role Theory. Concepts and Research*. New York: John Wiley & Sons, Inc., pp. 287–296. (Original work published 1958)

Harrison, R. (1972). Role negotiation—a tough minded approach to team development. In: W. W. Burke & H. A. Hornstein (Eds.): *The Social Technology of Organization Development*. Fairfax, VA: NTL Learning Resources, pp. 84–96.

Haug, F. (1994). *Kritik der Rollentheorie [Criticism of the Role Theory]*. Hamburg: Argument-Verlag. (Original work published 1972)

Herrmann, Th. & Kienle, A. (2003). Kolumbus: context-oriented communication support in a collaborative learning environment. In: T. J. van Weert & R. K. Munro (Eds): *Informatics and the Digital Society. Social, Ethical and Cognitive Issues*. Boston: Kluwer, pp. 251–260.

Herrmann, Th., Jahnke, I. & Loser, K.U. (2004). The role concept as a basis for designing community systems. In: F. Darses, R. Dieng, C. Simone, & M. Zackland (Eds.): *Cooperative Systems Design*. Amsterdam: IOS Press, pp. 163–178.

Ilgen, D. R. & Hollenbeck, J. R. (1991). The structure of work. Job design and roles. In: M. D. Dunette & L. M. Hough (Eds.): *Handbook of Industrial and Organizational Psychology*. Vol. 2. Paolo Alto, CA: Consulting Psychologists Press, pp. 165–207.

Jahnke, I. (2006). *Dynamik sozialer Rollen beim Wissensmanagement. Soziotechnische Anforderungen an Communities und Organisationen* (Dissertation, DUV/VS Springer, Wiesbaden).

Jahnke, I. (2009). Socio-technical communities: from informal to formal? In B. Whitworth & A. de Moor (Eds.). *Handbook of Research on Socio-Technical Design and Social Networking Systems*. Hershey, PA: Information Science Reference, IGI Global, pp. 763–778.

Jahnke, I. (2010). Dynamics of social roles in a knowledge management community. *Computers in Human Behavior*, 26 (4), pp. 533–546. doi:10.1016/j.chb.2009.08.010

Jahnke, I., Ritterskamp, C. & Herrmann, Th. (2005, November 3–6). Socio-technical roles for socio-technical systems: a perspective from social and computer science. In: *AAAi Fall Symposium: Roles, an Interdisciplinary Perspective*, Arlington, VA.

Krappmann, L. (1977). *Soziologische Dimensionen der Identität [Sociological Dimensions of Identity]*. Stuttgart: Klett-Verlag.

Linton, R. (1936). *The Study of Man*. New York: Appleton-Century-Crofts.

Luhmann, N. (1995). *Social Systems*. Stanford, CA: Stanford University Press.

March, J.G. & Olsen, J.P. (1975): The uncertainty of the past-organizational learning under ambiguity. *European Journal of Political Research*, 3(2), pp. 141–171.

Mead, G.H. (1934). *Mind, Self and Society*. London: University of Chicago Press. (Original work published 1934)

Merton, R.K. (1949). *Social Theory and Social Structure*. Glencoe, IL: Free Press/Macmillan.

Montgomery, J. (1998). Toward a role-theoretic conception of embeddedness. *American Journal of Sociology*, 104, pp. 92–125.

Nadel, S. (1969). *Theory of Social Structure*. London: Cohen & West. (Original work published 1957)

Nonaka, I. & Takeuchi, H. (1995). *The Knowledge Creating Company: How Japanese Companies Create the Dynamics of Innovation*. New York: Oxford University Press.

Nyanchama, M. & Osborn, S. (1999). The role graph model and conflict of interest. *ACM Transactions on Information and System Security*, 2(1), pp. 3–33.

Parsons, T. (1951). *The Social System*. London: Routledge & Paul.

Sandhu R., Coyne, E., Feinstein, H. & Youman, C. (1996). Role-based access control models. *IEEE Computer*, 29, pp. 38–47.

Sievers, B. & Beuer, U. (2006). Organizational role analysis and consultation: the organization as inner object. In J. Newton, S. Long & B. Sievers (Eds): *Coaching-in-Depth: The Organizational Role Analysis Approach*. London: Karnac, pp. 65–81.

Simon, R. & Zurko, M. (1997). Separation of duty in role-based environments. In: *Proceedings of 10th IEEE Computer Security Foundations Workshop*. Rockport, MA: IEEE Computer Society, pp. 183–194.

Stahl, G. (2006). *Group Cognition: Computer Support for Building Collaborative Knowledge*. Cambridge, MA: MIT Press.

Stahl, G. (2013). Theories of collaborative cognition: foundations for CSCL and CSCW together. In: S. Goggins & I. Jahnke (Eds.): *CSCL at Work*. Vol. 13 of Springer CSCL Book Series. New York: Springer.

Strijbos, J.-W., Martens, R. & Jochems, W. (2003): The effect of roles on group efficiency. In: B. Wasson, R. Baggetun, U. Hoppe & S. Ludvigsen (Eds.): *International Conference on Computer Support for Collaborative Learning 2003*. Bergen: Intermedia.

Turner, R. (2006). Role theory. In J. Turner (Ed.): *Handbook of Sociological Theory*. New York: Springer, pp. 233–268.

Turner, R.H. (1956). Role taking, role standpoint, and reference-group behavior. *American Journal of Sociology*, 61, pp. 316–328.

Whitworth, B. (2009). The social requirements of technical systems. In B. Whitworth & A. de Moor (Eds.): *Handbook of Research on Socio-Technical Design and Social Networking Systems*. IGI Global, pp. 3–22.

4

LEARNING AS REFLECTIVE CROSSACTION

The Example of Learning Expeditions

Things are not what they seem, and appearances are certainly not the whole of the story. This need to look behind appearances in careful, detailed and systematic ways is, of course, the common inspiration of all scientific and investigative work.

(B. Anderson, 1997)

In the earlier chapters, I proposed to see our digital networked world from the perspective of CrossActionSpaces where offline and online settings are smelting together. Such spaces are full of potential for communication; they are made through communication but also restricted and limited by roles that the actors play and the expectation patterns the actors have (Chapter 2). When human action is changing toward several cross-actions (Chapter 3), we can ask what learning is. Learning in such a world that is full of communication spaces is *reflective* doing and conducive of reflective cross-actions. In this chapter, I illustrate what this means, how it can be understood, how reflective multi-cross-actions can be characterized and what it requires to design for them. I use the example of learning expeditions to clarify reflective cross-actions, how it can be used in classrooms and how to design for learning expeditions. Since it is a highly dynamic set of cross-actions, the term 'multi-cross-action' refers to this phenomenon.

In recent years, learning has been understood as a process in which learners solve specific assignments in different steps and, at the end of their study, have completed several steps to get the degree of a study program. The term 'process' was important to viewing learning as a project that can be designed in different ways. Learning does not just happen to us; it is an active process of co-construction of new knowledge and skills. Learning is the development of competencies. However, the term 'process' often implies that all participants go straight ahead in order to reach the goal and neglects the fact that learning needs back-and-forth steps. Learning takes place in 'curves' and does not happen in straight lines. Detours are relevant for learning. We also learn by making mistakes and reflecting about them afterward. Sure, not all mistakes are useful for a learning progress; some of them are better to avoid. The point here is that learning might be seen from the viewpoint of designing for 'expeditions.' Learning processes evolve into learning expeditions that is grounded on the two levels of making and reflection.

Learning takes places in many different forms. For example, it is biochemical activity in the brain, it is remembering, it is conceptual change, it is a change in behavior, it is knowledge construction, it is social connectivity, and it appears in many other forms as well. "So what is learning? It is all of these" (Jonassen, Howland, Moore, & Marra, 2003). Therefore, it is crucial for every person who writes about learning to define learning or lay a focus. In this book, learning is understood as reflective communication; more specifically, it is reflective cross-action.

Learning in a networked world takes place across established systems, networks and communities. A learning expedition in the digital era is, then, the reflective making of CrossActionSpaces, which includes various steps and detours—and those detours are relevant for learning. A *learning walkthrough* presupposes a rather designed learning landscape more closely guided by teaching but with a greater variation and more student options for working and learning than the traditional course, while *learning expeditions* stand for more open-ended, problem-based learning paths and/or for goal/objective-oriented learning (to master X or understand the implications of Y) where the learning methods and instruments are very open (Jahnke et al., 2014).

In this book, I use reflection as a concept where people interact, connect to other resources, make choices and decisions, can explain why they are doing what and how they are doing it, and can say why this is useful for their learning progress, taking ethical considerations into account.

4.1 How Education Has Been Understood for Many Years

In 2000, Brown and Duguid delivered the message in their book *The Social Life of Information* that "we must look beyond mere information to the social context that creates and gives meaning to it." They made it clear that there is an urgent need to go "beyond the simplicities of information and individuals" by creating social interactions using new technologies. This insight is a great one, but has education so far developed in this direction?

The use of ICT has focused on "transportation for education" (Jahnke & Norberg, 2013). Education is understood as if it could be delivered to students. However, learning itself can never be delivered or transported from one person to another. We can only provide opportunities and conditions, more or less structured situations, in which students are able to learn; of course, it is possible to 'scaffold' learning.

> Distance learning made some motivated students happy to finally get access to education, but other students ended up lonely, with lost passwords and half-completed courses, ensuring they would never try again. . . . Teachers with older educational conceptions . . . had almost all learning drowned in a tank of water full of information. . . . But we all know, deep within, that this was all about *information*. It was not about learning and not about knowledge. Since long time, we had our bookshelves full of books and materials without knowing and being able to use the information therein.
>
> (Jahnke & Norberg, 2013)

We see the trend that teaching spaces are increasingly becoming learning spaces; for example, the flipped classroom is the inverted use of campus and personal learning spaces. The use of ICT in classrooms and courses is becoming more natural. To a greater and greater extent, ICT is being used for effectiveness and to support quality enhancements in a more profound way than at the beginning of the 21st century. ICT supports flexibility and gives qualitatively and quantitatively better access to education than in past years (Ehlers, 2013).

The expression 'distribution of education' is, however, unfortunate, as it does not accurately express the concept. It is not possible to deliver or distribute learning as products to households. 'Distance learning' is also a critical term; we do not learn *in* the distance, we learn in our heads and minds, while learning is often triggered via interaction. We have still not developed suitable words for what is happening. Our understanding is lacking. A new discourse has still to be constructed.

'Blended learning' is one of the few expressions that seem to allow a new teacher-created, bottom-up interpretation, using both the online environment and the physical surroundings (Sharpe, Benfield, Roberts & Francis, 2006). Some courses at universities are still a blend of places, focusing on the distribution of content online and teaching in classrooms as a kind of 'half-distance' education. Other educational developers go beyond this and concentrate on how ICT and interactive media can enhance the process of learning, using 'places' as designable and combinable tools.

Offline and online are still perceived as two worlds; one we inhabit, the other we visit by log-in procedures. But terms such as 'digital natives' and 'digital immigrants' are no longer such correct metaphors because the digital dualism is blurring. The online world is still sometimes, but not often, called virtual, in the sense of 'not real.' However, as Floridi argues, we are probably the last generation that makes a clear difference between on- and offline worlds (Floridi, 2007). How, then, does formally structured education look in the future? It is unlikely that higher education will be *in* the Internet as a place. It is unlikely that a search engine would take it all over and solve the problems of education. Business as usual is also unlikely. There is obviously a need to rethink how education works in time and space and to form new *process designs* (Jahnke & Norberg, 2013).

In 1995, Barr and Tagg wrote that there is a need to develop higher education from teacher-based approaches to more learning-centered designs. Since this statement, the plea is still there, but more and more teachers and educational developers can be found who do apply new learning designs (Jahnke & Kumar, 2014a, 2014b).

Adopting the concept of the social construction of reality by Berger & Luckmann (1967/1993), the digital natives are the next generation of digital immigrants who perceive the mediated reality as "objective facticity," which they cannot wish away. Web 2.0 and social media have become an external, compelling fact facing them. The use of new media such as Web 2.0 and the associated sociotechnical actions have evolved as habitualized actions and are taken for granted. New routines have been established. The Internet has become such an objective facticity for digital users who were born into this world of Internet and social media—as the older generations were born into a world of TV and radio.

To explain the social phenomenon of social media and its dynamics in a broader framework, the underlying theoretical approaches are useful. In particular, these are mediatization "media ecology" (Krotz, 2008; Lundby, 2009), media-constructed awareness and the sociotechnical approach (e.g., Herrmann, 2009; Fischer, 2007; Mørch & Skaanes, 2010). These approaches stress the duality of social processes and their interwoven structures as a "wicked problem" (Conklin, 2005). New media affects society, and "media is integrated into the operations of social institutions" (Hjarvard, 2008); on the other hand, society designs new forms of communication. Media is formed by society but also has become an active agent that influences human interactions (Giddens, 1984, "Duality of Structures"; structures are outcomes of the practice of society and serve as mediums). The Actor-Network-Theory (ANT; Latour, 2005) puts a third agent into play. Technologies and artifacts become an active agent in a network of human actions driven by different technologies.

The media-constructed social awareness approach underlines that people live in a media-constructed world with a difference between a socially constructed 'reality' and 'reality *given* by different media.' A given reality is perceived as a form of reality that is constructed by others, which the individual cannot wish away.

When new technologies transform over time into an 'old, already there object,' I call this objective facticity (adapted by Berger & Luckmann, 1967/1993); that is, people do not have influence or they do not have enough resources to change this object, although it is constructed by society and might be changeable.

Our school system serves as such an objective facticity. We see educational institutions as such an 'objective fact.' It is hard to change the routines, although these social institutions, structures and processes are changeable—regardless of what it would take to affect some changes. When we compare the Internet and social media structures with our established educational institutions, we perceive a difference; the first seem more vivid and actors are prosumers, while the second has established structures and defined roles, and change and development take longer.

In the past years, new forms of learning have emerged, as also argued by John S. Brown (2009), who writes: "Whatever your particular interest is, there is some niche community, already formed on the network you can join. . . . These resources not only provide facts. They are also tools you can use to build things to tinker with, to play with, to reflect on, and to share with others. And most importantly, you will learn from other people's comments and from what they do with your creations" (Brown, 2009, p. x).

Because complex societies need teams of workers, collaboration is one important aspect in learning today (Stahl, 2006). It is not possible anymore to collaborate efficiently without having social media; for example, think about how easy it is to share and create new information online.

> "Technological innovation is breaking out in administrative offices with data systems and among students with gaming, leaving the teachers behind to maintain their traditional classroom practices. The pressure to change the classroom with computing is coming from outside the classroom, in different forms from children and families and central offices."
>
> (Collins & Halverson, 2009, p. 127)

We currently do not know if formal schooling will be replaced or not, but new forms of both formal and informal learning will emerge around the edge of formal schooling (Brown, 2009). For example, read the project PLACES (Cerratto-Pargman et al., 2014) and our case of InPUD (Jahnke, 2010). InPUD is an informal online learning community and is part of a formalized computer science study at a university. Research showed a change in communication, distributions of information and shared knowledge, which together supported the formal study better than without it (read Jahnke, 2010, in detail). Social media affects the relationship between formal schooling, informal learning out of the school and collaborative learning in the workplace (e.g., Goggins, Jahnke & Wulf, 2013). These studies illustrate a transformation in education and learning through innovation in mobile computing (Tuomi-Gröhn & Engeström, 2003). Fischer (2011) stresses such new forms of lifelong learning as "cultures of participation." New questions emerge: to what extent and in what ways do actors in educational institutions in formal schooling reflect on their understanding of learning toward a culture of participation?

A new understanding of learning is also provided by George Siemens. In his concept surrounding "connectivism," he illustrates how existing information can be connected via an online network and its nodes; this is his central metaphor for learning. The idea is that any node (e.g., textual information, data, images, videos, figures) can be connected to another node. Learning in this approach is defined as "the process of creating connections and developing a network" (Siemens, 2005), where decision making is the central part of the learning. "Choosing what to learn and the meaning of incoming information is seen through the lens of a shifting reality. While there is a right answer now, it may be wrong tomorrow due to alterations in the information climate affecting the decision" (Siemens, 2005). With the idea of massive open online courses (MOOC), Siemens provides new ideas about an open model of education that is supported by new technologies.

Laurillard (2008) specifically discusses different pedagogical forms of mobile learning. She uses Kolb's "learning cycle" (1984), wherein learning includes a concrete experience, reflective observation, abstract conceptualization and active experimentation by learners. According to this cycle (Laurillard, 2007, pp. 163–164), designers and teachers have to ask if the design of mobile learning motivates and enables students to access content material, theory, ideas or concepts and ask if the design motivates learners to ask questions and offer their own ideas to the teacher or their peers; if the design motivates learners to use their understanding to achieve the task goal by adapting their actions; if the design motivates learners to repeat the practice by using feedback that enables them to improve performance; if the design motivates learners to share their practice outputs with peers for comparison and comment; if the design motivates learners to reflect on the experience of the goal-action-feedback cycle; and if the design motivates learners to debate their ideas with other learners and then reflect on their experience by presenting their own ideas and report designs (productions) to peers and to teachers.

This approach might be a good starting point for reflection on designs for teaching and learning; it is not restricted to a design for mobile learning. Mobile learning is a huge field, and different understandings of mobile learning are available. Some people conceptualize mobile learning in terms of devices and technologies, while others focus on the mobility of learners and the mobility of learning. Kukulska-Hulme (2012) provokes whether the devices are becoming smarter and people less smart. Further, others stress the learners' experience with mobile devices (Traxler, 2009). In addition, Sharples et al. (2005), Sharples (2006) and Pachler (2007) stress the importance of a theory of "mLearning" and a new research agenda. The approaches have in common that they argue that we have to look beyond the existing classroom concepts—and mobile learning is one possible concept to go in this direction.

4.2 Beyond the Concept of the Classroom

The studies on mobile learning (see for example the London Mobile Learning Lab) make clear that the classrooms and course concepts that underlie a room metaphor are blurring. Physical rooms are not the only space where we learn. For a long time, education has been seen like a 'house'; students went to this educational 'house,' and within these given structures and building blocks they created their own learning trajectories—but they could not revise the framework or the house. This has changed. In the age of digital media, it becomes clear that learners are not only part of the educational house, they also construct this house every day anew—especially when they use interactive mobile technology and media tablets.

Ilona Buchem's work on "open badges" (Buchem et al., 2012) shows how the students build their own educational house. In her words, we have to change the perspective. We look on schools and universities and see a fixed building with fixed structures; but when we change the perspective toward concepts such as Bring Your Own Device (BYOD), it becomes clear that the formal buildings are just empty. Instead, the students use different and diverse building blocks, in the forms of new Internet-based applications, and rebuild the university learning houses in their everyday interaction online and offline. The classroom-and-course metaphor has its limitations, as Anders Norberg wrote when examining the concept of "blended learning" (Norberg & Jahnke, 2014). Instead, educational actors need the support for creating more opportunities for learning processes.

When we start with the concept of CrossActionSpaces and see the world from these eyes (Chapters 1 and 3), we can see that new designs for learning are needed. When we shift the focus from traditional teaching aimed at *textbased learning or textbook learning* in the direction toward learning as reflective cross-action, we then need a new understanding and concept of learning that includes designs for learning when the answer is not known—designing learning for students 'as if' the answer is not known. Such a design not only focuses on content, where textbook reading is the aim, but creates learning expeditions. For example, a national-park event is not arranged around reading a textbook; it is rather an activity for students to connect with materials from the reality outside books, guided by some instructions for learning from exploring and studying specific questions within such an expedition. A design for learning transforms the metaphor of a national-park event to classroom learning. It is then built on several cross-actions, such as searching for information, findings first answers, searching for new information, exploring, studying, and reflecting and doing it again, whereas textbook learning is just one single action based on reading the book. In a learning expedition, textbooks could be part of the learning expedition, but using textbooks would never be a standalone activity.

New technologies and interactive media can be useful to foster this new type of learning expedition in a constructive alignment (Biggs, 1996; Jahnke, 2011; Mårell-Olsson & Hudson, 2008). Such new ways of teaching may include "networked scaffolding" (Tammets, Laanpere, Ley & Pata, 2013) and "collaborative reflections" (Prilla et al., 2013). An appropriate balance between content, creation and reflection transforms learning into a deeper learning experience. Reflection in social learnerships is the key. There is no learning without reflection (Kolb, 1984). Learning without reflection and without a social group is merely behavior without further development.

Although it is well-known that learning needs reflection, many designs for learning often do not include explicitly the layer of process-based reflections. My point here is that textbook learning is not enough, as we need classrooms where the *problem* is at the center and the students are able to learn what they want to learn rather than what they have to learn. With a *problem* at the center, students can become creative in order to solve this problem—they are able to perform reflective cross-actions. Teaching has then the function of designing and creating conditions for CrossActionSpaces, for making and for reflection. This fosters critical thinking and creative practices. With a problem at the center, learners develop a set of diverse skills in informal-*in*-formal settings (Jahnke, 2012; Hyllested, 2014).

However, that leads us to a new question. What is a real 'problem' that is useful for application in teaching for learning?

When the 'problem' is at the center, we have to answer what a 'problem' is. Students receive assignments to solve a problem in order to create skills, not to solve a routine task. A problem is a real problem where the students can use different ways to find a solution. The degree of problem solving depends on its difficulty. The solution is known to the teacher or there is no solution so far, the solution is unknown, and the students may express themselves in many different ways.

For example, in our study of Danish and Swedish tablet-classrooms, we saw some designs where the teachers created such assignments toward a learning expedition (Jahnke & Kumar, 2014a, 2014b). Teachers asked the students to create a product of what they learned; such products were, for example, short movies, digital book trailers, multimodal interactive books, digital paintings, Educreations videos, and videos from physical and chemical experimental settings. Students understood the possibility to be in a new role of producers and makers. The cases also illustrate how teachers created new conditions for learning. They used the media tablets in such ways that students were supported to 'do,' conduct and reflect their cross-action.

A routine task is when the students get an assignment in which they have to apply a given method to find the one and only correct solution. Although the task might be difficult for some students, it is merely a routine task requiring exercises and repetitions and does not need any creativity. Bergqvist and Bergqvist (2014) study shows the teachers' difficulties in designing such real problems. Teachers get no or little support in redesigning learning from routine tasks into 'real world problems.'

To define a real problem, the studies by Lave and Wenger (1991) are useful, especially their five characteristics of "situated learning" that help to define a real problem; it includes an authentic case. It is a complex case. Multiple perspectives on the case are supported and possible. Group interaction is required for solving the case. Articulation and reflection are needed to solve the case properly.

4.3 Who Learns? We All Do! And Who Has Knowledge? We All Have—It Depends on the Situation

Teachers are both owners of knowledge but also workplace learners.
Students are both learners and owners of knowledge.

Actors in and around education often think that the roles are clear: students are learners, and teachers are the experts. This might be true in some situations, but this perspective is too narrow. When we think like this, we have ideal 'roles' in mind but do not value the person who is in such a role. Another problem is that roles are not static; they change and blur.

The person in the student role is a learner, but the person also has knowledge; she is both owner and creator of knowledge and a knowledge giver. Students are not only learners. They are also experts in some areas. However, it is often unknown, or is not clearly seen, how much knowledge pupils and students have. It is one effort of the didactical design to recognize and value students as persons who have already gained experience. But, clearly, schools, students and teachers have expectations about the others, and such diverse expectations need to be made explicitly with the aim to discuss possibly contradictory expectations and how to solve those. To put roles and expectations on the table for discussion, at least to clarify them, might help to avoid social problems in the classroom.

The person in the teacher role is a knowledge scaffolder but also a learner, for example, when she develops new ways of learning enhanced by digital media. Teachers are not only experts; they are also workplace learners. They are designers of teaching processes and designers of learning opportunities. While creating activity-driven designs, they are learners on the way toward finding a suitable design for a classroom. When we see teachers as learners, there is much more potential to understand the different roles they take—they are not experts in everything; they are mentors for student learning, but they are also information seekers and need support in finding appropriate pedagogies and technology design in their desire to support student learning.

Who learns? We all do. It depends on the situation and the roles we take or have been assigned. What I wish to stress is that the conception of teaching and learning is too often too unidimensional. Humans tend to try to make it easy, but this misdirects the complex development of teaching and learning.

4.4 From Course-Based Learning to Learning Expeditions

Learning is an ongoing process of the construction of new knowledge. It is a proactive process of constructing rather than acquiring knowledge (Duffy &

Cunningham, 1996). Individuals create a sense of their own world and give meaning to it. They make sense of the information around them: they are meaning makers. Everything with which they come into contact is constructed by their own models of their experience. Hence, learning is not defined as simply the transmission of data from one individual to another but a social process whereby knowledge is coconstructed in a situation within an offline and online community. Learning is about moving from peripheries into the core of a "community of practice" (CoPs) where the learners have different learning trajectories (Wenger, 1998; Stewart, 1996).

I build on the idea of a learning trajectory by Etienne Wenger (1998). From an education viewpoint, a learning trajectory can be supported by a learning walkthrough (Jahnke et al., 2010) that develops into a learning expedition (Jahnke et al., 2014).

Learning trajectories and learning processes are cognitively constructed and socially framed. Teaching processes and instructions support and scaffold such a learning construction (Bruner, 1961, 1967). We cannot deliver learning; educational institutions may provide conditions and opportunities to foster, scaffold and enable learning. Current discussions in education concentrate on shifting the focus from the teacher's teaching to the student's learning, e.g., in adopting e-portfolios, creating personal learning environments (PLE), and using learning badges and learning expeditions where the student becomes a prosumer.

Promoting concepts for the shift from teacher-centered to student-centered learning concepts is not new. However, discussions about pedagogical learning approaches received a new drive as new community platforms based on Web 2.0 technologies emerged. For instance, platforms for user-generated content such as Wikis, blogs and social networking platforms (Jahnke, 2009) provide new opportunities to bring the real world outside a classroom into the learning situation. Through web-enabled technology, educational institutions (schools, universities) are able to connect learning to the real world; it is easier to connect the 'two' worlds.

An often-used expression is blended learning, which tries to mix between offline and online learning situations. In fact, it never was pure distance or online learning; it is rather distance and online teaching. Blended learning has often been used as an approach that combines individual and cooperative learning with opportunities to interact with other course members online and face to face, but, as Norberg and Jahnke (2014) explored, what elements can really be blended and mixed? In a small European study, we asked researchers and instructors for their views on blended learning. One reply was, "Are you working in the kitchen?" A European researcher replied to us, asking what blended learning meant (Norberg & Jahnke, 2014). The study discusses the different perspectives on blended learning; on the one hand, it is not a useful term for researchers because it is not clear enough, while on the other, this term makes it open and useful for teachers as it stresses a mix of traditional processes and new pedagogies. Besides blended learning, there are several other terms that are also not clear enough, for example, online learning and e-learning. What all have in common is that they underlie a course-driven concept—teaching is organized around meetings at a special time and place, offline or online. Those concepts have in common that they stop here and do not integrate how to support learning. Instead, teaching *becomes* learning—which is a problem because teaching does not mean that students learn. Those concepts neglect the potential for creating conditions for learning processes and learning expeditions. Instead of arranging learning around meetings (lectures, seminars or workshops), it might be fruitful to organize learning from the perspective of a 'process.' Then, the question is not how often do teachers and students meet but what teachers need to do to support student learning.

In a modern networked world, in which information is almost everywhere and available online, the 'course' concept is old-fashioned. Instead of thinking in 'courses,' a new term is more appropriate. We call it a 'learning expedition' (Jahnke & Norberg, 2013).

4.4.1 A Candidate for Learning Expeditions: Research-Based Learning Situations (Inquiry-Based Learning)

With the newer concept of research-based learning, the idea was born to rethink learning toward a more student-centric learning approach with more actions and activities, instead of focusing too much on information consumption. Research-based learning, according to Jenkins and Healey (2010), is divided into four types of learning. *Research-led* learning is learning about current research in the discipline, *research-oriented* learning is developing research skills and techniques, *research-based* learning is undertaking research and inquiry, and *research-tutored* learning is engaging in research discussions.

Research-based learning is a pedagogical approach, which includes scaffolding for teaching and learning along with research processes where students undertake research and inquiry (Jenkins et al., 2007). When we see learning through those eyes, teaching and learning needs to be structured by the process of research phases of creating hypotheses and a theoretical framework, creating a research design, performing inquiry, describing results and making conclusions. Such research-based learning process is then the foundation for designing reflective cross-actions.

The difference between research, what science does, and research-based learning *is* the key element of feedback and reflection that is included in each research step that the learner has carried out (Wildt, 2007). To every step in research-based learning, feedback, formative assessment and guided reflections are essential to support the learners in their learning progress. Without such feedback, it is just a traditional research circle and not research-based *learning*.

In traditional classrooms, learning is organized around meetings of teachers and students, and it is not organized around cross-actions (Chapter 1). With the concept of research-based learning, we have an approach at hand that can be used for designing reflective cross-actions. Instead of focusing on synchronous meeting spaces, the focus lies on the research-based 'process.' The foundation for designing for learning is then the 'process' rather than a location.

The approach of exploratory learning also tries to make a difference in the traditional course concept. Although it was invented originally as a theory for learning outside institutions, this concept is very rare in teaching practices in schools and universities. Exploratory learning is an active process in which a learner constructs her own meaning based on her own experience; this means that learners explore something (e.g., artifacts, hypothesis, ideas and results) without having or giving a solution formulated by the teachers. Learners "interact with the world by exploring and manipulating objects, wrestling with questions and controversies, or performing experiments" (Bruner, 1961). However, exploratory learning does not mean unguided learning (Kirschner, Sweller & Clark, 2006).

Exploratory learning concepts, also known as discovery learning, encourage the learner to carry out experiments and to uncover relationships. Learners have the opportunity to discover unknown and unexpected object properties, characteristics and theoretical models by following various learning paths. What exploratory learning is missing, or at least it is not explicitly mentioned, is the role of reflection. A relevant contribution is therefore made by Kolb's "experiential learning theory" around 1994 (Kolb & Boyatzis, 2000) that says that learning takes place in four steps: concrete experiences (being involved in a situation, doing something), active experimenting (testing a theory by making a plan and following it), reflective observing (looking at an experience and thinking about it), and abstract concept making (forming theories about why an experience happened the way it did).

In one of our studies called PeTEX, we studied and designed a learning expedition, although we did not call it that from the beginning. In our EU-funded PeTEX project called Platform for eLearning and Telemetric Experiments from 2009 to 2011 (e.g., Terkowsky et al., 2011), we developed a platform for teaching and learning in remote laboratories for engineering students in higher education. The labs are physically located in Sweden (at KTH University), Italy (Palermo University) and Germany (Dortmund University). These labs have different machines that do different things such as testing the quality of materials. Those machines are quite expensive, and not every university wants to buy the same machines, so PeTEX started a remote lab to create access to machines throughout Europe. An aim was that students receive a range of possibilities in their studies by gaining access to a range of different machines without traveling to those countries. The design of a learning expedition is grounded on experimental, research-based learning that takes place within remote laboratories using web-enabled technology. PeTEX started with the question of how such experimental learning expeditions can be supported and what kind of conditions are needed that enable, create and foster knowledge sharing in such remote labs for engineering education. The guiding question of involved designers and experts from sociotechnical and pedagogical areas was, "What does the design need that students are able to learn? What do students learn when the experiments fail?" It became clear that a sociotechnical prototype requires several possibilities for learning walkthroughs because different students have different needs and different problems. A walkthrough for beginner, intermediate and experts have been conceptualized, but these walkthroughs are flexible; they have a high degree of freedom, and learners are able to switch between different layers. The layers include individual learning sessions, a session where students plan and conduct the remote experiments in engineering and a reflection activity in which students also write reviews for their peers. The different layers and walkthroughs offer different instructions but also offer freedom of doing different activities to ensure that students are able to 'do' their own cross-actions.

4.4.2 No Learning Expedition Without Creating Conditions for Creativity

The design of learning expeditions as exemplified in PeTEX gives a hint that such a learning approach is not possible without having the freedom of being creative. When students get the chance to explore or create something, creativity is required that helps a learner solve a problem or explore an issue.

I do not want to open that 'can of creativity worms' here. There is plenty of knowledge out there that shows how to support creative learning and what conditions might limit creativity. I only want to shed light on a study that is called DaVinci. In this study, we asked university teachers about their understandings of student creativity. More precisely, we asked them to illustrate in what ways they look at student creativity. Six facets could be clustered that help to open and reflect designs for learning toward creativity. Creating conditions for creative learning expeditions involve 1) students' self-reflections, 2) that they can make autonomous and independent decisions during the learning process, 3) design fosters engagement, curiosity and motivation, 4) students are able to produce something, 5) multiperspective thinking (students show more than one perspective, contradictory views, on the same topic), and 6) developing original, new ideas (Jahnke & Haertel, 2010; Jahnke, 2013).

Creative designs are closely related to the notions of learner-centeredness, autonomy, ownership, making one's own decisions, curiosity, the freedom of continuing learning when and where it suits the learner, playfulness and creating new artifacts (Jahnke, 2013).

A course or classroom that is only focusing on lecturing or presenting information lacks in creativity. Instead of 'giving' information to students, a design for learning expeditions helps students to perform and learn in experiential and reflective ways. For example, in math, students explore and discuss different strategies to solve a task. They even create small videos to illustrate pros and cons. In language, students do not only read about grammar. They create web-tours for other students with questions and answers about grammar. In physics and chemistry, they invent experiments, record them and watch them to understand what went wrong and how to improve it. These examples are not only examples on paper. I have seen them in the practice of schools in Denmark, Sweden, Finland and the United States.

The question is, how to design for them? And are there any recommendations? Yes, there are some key features. The conditions for such designs toward reflective cross-actions will be discussed in the next chapter.

4.4.3 Beyond Courses—Thinking of Learning Expeditions in Groups and Communities

In a former, typical one-room schoolhouse a hundred years ago, "learning was social, not didactic," writes John Seely Brown (2009). Students had to go to the information. Today, the availability of information through web access from anywhere at any time has made it easier to engage students in learning communities and can also link weakly coupled learners. But still, schools and higher education do not use this potential. Concepts of problem solving are still rare that do not focus on having a right answer but offering several possibilities for many different answers.

This is different when designing learning from the view of learning communities such as communities of practice, introduced by Lave and Wenger (1991) and later Wenger, McDermott and Snyder (2002). Learning expeditions can be designed as an event of such communities. Such communities of practice are characterized through social relationships among individuals "who share a concern, a set of problems, or a passion about a topic, and who deepen their knowledge and expertise in this area by interacting on an ongoing basis" (Wenger et al., 2002, p. 4). In other words, a design for learning expedition has to answer the question of how to create such a community feeling where learners want to share and learn together.

When we go into details here, the creation of a design for learning expedition can start with analyzing the size of the learning group, the primary content, lifespan and degree of presence (Preece, 2000). The group size may range from small groups with 25 members to large groups with 100,000 actors and more, where the participants are more or less active. Different sizes need different designs, for example, the design for social relationships differs from small to large groups. The primary content of the learning expedition varies. In schools and universities, the content depends on the curriculum. Relevance of designing of learning expedition is also the lifespan. Is it just a course for six weeks, or is it arranged over a period of months or several years (such as doctoral study programs)? The lifespan matters for the design. A six-week learning expedition is probably planned differently than a four-months learning community. The design of the degree of presence also has an effect. Is it just pure online communication, where people cannot meet due to different reasons, or is it a mixed communication with online and offline parts?

Learning expeditions organized in educational institutions and online groups outside such institutions differ in their concepts toward private identity and public accessibility (van de Sande, 2010; Brandon & Hollingshead, 2007). Private identity means that the users can use anonymous nicknames and keep their identities private, whereas the information that they share is public. In discussion boards (forums), the content has public access, and people often do not reveal their private identity. This differs from social networking sites, where a special degree of the private identity is shown. In schools and higher education, the identity of learners is almost always available. Administrators of learning management systems or Intranet application in schools and universities often give the user a single-sign account, which means that the account name is linked to the enrolled person and that is connected to the private identity. This difference has an effect of designing for learning expeditions.

The benefit aspect of learning in such a community of practice is that the learners are not only part of a group to learn specific content or to explore a topic. The key principle is that learners get access to a kind of guided reflection so as to develop from lonely reflective practitioners (Schön, 1983) to a community of reflecting peers. Such a community approach is a form of peer-reflective learning. Learners develop their topic together; they are able to construct meaningful learning in a group where collaborative reflections help them to proceed and make progress (Jonassen et al., 2003).

How are communities of practice linked to learning expeditions? We suggest two concepts that might be a useful place to start. The learning walkthrough presupposes a rather designed learning landscape more closely guided by teaching but with a greater variation and more student options to work and learn than the traditional course. Our PeTEX project is an example of such a learning walkthrough. The learners have several options to walk through content (called LearnBar modules in Moodle); they plan, prepare and conduct engineering experiments in remote-controlled laboratories online (online access to three labs in three European countries), and they reflect with their peers (using blogs and Wikis). There are two learning approaches that guide where students start. Students start with the engineering experiments, and then they go to the content to give meaning to the observation they made. Other students want to have first the content knowledge, and then they prepare for the experiment (Terkowsky et al., 2011).

A learning expedition differs from the learning walkthrough. A learning expedition stands for a more open-ended and problem-based learning path. It might include goal-oriented learning to master X or understand the implications of Y, but the learning methods and instruments are very open. Both of the approaches need a design that includes guided reflections by teachers or peers with the aim to reflect the 'doing' and performance of cross-actions so as to proceed in learning.

When we use the concept of cross-action and transform it to teaching and learning in educational institutions, it is important that teachers and instructors scaffold the process of peer-reflective learning, guided reflections and social partnerships. It is not enough just to give the students assignments and put them into a community; they need guidance and support in the form of microreflections and process-based feedback. When transforming the approach of communities of practice of communities of interest (Fischer, 2011) into educational institutions, designing for reflection is key. Guided reflections in social partnerships, and reflections on roles, are key to succeed in learning. There is no learning without reflection. Outside educational institutions, self-reflection takes place in forms of the outcome. A person wants to improve his swimming style; he watches several videos online, and in the swimming hall later, he transforms theoretical knowledge into practice. He gets immediate feedback while swimming. In schools and universities, however, there is often a lack of immediate feedback because it is not included in the design. The other problem is that students often expect that the teachers have to give them feedback instead of self-reflections. The design of school and university system is arranged so that we always wait for external feedback from the teachers. Here, the learning expedition design wants to make a difference.

Based on the principles of learning in a community of reflecting peers, the nature of learning expeditions can be described as follows: learning expeditions are processes and loops, which are blended in different spaces and support each other to help students in their learning; they happen in CrossActionSpaces via web-enabled media; and they are grounded on research-based learning, in which process-based feedback, guided reflections and process-based formative assessment (feed*forward*), networked scaffolding and self-boosted learning are key principles in a community of reflective peers. When we see learning in schools and universities from these eyes, then the relevant question is, how do we design for such learning expeditions? The next chapter gives answers.

4.4.4 Schools and Universities of the Future—Beyond Courses Toward Learning Expeditions

Reimagining schools and universities of the future, where learning expeditions are 50% of the credit points, 50% of the credit points cover the content and follow the traditional understanding of curriculum-driven and course-driven concepts; this is the obligatory content. The other 50% of the credit points are for these learning expeditions, a *format* that takes place in different formats depending on what the student wants to learn, across the university boundaries and within a universe of universities. A possible scenario is that the student has a choice between the format such as a traditional lecture, a MOOC, a creativity workshop, a project, a research-based learning expedition and the participation at communities of interests (Fischer, 2011). The student makes a choice of 'what s/he wants to learn.' Then, s/he creates an e-portfolio in which she explains why she had chosen those formats and not others, and she makes the learning outcomes visible, for example, while using open badges for microassessment (Buchem et al., 2012). In such a form, the student develops her own study program, "My degree—my way" (Boyer, 1990). The study program becomes a personalized, individualized study program. For example, the OpenUniversity (UK) already started to offer the use of Open Badges called BOCs—"Badged Open Courses"—as seen on February 13, 2015, on Twitter. In such a situation, the teacher turns into a learning companion; he or she is a supporter and a coach for students if the students want to have support.

Why do I propose 50% and not 100% learning expeditions? Sometimes the students do not know what to study and why. It is not that I say the students are not capable of making decisions; it is rather that I have observed that students expect the formal system of education to know what is best for them. Thus, in order to help them in their learning to learn what they want to learn and why, I argue that it would be best to have a 50–50 structure. Fifty percent is made by the educational system; then the students receive inspiration as to what they want to do with the other 50% that finishes the degree. Of course, a 70/30 or 40/60 split could also work; design-based research is needed here in order to figure out what could be an optimal rationale for students.

Readers could argue now that we should let learners learn in communities of interests (COIs) because in such formats they find other learners with same or similar interests. Yes, this is possibly part of such a 50–50 model. I tend to argue, however, that the focus on an exclusive peer-learning model, and the emphasis is 'not peer-learning only,' never can be more effective for learners than other forms of learning where a teacher is part of the learning—a range of learning models is required. The Khan Academy is a nice example of how peer-learning, learning processes and learning projects are combined with subject classes where the subject topics only get a small amount of time.

What I want to say is that peer learning is a great model but not exclusively and not alone. Why? Observe peers when they are gathering, such as younger students, postdoctoral researchers, senior professors or others. What we see in those groups is that they build expectations and small interaction patterns such as power roles, clown roles, opinion makers, a person who has always claims s/he is right (at least s/he thinks that way), and so forth (Bales, 1950). This kind of group dynamics can be sometimes very annoying for learners, and this limits learning. Second, learners are searching for mentors or people with experiences so as to learn from them. Humans do not search for mentors, coaches, learning companions or teachers in all types of situations, but they do it in some situations. Some learners do more and want more, and some search less and want to try without such an experienced person. Since learners start their learning journey and learning expeditions from very different departures, they need different support, and, therefore, a model such as 50–50 could be an interesting starting model in schools and universities. And, perhaps, in 50 years, we will only have such Badged Open Courses or e-portfolios.

4.5 References

Anderson, B. (1997). Work, ethnography and system design. Technical Report EPC-1996-103. In: A. Kent & J. G. Williams (Eds.): *The Encyclopedia of Microcomputers*, Vol. 20. New York: Marcel Dekker, pp. 159–183.

Bales, R. F. (1950). *Interaction Process Analysis. A Method for the Study of a Small Group.* Chicago, IL: University of Chicago Press.

Barr, R. & Tagg, J. (1995): From teaching to learning. A new paradigm for undergraduate education. In: D. DeZure (Ed.): Learning from change, *Change Magazine*, S198–200.

Berger, P. & Luckmann, T. (1993). *The Social Construction of Reality.* Frankfurt: Fischer. (Original work published 1967)

Bergqvist, E. & Bergqvist, T. (2014). Teachers' interpretations of the concept of problem— a link between written and intended reform curriculum. Manuscript submitted for publication.

Biggs, J. (1996). Enhancing teaching through constructive alignment. *Higher Education*, 32(3), pp. 347–364.

Boyer, E. (1990). *Scholarship Reconsidered: Priorities of the Professoriate.* Princeton, NJ: Carnegie Foundation for the Advancement of Teaching.

Brandon, D. P. & Hollingshead, A. B. (2007). Characterizing online groups. In A. Joinson, K. McKenna, T. Postmes & U.-D. Reips (Eds.): *The Oxford Handbook of Internet Psychology.* Oxford: Oxford University Press, pp. 105–119.

Brown, J. S. (2009). Foreword. In A. Collins & R. Halverson (Eds.): *Rethinking Education in the Age of Technology.* New York: Teachers College Press, pp. ix–x.

Brown, J. S. & Duguid, P. (2000). *The Social Life of Information.* Boston, MA: Harvard Business School Press.

Bruner, J. S. (1961). The act of discovery. *Harvard Educational Review*, 31(1), 21–32.

Bruner, J. S. (1967): On Knowing: Essays for the Left Hand. Cambridge, MA: Harvard University Press. Retrieved February 2010 from http://www.learning-theories.com/discovery-learning-bruner.html

Buchem, I., Cochrane, T., Gordon, A. & Keegan, H. (2012). M-Learning 2.0: the potential and challenges of collaborative mobile learning in participatory curriculum development. In *Proceedings of the IADIS Mobile Learning Conference 2012,* Berlin, Germany.

Cerratto-Pargman, T., Otero, N., Milrad, M., Spikol, D., Kutsson, O. & Ramberg, R. (2014). Purposeful learning across collaborative educational spaces. In *Proceedings of ICLS'2014, Learning and Becoming in Practice,* Boulder, CO.

Collins, A. & Halverson, R. (2009). *Rethinking Education in the Age of Technology: The Digital Revolution and Schooling in America.* New York: Teachers College Press.

Conklin, J. (2005). Wicked problems and social complexity. In: *Dialogue Mapping: Building Shared Understanding of Wicked Problem: Building Shared Understanding of Wicked Problems.* West Sussex: Wiley.

Duffy, T. M. & Cunningham, D. J. (1996). Constructivism: Implications for the design and delivery of instruction. In: D. H. Jonassen (Ed): Handbook of Research for Educational Communications and Technology. New York: Simon & Schuster Macmillan, pp. 170–198.

Ehlers, U.-D. (2013). *Open Learning Cultures. A Guide to Quality, Evaluation and Assessment for Future Learning.* New York: Springer.

Fischer, G. (2007, July): Designing socio-technical environments in support of meta-design and social creativity. *Proceedings of the Conference on Computer Supported Collaborative Learning* (CSCL 2007), Rutgers University, New Brunswick, NJ, pp. 1–10.

Fischer, G. (2011, October). Social creativity: exploiting the power of cultures of participation. In *Proceedings of SKG2011: 7th International Conference on Semantics, Knowledge and Grids*, Beijing, pp. 1–8.

Floridi, L. (2007). A look into the future impact of ICT on our lives. *The Information Society: An International Journal*, 23(1), pp. 59–64.

Giddens, A. (1984). *The Constitution of Society.* Cambridge: Polity Press.

Goggins, S., Jahnke, I. & Wulf, V. (2013). *CSCL@work, Computer-Supported Collaborative Learning at the Workplace.* New York: Springer.

Herrmann, Th. (2009). Systems design with the socio-technical walkthrough. In B. Whitworth & A. de Moore (Eds.): *Handbook of Research on Socio-Technical Design and Social Networking Systems.* Hershey, PA: Idea Group, pp. 336–351.

Hjarvard, S. (2008). The mediatization of religion: a theory of the media as agents of religious change. In: *Northern Lights 2008. Yearbook of Film & Media Studies.* Bristol: Intellect Press.

Hyllested, T. (2014). Out of school environments as resources for learning. In *Designs for Learning*, 4th Conference in Stockholm. Retrieved May 11, 2014, from http://www.designsforlearning.nu/conference/program/pdf_webb/hyllested.pdf

Jahnke, I. (2009). Socio-technical communities: from informal to formal? In B. Whitworth & A. de Moor (Eds.): *Handbook of Research on Socio-Technical Design and Social Networking Systems.* Hershey, PA: Information Science Reference, IGI Global, pp. 763–778.

Jahnke, I. (2010). A way out of the information jungle—a longitudinal study about a socio-technical community and informal learning in higher education. *International Journal of Socio-technology and Knowledge Development*, 4, 18–38. doi:10.4018/jskd.2010100102

Jahnke, I. (2011). How to foster creativity in technology enhanced learning. In B. White, I. King & Ph. Tsang (Eds.): *Social Media Tools and Platforms in Learning Environments: Present and Future.* Springer, pp. 95–116. doi:10.1007/978-3-642-20392-3_6

Jahnke, I. (2012). Technology-embraced informal-*in*-formal learning. In A. Ravencroft, S. Lindstaedt, C. Delgado Kloos & D. Hernandez-Leo (Eds.): *21st Century Learning for 21st Century Skills. 7th European Conference on Technology Enhanced Learning.* Berlin: Springer, pp. 395–400.

Jahnke, I. (2013, July–September). Teaching practices in iPad-classrooms: alignment of didactical designs, mobile devices and creativity. *International Journal of Mobile and Blended Learning* (ijMBL), 5(3), 1–17.

Jahnke, I. & Haertel, T. (2010). Kreativitätsförderung in der Hochschule—ein Rahmenkonzept. (Fostering creativity in universities—a framework). In *Das Hochschulwesen.* 3/2010, pp. 88–96.

Jahnke, I. & Kumar, S. (2014a). Digital Didactical Designs: teachers' integration of iPads for learning-centered processes, *Journal of Digital Learning in Teacher Education*, 30(3), pp. 81–88. doi:10.1080/21532974.2014.891876

Jahnke, I. & Kumar, S. (2014b): iPad-didactics—didactical designs for iPad-classrooms: experiences from Danish schools and a Swedish university. In: Ch. Miller & A. Doering (Eds.): *The New Landscape of Mobile Learning: Redesigning Education in an App-based World.* New York: Routledge.

Jahnke, I. & Norberg, A. (2013). Digital didactics—scaffolding a new normality of learning. In: *Open Education Contributions to the JRC-IPTS Call for Vision Papers.* Part III: Higher Education, pp. 129–134.

Jahnke, I., Svendsen, N. V., Johansen, S. K. & Zander, P.-O. (2014). The dream about the magic silver bullet—the complexity of designing for tablet-mediated learning. In *ACM GROUP 2014 Conference Proceedings.*

Jahnke, I., Terkowsky, C., Pleul, Ch. & Tekkaya, A. E. (2010). Online learning with remote-configured experiments. In M. Kerres, N. Ojstersek, U. Schroeder & U. Hoppe (Eds.): *Interaktive Kulturen, DeLFI 2010*, pp. 265–277. Proceedings of 8. Tagung der Fachgruppe E-Learning der Gesellschaft für Informatik e.V.

Jenkins, A. & Healey, M. (2010, Spring). Undergraduate research and international initiatives to link teaching and research. *Council on Undergraduate Research Quarterly*, 36–42.

Jenkins, A., Breen, R., Lindsay, R. & Brew, A. (2007). *Re-shaping Higher Education: Linking Teaching and Research.* London: Routledge Falmer/SEDA.

Jonassen, D. H., Howland, J., Moore, J. & Marra, R. M. (2003). *Learning to Solve Problems With Technology: A constructivist Perspective* (2nd ed). Columbus, OH: Merrill, Prentice Hall.

Kirschner, P. A., Sweller, J. & Clark, R. E. (2006). Why minimal guidance during instruction does not work an analysis of the failure of constructivist, discovery, problem-based, experiential, and inquiry-based teaching. *Educational Psychologist*, 41(2), 75–86.

Kolb, D. (1984). *Experiential Learning: Experience as the Source of Learning and Development.* Englewood Cliffs, NJ: Prentice-Hall.

Kolb, D. & Boyatzis, R. (2000). Experiential learning theory: previous research and new directions. In R. J. Sternberg & L. F. Zhang (Eds.): *Perspectives on Cognitive, Learning, and Thinking Styles.* Mahwah, NJ: Lawrence Erlbaum.

Krotz, F. (2008): Media connectivity. Concepts, conditions, and consequences. In: A. Hepp, F. Krotz, S. Moores & C. Winter (Eds): *Network, Connectivity and Flow. Conceptualising Contemporary Communications.* New York: Hampton Press, pp. 13–31.

Kukulska-Hulme, A. (2012). Smart devices or people? A mobile learning quandary. *International Journal of Learning and Media*, 4(3–4), pp. 73–77.

Latour, B. (2005). *Reassembling the Social—An Introduction to Actor-Network-Theory.* Oxford: Oxford University Press.

Laurillard, D. (2007). Pedagogical forms for mobile learning: framing research questions. In: N. Pachler (Ed.): *Mobile Learning: Towards a Research Agenda.* London: WLE Centre, IoE, pp. 153–175.

Laurillard, D. (2008). Technology-enhanced learning as a tool for pedagogical innovation. *Journal of Philosophy of Education*, 42(3–4), pp. 521–533.

Lave, J. & Wenger, E. (1991). *Situated Learning: Legitimate Peripheral Participation.* New York: Cambridge University Press.

Lundby, K. (2009). *Mediatization. Concept, Changes, Consequences.* New York: Peter Lang.

Mårell-Olsson, E. & Hudson, A. (2008). To make learning visible: in what way can ICT and multimedia contribute? *Tidskrift för lärarutbildning och forskning*, 3–4, pp. 73–90.

Mørch, A. I. & Skaanes, M. A. (2010). Design and use of an integrated work and learning system: information seeking as critical function. In: S. Ludvigsen, A. Lund, I. Rasmussen and R. Säljö (Eds.): *Learning Across Sites: New Tools, Infrastructures and Practices.* London: Routledge, pp. 138–155.

Norberg, A. & Jahnke, I. (2014): "Are you working in the kitchen?": European perspectives on blended learning. In A. G. Picciano, C. D. Dziuban & C. R. Graham (Eds.):

Blended Learning—Research Perspectives, Vol. 2. New York: Routledge/Taylor & Francis, pp. 251–267.

Pachler, N. (2007). *Mobile Learning: Towards a Research Agenda.* London: WLE Centre, IoE.

Preece, J. (2000). *Online Communities: Designing Usability, Supporting Sociability.* Chichester: John Wiley & Sons.

Prilla, M., Herrmann, Th. & Degeling, M. (2013). Collaborative reflection for learning at the healthcare workplace. In: S. P. Goggins, I. Jahnke & V. Wulf (Eds.): *Computer-Supported Collaborative Learning at the Workplace—CSCL@Work.* New York: Springer, pp. 139–165.

Sharpe, R., Benfield, G., Roberts, G. & Francis, R. (2006). The undergraduate experience of blended e-Learning: a review of UK literature and practice. A report to the Higher Education Academy. Retrieved October 15, 2014, from https://www.academia.edu/188000/The_undergraduate_experience_of_blended_e-learning_a_review_of_UK_literature_and_practice_undertaken_for_the_Higher_Education_Academy.

Sharples, M., Taylor, J. & Vavoula, G. (2005). Towards a theory of mobile learning. *Proceedings of mLearn 2005 Conference*, Cape Town, www.mlearn.org.za/CD/papers/Sharples.pdf

Sharples, N. (2006). Big Issues in Mobile Learning. *Report of a workshop by the Kaleidoscope Network of Excellence Mobile Learning Initiative.* LSRI, University Nottingham. Retrieved January 14, 2012, from http://www.lsri.nottingham.ac.uk/msh/Papers/BIG_ISSUES_REPORT_PUBLISHED.pdf

Siemens, G. (2005). Connectivism: A learning theory for the digital age. *International Journal of Instructional Technology & Distance Learning* Retrieved March 24, 2014, from http://www.itdl.org/Journal/Jan_05/article01.htm

Stahl, G. (2006). *Group Cognition: Computer Support for Building Collaborative Knowledge.* Cambridge, MA: MIT Press.

Stewart, T. A. (1996, August 5): The invisible key to success. Shadow groups called communities of practice. *Fortune Magazine*, pp. 173–176.

Tammets, K., Laanpere, M., Ley, T. & Pata, K. (2013). Identifying problem-based scaffolding patterns in an online forum for construction professionals. *ECTEL 2013*, pp. 526–531.

Terkowsky, C., Pleul, C., Jahnke, I. & Tekkaya, A. E. (2011). Tele-operated laboratories for online production engineering education. Platform for e-Learning and telemetric experimentation (PeTEX). *International Journal of Online Engineering (iJOE)*, 7, Special Issue: Educon 2011, pp. 37–43. Vienna: IAOE.

Traxler, J. (2009). The evolution of mobile learning. In R. Guy (Ed.): *The Evolution of Mobile Teaching and Learning.* Santa Rosa, CA: Information Science Press, pp. 1–14.

Tuomi-Gröhn, T. & Engeström, Y. (2003). *Between School and Work: New Perspectives on Transfer and Boundary Crossing.* Amsterdam: Pergamon.

van de Sande, C. (2010). Free, open, online, help forums: convenience, connection, control, comfort, and communication. *International Journal of Sociotechnology and Knowledge Development*, 2(4), 1–17. doi:10.4018/jskd.2010100101

Wenger, E. (1998). Communities of practice. Learning as a social system. *Systems Thinker*, 6.

Wenger, E., McDermott, R. & Snyder, W. M. (2002). *Cultivating Communities of Practice: A Guide to Managing Knowledge.* Boston, MA: Harvard Business School Press.

Wildt, J. (2007). On the way from teaching to learning by competences as learning outcomes. In: A. Pausits & A. Pellert (Eds.): *Higher Education Management and Development in Central, Southern and Eastern Europe.* Münster: Waxmann, pp. 115–123.

5

TEACHING CREATES CONDITIONS FOR LEARNING AS REFLECTIVE CROSS-ACTION

Digital Didactical Design

The future is not out there to be discovered, but will be designed.
(Gerhard Fischer—not alone but together, socially framed [Isa Jahnke])

Reflecting the aforementioned chapters toward a complementary understanding of teaching and learning from the perspective of CrossActionSpaces (Chapter 1), how do we approach and work our way toward achieving the new challenges in education? The European way of trying to understand and design education, 'didaktik,' is a useful approach, although it is often not clear what it contains. I want to shed light on this model and how we use it in our studies of creating, developing and evaluating technology-enhanced designs for learning.

In CrossActionSpaces, learning is not only dependent on traditional human action and interaction; learners perform several actions and interactions across existing spaces and also create new spaces for communication. Humans use the traditional rooms for asking questions, sharing information and learning from others, but they also use off- and online channels and web-enabled technology to engage with the world around them. The world provides hundreds and thousands of existing and new, emergent communication spaces—made by humans and bots.

When we see today's networked world from the eyes of CrossActionSpaces, in which learning can be understood as reflective cross-action, we are able to derive some criteria and conditions that are relevant for teaching and learning designs in schools and higher education.

In a networked world, a design for teaching and learning creates conditions in which learners are able to walk through such co-expanded spaces; educators and learners even create new spaces and reflect during their walkthroughs. Teaching and learning designs support learners to become reflective makers (prosumers);

a design scaffolds and guides them and creates conditions for reflective learning expeditions (Chapter 4). Since cross-actions are affected by the roles the individual takes, a design also needs to include reflection about roles and even support teachers and learners to be in diverse roles; roles will be made to a topic that teachers and learners discuss.

In the next sections, I introduce designs for teaching and learning from the perspective of didaktik and Digital Didactical Design. Teaching is creating conditions and processes for learning. Digital Didactical Design is an approach for creating, developing and reflecting on teaching toward technology-enhanced designs for learning.

The term 'didaktik' comes from the Greek word meaning, in a broader context, the theory and science of teaching and learning, whereas pedagogy and pedagogical competence draw on 'educating someone' (Bildung) in the sense of nurturing children. It is obvious that both pedagogy and didactics are strongly connected. A new term bringing both concepts together seems to be needed: didagogy—didactics and pedagogy. However, I decided to use 'didactics' (didaktik) over 'pedagogy' because, in a German and Scandinavian context, it implies the science of form and practice for planning and performing both together teaching and learning as a social practice (Lund & Hauge, 2011). Pedagogy has a broader view. It also looks on situations outside educational institutions. Research on those designs has the purpose, for example, to inform the practice of developing learning technologies and educational technology (Olofsson & Lindberg, 2012).

Didaktik draws on Vygotsky's studies on the "Zone of Proximal Development" (1978), meaning that student learning can achieve longer and deeper outcomes with teacher and peer interaction. Vygotsky studied how young children learn languages and found that the learners achieve significantly better results when they are with peers or teachers together.

Digital Didactics claims to make a difference in 1) student learning, compared to self-directed individual learning; 2) institutional effectiveness, upgrading the teacher role by reinventing it, for example, the teacher is part of the networked scaffolding culture; and 3) the value of education for society, by an increased access and worthy concepts of lifelong learning, which draw on a close cooperation with the public and corporate sectors. Digital Didactics has the purpose of critically questioning everything in the search for such appropriate processes, going beyond the course concept, beyond the isolation of teaching and learning from society, beyond the student homogeneity ideal, beyond current forms of grading and feedback (assessment and reflection), beyond separation of formal and informal learning, and beyond designs of 'boring' learning environments.

Digital Didactical Designs is based on Peter Hinssen's "new normal" idea (2010) that claims we are now about halfway in the implementation of ICT in society and that from now on we will see more benefits from ICT. ICT tools work well enough to make ordinary activities easier and more effective in a significant way. When we apply the new normal idea to education, there has been a lot of experimenting in the past, with half-successes and technical troubles when trying to use ICT, but we can expect a more rewarding use of ICT in the near future. ICT-supported open educational resources, Digital Didactics, teaching and learning will be intertwined and will shape a new educational entity.

In Jahnke & Norberg (2013), we ask, "what is the place for education, if we have to call it something?" It will no longer be called the 'teaching place' (e.g., lecture halls) nor the 'classroom as learning place' (that was a valid expression a long time ago). The place for education will not be called a 'student collaboration place,' and it is not really in the 'cloud' (we have physical bodies as well), but there will probably be a sort of ICT-supported social information sphere between teachers and learners, using places, tools, books and Open Educational Resources (OER).

Looking to the future, the traditional teaching space may not be the central metaphor for education, nor be meaningful to augment with technology. It might be more suitable to focus on learning processes than on places. More precisely, future learning requires a design that includes reflective cross-actions, for example, in forms of learning expeditions (Chapter 4).

I follow the approach by Jahnke & Norberg (2013), where we propose the terms 'learning walkthroughs' and 'learning expeditions' (a time and process metaphor) happening in Arena X (space metaphor). Here, I propose to call it CrossActionSpaces in which learning takes place as reflective cross-actions that includes the support of individual and group learning in networked scaffolding processes.

ROLE-CONSTRAINED LEARNING HINDERS THE OPENING UP OF EDUCATION

Digital Didactics for teaching and learning takes place in educational institutions; these are sociotechnical systems and "objective facticities" (Berger & Luckmann, 1967/1993), hard to wish away but changeable, where actors in these institutions have adopted roles and the interactions of the actors are grounded in their taken and assigned roles. These structures make education into rather closed systems, instead of open ones. This is bad news. Human interactions, the interactions of teachers and students, rely on their roles. The good news is that we can educate about these structures and systems, and when we have achieved knowledge, we have the potential to make a difference and to make a change in our everyday, role-constrained learning. We cannot wish the roles totally away, although we want to, but we can work on the role perception, role behavior and role performance—we can change the expectation and the roles; we can change the patterns.

5.1 Digital Didactics—Three Interwoven Layers

The use of ICT—web-enabled, small, flexible devices in education—affects many layers of education including content, activities and actions in classrooms, as well as local, national and international wide decision-making. The new

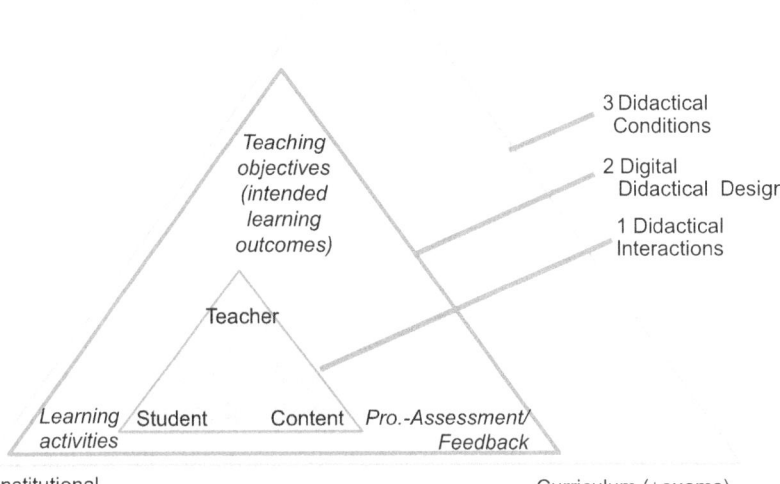

FIGURE 5.1 Digital Didactical Design layers in educational institutions—obstacles and spaces for negotiation and development (from Jahnke et al., 2014)

situation affects three levels of didactics: 1) the relation between teacher, students and content; 2) the didactical design (teaching aims, learning activities, assessment, social relations and roles); and 3) organizational development, curriculum development and academic staff development; see Figure 5.1. Each of the layers gives a frame but also affects the other layers. Teachers who are designers for learning are affected by all layers. Their developed designs are in a tension between didactical interactions and didactical conditions. The designs are only as good as the strategies of institutional, curriculum and staff development. For example, little or no development of curriculum probably means no new designs for cross-actions and no tablet-mediated learning designs, whereas a school strategy toward digitalization can mean that teachers will be supported by the management to develop new designs and teachers receive services in the forms of workshops, etc. on how to created new tablet-mediated designs for learning.

Triangle 1. The Inner Layer—Content-Student-Teacher— Didactical Interactions

In the inner layer, there is the embedded triangle, the concept of the relationship between content-student-teacher based on Klafki's concept (1963). This triangle is named *didactical interaction*. The relation of the two roles, teacher and student, to content and vice versa can be designed. The concept makes the interaction between the actors and content visible. In earlier years, content was in the text-book; nowadays, content is also made in collaboration using web-enabled technology. In the era of interactive technology and disruptive education (Hyman, 2012), the design of content takes on a new meaning. Educational resources and the uses of other content and materials are much wider than those of years ago. The range of material runs from podcasts, videos, slide-share and social networking sites to traditional books, which are increasingly available online. There is potential for designing of reflective cross-action.

Triangle 3. The Outer Layer—Didactical Conditions

In the outer layer, the three elements of organizational/institutional strategies, curriculum development (study programs) and academic staff development are illustrated. This layer is called *didactical conditions*.

The issue of 'academic staff development' deals with the challenge of giving enough support to the teachers and instructors in educational institutions. Here we need radical new thinking. Teachers are learners in the workplace—school or university workplace. Currently, many universities offer workshops but do not help the teachers to solve a problem when it occurs. Workshops are often conducted separately and need external days; they are not connected to the teachers' workplaces. In New Zealand (Cochrane & Narayan, 2011), there is another approach: they create teacher groups so as to help them to grow in their teaching practice and pedagogy, planning and performance of teaching and designing for student learning. Cochrane focuses on a cultural change where the teachers work in a community of reflecting peers. His groups move from a teacher-students-loneliness constellation to an open community of practice. The similar idea is seen in the concept of Scholarship of Teaching and Learning (SoTL), well known in the UK, where teachers build communities, publish their teaching reflections and discuss further developments.

The issue of 'organizational and institutional development' deals with existing structures and strategies in educational institutions. Are the organizational structures in schools and universities helpful for the teachers in their work of creating Digital Didactical Designs, and what traditions actually support and hinder the teachers in performing creative work and trying new pedagogies? This issue also deals with resources that the organization gives or does not give to teachers for development.

The 'curriculum development' deals with scrutinizing existing structures of study programs including existing forms of exams. What is the content of the programs, what are their structures and processes and how can one change these programs toward learning expeditions while avoiding the thinking of course metaphors? Study programs focus on content and neglect the integration of creativity. What we often see is that study programs give a grade at the end of the program, to judge the student's learning outcome, and neglect the potential of student development over time. Formative assessment for supporting learning progress is missing. For example, teachers create new forms of learning expeditions where students are creative, but the curriculum does not ask for creativity and the written exams do not reflect on student creativity. That can be interpreted as a mismatch between layer 2 and layer 3. In such a case, either the curriculum or the teacher's applied designs need a change.

The three components influence each other. The teachers' development (academic staff) is dependent on the other two issues and vice versa. The teachers' development can only be as 'good' as the organizational resources allow them to be, and the curriculum structures can hinder the innovative teachers and their designs to try new pedagogies because the curriculum or rules of the written examination may not allow new designs. Or, the curriculum fosters new designs, but the teachers cannot do it because the resources are not enough to help them to develop new skills, such as digital competencies.

5.2 The Middle Layer—Digital Didactical Design (Theory and Process View of Triangle 2)

In the middle of the three layers, there is triangle 2 of the Digital Didactical Design (DDD). It is affected by the outer and the inner circle and affects the other two layers. It is the key layer of Digital Didactics, which embraces the others. This layer focuses on enabling student learning and creating conditions for enabling learning. A researcher may use the layer to study the practice in schools and universities; a teacher may use it to start to redesign and reorganize teaching and learning.

Following the constructivism approach, learning is knowledge construction defined as the creation of new knowledge that is "an active process of constructing rather than acquiring knowledge" (Duffy & Cunningham, 1996, p. 171)—learning is socially framed. The term 'socially framed' refers to the concept of communication; learning is communication (Chapters 2 and 3). To reach a deeper learning level, human interaction is necessary to move into the zone of proximal development (Vygotsky, 1978). Deeper learning takes place when there is support for communicative interactions by peers, a teacher or a community.

This learning approach represents a shift in designing teaching toward learner-centered approaches (Barr & Tagg, 1995), which support deeper understanding and reflections and boost several other skills such as critical and creative thinking. Such 'active learning' is related to the role of learners, where they are not only consumers or surface learners but also active agents and producers in their construction of new knowledge: *prosumers and reflective makers*. Teaching practice then contributes to a form of deeper learning, not surface learning only, and can integrate opportunities for learning, when learners get support to expand their thinking beyond consumptive behavior and beyond traditional reproduction of existing knowledge—a "conceptual change" of student thinking and doing (according to Kember, 1997). Learners shift from being consumers to becoming critical-reflective producers.

I decided to use the term 'didaktik' (didactical design) over instructional design since didactical design has its roots in the understanding of didactics that not only includes methods, 'how' to teach, but also embraces the question of 'what' to learn including the development of curriculum (and content), 'why,' and 'when/where' (in what kinds of situations). In particular, a didactical design focuses on learning outcomes as competence development; students get the opportunity to develop several skills and different kind of competencies to solve complex problems. Didactics is neither limited to methods of teaching nor to the social practices of pedagogies. Didactical design (middle layer) includes in a broader sense the layers of didactical conditions (outer layer) and didactical interaction (inner layer) and provides a framework for studying and designing those interwoven layers and their key elements. Andreas Lund makes it clear:

> Didactics can be understood as the design of social practices in which learners, teachers and (social and material) resources are configured and re-configured in activities that make knowledge domains and knowledge advancement visible, and that continuously create teach|learn opportunities for reflective participation in such activities.
>
> (Andreas Lund, 2013, presentation in Norway)

This understanding of didactics also stresses the importance of social relationships. The adoption of pedagogical means in teaching practices has the aim of design for social partnerships ("the social organization of classroom instruction," Mehan, 1979).

The term 'design' focuses on specific actions and parts of activities by teachers in educational institutions. A design focuses on certain elements but does not take the whole reality into consideration. A design shapes a focus and key points and provides and gives a form (Gestalt). A design has both a planned component and an operative doing of social practices.

Design is the act of giving a form to something (Bonderup Dohn & Hanssen, 2014); a design is the act of modeling and forming learning; the teacher gives a form to sociotechnical-pedagogical processes for different kinds of quality learning. The teacher's applied designs-in-practice is process and product, plan and use (Wasson, 2007)—it is a plan but also a design in action.

Teaching is creating conditions for learning. Such conditions can be formed and shaped via the design of teaching and learning processes. Then, teaching is both planning and conduction of sociotechnical-pedagogical processes. Teaching is process design for learning. Such a dynamic design in action can be used in practice and research studies, for example, helping the teachers to reflect on their practice *in situ* and pointing to improvements for learning.

The term 'didactical design' is inspired by the European understanding of 'didaktik' and 'Bildung' (education), inspired by Hudson (2008), Fink (2003) and Lund & Hauge (2011), who distinguish between teaching concepts and learning activities, calling them designs for teaching as well as designs for learning. This view on didactics and design puts teaching and learning into a new light. Teaching is not only a tool to reach the cognitive dimension; teaching is also an activity-driven design for enabling learning as a process and is an activity for knowledge production for the students' activity designs for learning (Hauge & Dolonen, 2012).

However, what the teachers plan and what they do can differ due to different reasons. Therefore, to study a Digital Didactical Design, researchers and educational developers have to go into the practice of teaching and learning. Here, I use the model of a Digital Didactical Design (DDD) for empirical studies in both schools and universities. I want to understand how teachers design for learning when they use digital media. What are their teaching practices, defined as sociotechnical-pedagogical processes, and do they use the potential of the web-enabled technology for teaching and learning? If yes, how and in what ways, why and for what purposes?

A Digital Didactical Design includes planned activities and involves different elements and their relations in a constructive alignment (Biggs, 1996) named as teaching aims (nowadays transformed into intended learning outcomes), learning activities, process-based assessment, social relations and technology support such as digital media (Figure 5.2):

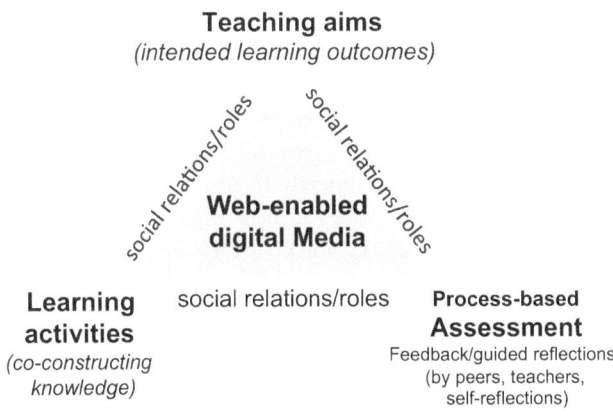

Teaching aims
(intended learning outcomes)

social relations/roles

**Web-enabled
digital Media**

social relations/roles

**Learning
activities**   social relations/roles   **Process-based
Assessment**
*(co-constructing
knowledge)*   Feedback/guided reflections
                                                  (by peers, teachers,
                                                  self-reflections)

FIGURE 5.2 Digital Didactical Design—elements and relations (from Jahnke & Kumar, 2014, p. 82)

Figure 5.2 shows that in an ideal world, an applied Digital Didactical Design includes different design elements such as:

1. Teaching aims and intended learning outcomes (ILO) that are clear and visible (McCormick & Scrimshaw, 2001);

2. Learning activities for students that they can achieve the teaching aims and ILO; it includes the plan of how the students achieve these aims in such a way that they are able to develop competences and skills (ILOs) (McCombs, 2000)—meaningful learning, from surface to deep learning (Jonassen, Howland, Moore & Marra, 2003);
3. Different forms of feedback and formative assessment (Chapman, 2003) to support the student learning progress, especially process-based guided reflections and assessment and (Bergström, 2012);
4. The development and reflection of social roles for teachers and students ("dynamics of social roles," Jahnke, 2010); and
5. Interactive, web-enabled technology in the forms of multimodal resources that help to create new communication spaces (Selander & Kress, 2010; Loveless, 2007, Conole, 2013).

The five elements are not totally new. Different researchers in the field of educational sciences mentioned those pedagogical elements, among many other dimensions, years ago. For example, McCormick & Scrimshaw (2001) adapted the model by Banks, Leach & Moon (1999), which includes goals and purposes, a view of learning, a view of knowledge, the classroom discourse and the roles of learners and teachers. For a *design perspective*, for which I argue, I selected these five elements (1 to 5, above) that are the most relevant ones with which to start when creating a design. This is the basic assumption.

The five elements support each other to foster student competence development. When all the elements fit together, then it is like the feeling at a warm, nice home, a strong building; learning is enabled, and the design increases the likelihood that learning really takes place. When the elements are not aligned and do not fit to support each other, then they are just building blocks, the home is cold, and learning is difficult or happens merely by accident. The assumption is that the five components of the DDD foster student engagement. As we know from other studies (e.g., Chapman, 2003; Northcote, 2009, Roschelle, 1992), student engagement supports deeper learning outcomes.

Behind the one triangle in Figure 5.2, two hidden triangles are actually involved (Figure 5.3); one represents the teacher, while the other shows the student perspective. As Northcote (2009) shows, there are different educational beliefs and pedagogical attitudes (Norqvist, Leffler & Jahnke, 2015) that represent different views on teaching and learning. Northcote's empirical study collected beliefs by teachers and learners. For example, she asked about "what is your view on effective learning"; "how do you believe learning takes place"; and "what is your view on the nature of knowledge."

Figure 5.3 illustrates the two different views on the design. In an optimum design, both designs have great overlaps; in weak designs, there is no overlap at all, and this provides an indicator that the teacher does not support learning from the student perspective.

FIGURE 5.3 Teachers' and students' views on the Digital Didactical Design

5.2.1 For Empirical Studies—Transforming the DDD Into a Five-Layer Pentagon

For using the DDD model in practice (Jahnke et al., 2014), for analyzing technology-enhanced teaching and learning, the Digital Didactical Design has been transformed into a five-layer pentagon. The five elements of the DDD are illustrated on a scale from 1 to 5 inspired by the Likert scale and translated into five layers (Figure 5.4). The data comes from classroom observations, interviews with teachers and group interviews with students. The inner circle of the pentagon

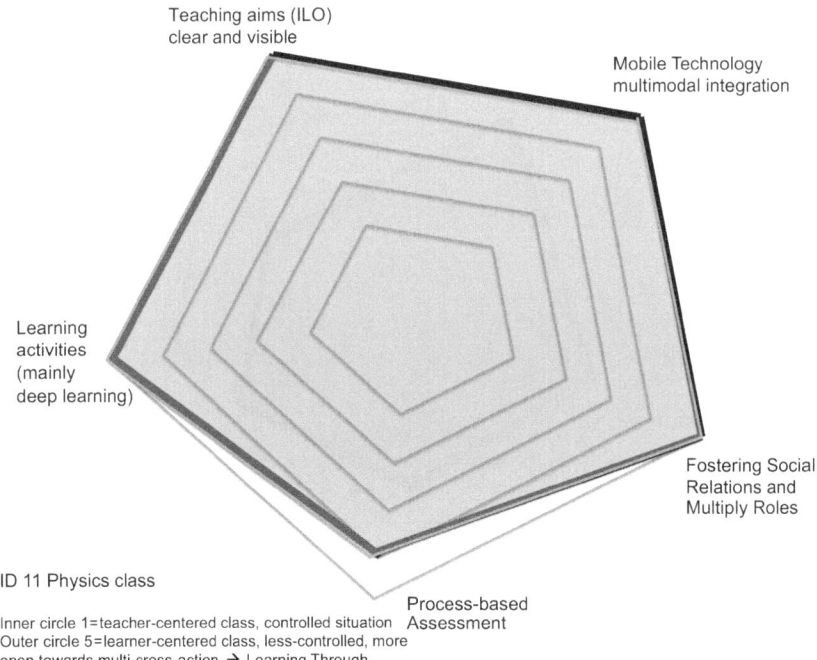

FIGURE 5.4A Example A of a Digital Didactical Design

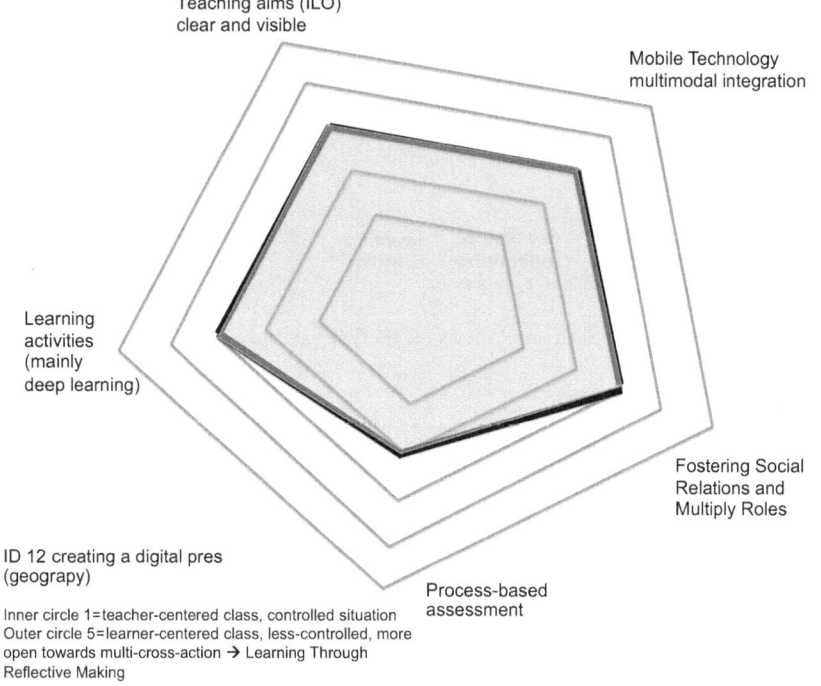

FIGURE 5.4B Example B of a Digital Didactical Design

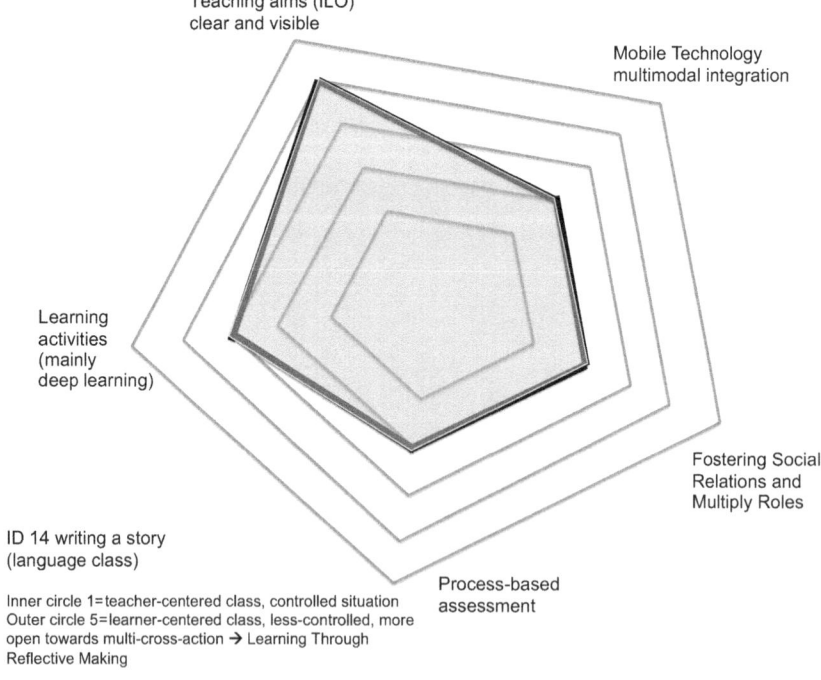

FIGURE 5.4C Example C of a Digital Didactical Design

model is rather teacher centered, with a focus on short-term repetition of what has been learned; the students act as consumers. The outer circle illustrates more learner-centered approaches; e.g., reflective, creative learning where the learners are producers (read further after Table 5.1).

As we know from previous studies (Jahnke, Norqvist & Olsson, 2014), learner-centered approaches are useful for deep learning (Kember, 1997), whereas teacher-centered classes support surface learning, such as remembering facts. A suitable balance in which both surface learning and deeper learning takes place is desirable for educational institutions. More research is required into what a 'good balance' might be.

With this analysis tool (Table 5.1), classrooms in schools and courses in higher education are observable; some might have a teaching-centered learning

TABLE 5.1 Using the DDD for empirical studies (researchers) and for reflecting learning practices (teachers and learners)

DDD component: Designing learning and fostering student engagement	Description understood as examples (not to be seen as a complete list)
Character of **teaching aims and ILO** (Intended Learning Outcomes): clear and visible; character of aims and learning outcomes? Focus on content— Focus on skills	1 = Not clear, not visible, no communication about teaching aims or learning intentions; focus on content 2 = 3 = Oral communication 4 = 5 = Teaching aims are clear and visible for teacher and students; intended learning outcomes in forms of development of skills; there is a source somewhere where the students can go back and read the aims and outcomes; at best, co-aims of students are included, students know the criteria for learning progress (available right from the start)
Character of **learning activities:** students as reflective makers?	1 = Students hear what teachers read from the textbook (surface learning only; e.g., remembering/repetition of facts); theoretical problems without connecting it to a real world problem 2 = 3 = In-between (. . .)—signs are: students are not so engaged, too much time for doing other things (e.g., playing cards instead) 4 = 5 = Learning activities have a range from surface to deep learning: prosumers, engaged classrooms, collaboration with peers; the activities are connected to the students world and include a real-world problem (e.g., everyday experience); a real audience, students produce something and critically reflect on it (e.g., evaluating/creating/making), relate knowledge to new knowledge; "organize and structure content into coherent whole" (Marton & Säljö, 1976), students are engaged as reflective makers

(Continued)

TABLE 5.1 (Continued)

DDD component: Designing learning and fostering student engagement	Description understood as examples (not to be seen as a complete list)
Character of **assessment:** process-based?	1 = Feedback only at the end (summative feedback); character of the feedback is rather summative, not formative 2 = 3 = Feedback during the class (not only technical help) by coincidence; teacher only gives feedback when they ask for support; passive support 4 = 5 = Criteria for a learning progress are visible for students since the beginning of the learning process; Feedback/feedforward at the end but mainly process-based assessment for learner's development; a plan exists for how the teacher creates pro-assessment (formative evaluation); a range of forms such as self-assessment; peer-reflective learning and feedback by the teacher, e.g., students document learning (electronically; a map or text, etc.), and the teacher asks them to go back and reflect
Character of Social relations: **multiple roles?**	1 = Teacher is in the traditional role of the expert only; students are only seen as consumers (of solving closed questions and tasks where only one correct answer is possible) 2 = 3 = Teacher is in 1–2 roles but spends majority of time as expert; teacher does not support student engagement to be active 4 = 5 = Teacher plays different roles such as expert, process mentor, learning companion, coach, consultant; she fosters the students to be in different roles such as consumers, producers, collaborators, critical reflectors, etc.; teacher engages the students; teacher activates the students to change their roles; students are in several roles, e.g., teachers for their peers, finding own learning aims, creating own learning tasks, etc.; teacher supports the student reflection of roles and development of new roles
Character of **web-enabled technology/ digital media for cross-actions?**	1 = Low extent, drill and practice; students work primarily alone when using technology, not related to the real world (e.g., technology is substitute for pen and paper) 2 = 3 = Medium extent (e.g., new technology is substitute for existing media; for example, tablet substitutes a laptop) 4 = 5 = High extent, multimodal such as writing texts, camera app, digital paintings, using apps for collaborative creation; students construct, share, create and publish their knowledge to a real audience; students use online resources, actively select topics beyond the limitations of even the best school library, etc.

approach, whereas others apply a rather learner-centered learning approach (Barr & Tagg, 1995). With this tool, we look at the 'real' applied designs-in-practice. Instead of asking what the educational actors have in mind or want to do, we look at the practice. This serves as a door opener to starting conversations about different teaching and learning practices with the educational actors.

5.2.2 A Typical Example From Our Classroom Studies—Process Design View

In this section, a typical tablet-mediated classroom will be described, which we observed as part of our research projects. We started observations in tablet-classrooms and tablet-courses in 2012 with Danish classrooms and a Swedish university, and we observed almost 40 classrooms (more will come). In this section, I describe first a typical tablet-mediated classroom from a didactical design view; then, I show the same classroom from a process design view.

The classroom was a 9th grade physics class of 15 students (8 girls and 7 boys) that was conducted in the early morning of a normal school day in 2012 (Jahnke & Kumar, 2014).

Teaching aims/learning intention: The teacher communicated the teaching aims and intended learning outcomes on two levels: content level and developing competencies (skills). With regard to the content, the aim was to apply theoretical knowledge of physics that the students learned in former lessons. With regard to skill development, the students got the learning opportunity to conduct experiments in physics "to show what they have learned" (as the teacher added later in the interview).

Learning activities: The students received the assignment to plan and conduct an experiment that demonstrated the application of recently learned knowledge in physics on light or sound. Students chose groups and started to work on the assignment; the number in each group varied from seven students in one group, three to four students in some groups and two students in another group. Some groups created mind maps on the tablet; others used a mix of resources, such as the Internet access provided by the media tablet, a book, or pen and paper, to plan the idea. Students used the media tablet in many different ways, such as:

- Searching for information on the Internet
- Using mind map apps to visualize what they know, to mark what they don't know, and where they need advanced knowledge
- Watching videos
- Using camera and video-recording features to take photos and videos while preparing and conducting the physics experiments
- Using an app that included many textbooks for physics education
- Using tuning apps for sound experiments

- Uploading the plan and later the conducted experiments to the school Intranet and the school's YouTube channel
- Sharing and discussing with students from the university online.

The students documented first the preparation process of creating the experiment, and then they video-recorded the physics experiment. In almost all groups, the experiment failed the first time; the recorded short videos were useful in order to reflect together how to improve the experiment. That can be seen as a kind of "collaborative reflection" in school settings (Prilla et al., 2013). After watching the videos, the students came up with new ideas about what to improve for the next round. Some groups decided to carry out these reflections without the teacher, and other groups requested the teacher for support. The teacher helped the students by asking them questions without giving them the answer. He added later in the interview that he wants the students to find the solution themselves, but, of course, he guides them when the students need guidance. The teacher also created the opportunity for the students to discuss and share their ideas online with students in physics from a university. He connected the classroom situation to a 'real audience' (university students).

Feedback/assessment: In this class, the assessment was process based and part of the learning process. The teacher gave criteria in the beginning, such as creating a successful experiment in the fields of sound or light. Process-based assessment was supported in the form of documenting the learning progress and looking back to the documentation for a critical reflection with the aim of improving the second experiment. It was not only feed*back* but also feed*forward*. The teacher explained his reasoning as: "How do I know when the students have learnt something? When they can apply it to the real world." He wanted students to learn to "test their theories through experiments within a given field (e.g., sound, light)" and "learning by mistakes." To support this outcome, he also checked the experiment results with the groups and gave them feedback in the form of guided questions to help them to find the mistakes by themselves. In doing so, the groups experienced 'aha moments.' Later in the process, the students shared their results with their peers by uploading the results and videos on the Intranet and to the school YouTube channel. In the interview, the teacher stated, "I want to set the knowledge of my students free."

Social relations and multiple roles: All the students were engaged; they did communicate and interact with each other. This corresponded to the teacher's philosophy of "informal teaching." He said he wanted students to experiment and wanted to foster a role change in which students teach other students, while he could focus on the process of learning and providing personalized feedback to students. He added, "I have more time for my students for individual guiding" and stressed the benefit: "The students are equal now, all of them now have access to knowledge." The teacher played several roles; he was expert but also process designer, didactical designer and mentor for the students. The students were consumers but most of the time in the role of reflective makers and even teachers for their peers. The teacher was engaged, and he engaged the students. He also reflected and mentioned problems: "The biggest challenge for us teachers is to know when to shut off the media tablets; when should we use media tablets, when shall we use other things?"

Tablet-integration: The media tablets were used in forms where even the best school library cannot support this kind of learning. The media tablet was used as a multimodal device and in a flexible way that today no other device offers. The web-enabled mobile technology was used to collect information online; students read digital books, planned the experiments, recorded the experiments, watched the video in case the physics experiment went wrong, documented the experiments and distributed them via the school's YouTube channel. In the written exams later, the students were even allowed to use their produced videos as a resource.

Figure 5.5 shows the Digital Didactical Design from the viewpoint of the process design where all five components of the DDD—teaching aims (learning intentions), learning activities, process-based assessment, roles and technology (resources)—are illustrated.

The process view makes visible the ways the five components of the Digital Didactical Design model have been modeled and 'formed' in classroom ID11. It is a degree of complexity of modeling roles, activities and resources over time. When teaching is understood as *process design*, it helps to make decisions such as pedagogical reasoning; forming sociotechnical-pedagogical processes; and which activities, resources and roles to include and which not to include.

The process view in Figure 5.5 is very simplified. In detail, it was a back and forth of activities. Nevertheless, the model gives an idea of what I mean when I call it a 'process design view' and how designs for learning can be designed from a sociotechnical-pedagogical process perspective.

With the process view, it becomes clear why it is difficult to *differentiate* between teaching and learning activities in the practices of schools and universities. When the practice of teaching and learning is designed as a *process*, then the design starts with a focus on the outcome (learning intentions, teaching aims) and the student activities (marked as rectangles in Figure 5.5). Then, resources, roles and process-based assessment activities can be designed. A redesign, and a *redesign* of the redesign, starts. From a design perspective, teaching is the act of giving a form to the sociotechnical-pedagogical processes; teaching has the purpose and is the act of 'translating' the digital didactical design into a process design.

Teaching Is Process Design for Learning. Teachers 'Juggle' Well.

From our projects and empirical studies in schools (read Chapter 7), we were inspired to rethink the clusters of the innovative teachers. They are different in

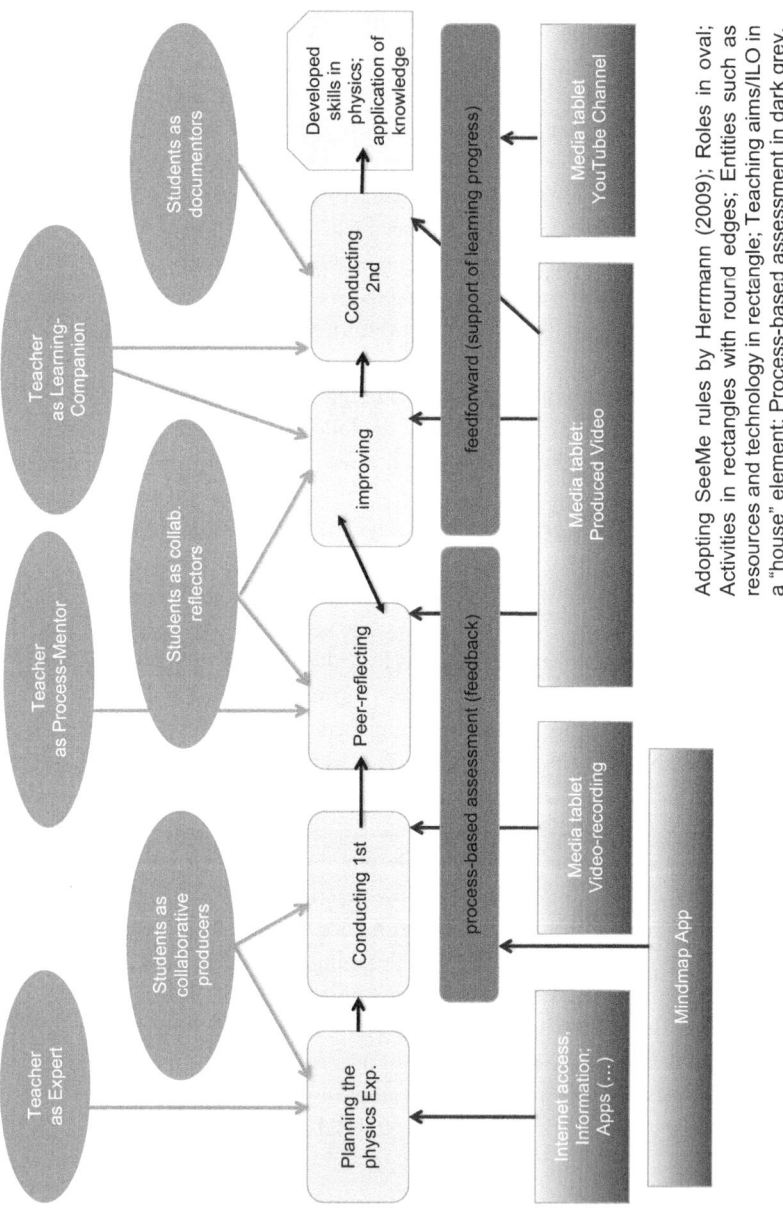

FIGURE 5.5 Digital Didactical Design of classroom ID11 from the process design view

Adopting SeeMe rules by Herrmann (2009): Roles in oval; Activities in rectangles with round edges; Entities such as resources and technology in rectangle; Teaching aims/ILO in a "house" element; Process-based assessment in dark grey.

terms of that they 'juggle well' (i.e., keep all the balls in the air) and have an idea of a process for the classroom in mind. Of course, it is unknown what will happen in reality, but the innovative teachers could be able to tell the observer about the classroom process, especially what follows on what in terms such as:

* What kind of learning intentions (teaching aims) are formulated for this classroom;
* What the plan is regarding what activities happen when to support the learning intentions
* Which roles are involved when and for what learning activity;
* Which resources are needed for what and when (e.g., what apps, what books); and
* What kind of process-based assessment activities will be done and when.

Such a sociotechnical-pedagogical process is informed by the Digital Didactical Design components. Teaching is the ability to translate the five components of the DDD into a procedure and process. Teaching is process design informed by the Digital Didactical Design. Teachers are jongleurs. Since the process is a plan, and the future is unknown, the teachers are jongleurs within such process designs. However, they are prepared for the unknown and have anticipated what could be wrong and have a plan B or C in mind. That makes a good juggler.

5.2.3 Design for Teaching Aims and Learning Intentions

Teaching aims are not only those that are derived from the curriculum. Teaching aims include both a form of measurable items that the teacher has translated from the curriculum and those that she constructs so as to foster student competence development. Aims can be described in the form of learning outcomes, skills and competences, which the student is able to develop *in and through* engaged learning situations. The teacher designs an opportunity to learn in which the students are able to achieve the aims and develop intended learning outcomes in the form of competences (e.g., skills to deal with and analyze online information and the different sources).

When we look at education that includes skills such as 'remembering' what is in the textbook, but also deep learning such as critical-reflective producers in social interactions (technology mediated or not), then it becomes clear that not all learning is measurable. It is a problem that not all learning outcomes are measurable, or at least they are not so easy to measure accurately after the class is over. When we, the readers of this book, reflect on what we learned from our childhood in order to become grown-ups, then we know, sometimes we learn years later, that the 'aha!' moment was suddenly there many years after finishing school. The time between inputs (such as information and learning activities given in schools and universities) and the outcomes vary; sometimes there are years between the 'aha!' moments. However, that does not mean it doesn't count.

When using the Digital Didactical Design framework, the question is whether the teaching aims are clear and what qualities they address—for the teachers themselves and for the students.

Formulating teaching aims as intended learning outcomes (learning intentions) by a teacher seems straightforward, but it is not. Consider Bloom's taxonomy (1956; revised by Anderson & Krathwohl, 2001); describing the possible learning outcomes on the level of "remembering, understanding, applying" is easier than on the other levels of "analyzing, evaluating, creating":

- My students remember (repeat) and understand (can explain) Topic X.
- My students are able to apply Topic X to Y.
- My students are able to analyze and evaluate Topic X. My students are able to create critical thinking in the form of different multiperspectives on Topic X.
- My students are able to create something new using Topic X.

Furthermore, many schools and universities focus on the development of competences such as 'ability to handle digital information' (e.g., online source critique). In the age of technology, where access to information is no longer a problem, there is a new need to reflect on teaching aims and intended learning outcomes:

- To know about the information is a main outcome on the surface learning level.
- To bridge textbook-driven learning and learning 'when the answer is not known' is useful in supporting a deep-learning approach.

Furthermore, there are also the learning outcomes from the students' perspectives. Do the students want to learn what the teachers expect, or do they have their own intended learning outcomes; and if 'yes' to the latter, can they make these visible to themselves and to the teachers? Could the teachers integrate the students' co-aims into the teachers' teaching aims?

I argue that curricula and study programs need a balance of what experts think is relevant for learners and what learners expect to learn and what they want to learn. It cannot be only the responsibility of the students to say what they want to learn (because sometimes they don't know what they want to learn and guidance might be useful), but the existing curricula are not flexible enough to have specific spaces for the learners' wishes. It is hard to say what a 'good' balance between curriculum learning outcomes and student wishes might be: whether 50:50, 70:30, 40:60 or something else, this question cannot be answered here. It depends on the design of the curriculum and may differ in different contexts. But we should start to try something out, reflect and learn from those experiences. Further research is required.

The importance of discussing and describing teaching aims as intended learning outcomes is not a stand-alone activity; rather, it is the possible starting point for creating learning activities. Once educational actors and teachers have the first teaching aims documented, the next step is to think about how to design activities for learners so as to achieve these teaching aims. Are the teaching aims and intended learning outcomes (ILO) aligned and related to the learning activities? This design question needs an answer from every teacher.

- Are the teaching aims and learning intentions created by teachers and students? If the aims are developed by someone else, such as an external committee, are teachers and students able to adopt them for their needs?
- Are the teaching aims and ILOs visible, and are these aims explicitly written and accessible somewhere online or offline? Are the teaching aims visible to the students, to other teachers, to the educational institution?
- What is the character of the teaching aims and ILOs: do they refer to surface levels only, while neglecting deeper learning skills? Do they focus on acquiring content or skill development?
- Are there new teaching aims and ILOs included with regard to the digital world such as the ability to handle digital information, being critical about the sources, how to interact online (ethics and values)?
- Is the purpose of the teaching aims and ILOs clear? What is the actual meaning behind them; what have students really learned?
- Do the teaching aims and ILOs include *co-aims* created by the learners? Are the aims and ILOs flexible that students can add their own ILOs?

If the answer to these questions is 'no,' then the educational actors have the responsibility to make the teaching aims and ILOs clearer, more understandable and visible for learners.

5.2.4 Design for Learning Activities (Individual, Collaborative, Community Learning)

One unsolved problem in the learning sciences is whether we can measure learning or not. It is a matter of the definition. What is learning? We can measure what a student remembers from the textbook, but it is more difficult to measure higher levels on Bloom's taxonomy, such as student creativity and the conceptual change of learners (see our research on teachers' conceptions of student creativity; e.g., Jahnke, 2011). Some researchers even argue we cannot measure deeper lifelong learning at all. I want to stress that there are several understandings of learning, such as those mentioned in Chapter 4. Instead of asking about the 'one and only' possible definition of learning, and what learning is, there is a need to argue for a pluralism that includes various understandings of learning for different situations in various spaces and for different learning processes.

Nowadays, actors in the interdisciplinary fields framed by the learning sciences and educational institutions want to have results showing if learning took place and the quality of it. Often this turns into the measurement of how well a student repeats the textbook or other content. However, this is merely a tiny portion of learning; such learning is learning on the surface, which might be still important, and we need it because we do not want to reinvent the wheel. However, it seems that educational institutions currently focus too much on this level of repetition. In the pressure to measure learning and to create rankings, and establish national and international tests for schools and universities, deeper learning has been neglected. One explanation is that it cannot be measured as easily as surface learning. Approaches such as critical-constructive collaborative reflections and the production of new things, creativity and social innovations are difficult to measure (if measurable at all). Can we actually really measure deeper learning in its entirety?

A Digital Didactical Design makes the teaching aims and learning intentions clear and designs learning activities for students to achieve these teaching aims. This is the start for what I call designing *of* and *for* engaged learning activities. A design for learning activities can include many of different activities, individual and collaborative actions. Learning as a cognitive effort is framed in a social process and takes place in social interactions such as in communities of learning expeditions in several communication spaces. However, it also needs individual learning phases because learning is also a cognitive construction process over time.

Over the last years, *didaktik* has argued that a shift is needed from teaching toward learning (e.g., Barr & Tagg, 1995); 'shift' means that learning opportunities are enabled, offered and creatively designed *through the eyes of learners*. When learning is constructed of knowledge building and development of competences, then the teacher's task is the creation of sociotechnical-pedagogical processes where the learner is capable of making a 'construction' and of giving meaning to information and activities. Learning is a process, knowledge and competences are intertwined results, and at the same time they are the start for the next learning process—it is a highly intertwined connection, a wicked situation. A knowledge-building process is a learning process.

When learning is a cognitive and social activity embedded into "situated actions" (Roschelle, 1992), then knowledge is also a constructive activity in which a person creates and develops a theoretical or practical understanding of something. Knowledge cannot be transported from Person A to Person B. From a person's viewpoint, knowledge is the act of interpreting new information and putting this information into the person's own context; context includes, for example, experiences that a person has already had and concepts she has about a subject. Knowledge is the interpretational process of connecting information into a person's own context and concepts. This means that the Internet and digital media world consists of information, and what people make out of it can become knowledge when they use the information and intertwine it with their own context and cognitive concepts.

The shift from teaching toward learning also argues that not the teaching aims but rather the intended learning outcomes (learning intentions) should be the start for designing learning (read Section 5.2.3 on teaching aims and learning intentions).

A deeper learning activity includes activities for problem solving that is connected to a real-world problem. To do this, teachers can create and define what an appropriate problem is. A problem is not a routine task that can be learned through exercises and repetition. A problem is a 'real' problem, related to a real audience, where the students are motivated and engaged to use different ways to find a solution. The degree of problem solving and its difficulty depends. The solution is known to the teacher, there is no solution so far, or the solution is unknown (read Chapter 4 and Section 4.2 in particular for discussion of what a good problem is, especially the text under "What is a real 'problem' that is useful for application in teaching for learning?").

Reading a textbook is not a learning activity per se; it is merely a task of informing students about existing facts. Textbook reading is often designed as an *information activity*. In order to trigger learning, the design of other forms of learning activities is required. For example, the teacher could design questions about the text or, better still, show a problem first; then the textbook is just one resource for solving the problem. Then, the content of the textbook is not the main aim, but when solving the problem the students learn how to use the content. Collaborative reflections and collaborative creativity (Herrmann, 2009; Prilla et al., 2013) may support an active learning expedition.

When using Kember's approach (1997) on how teachers understand themselves and their teaching practices, it allows different quality levels of teaching and learning to be revealed. The textbook learning model is a kind of 'information delivery,' whereas on the deeper level the facilitation of understanding is one example. This means that students not only learn what is in the textbook but also reflect on (and become critical about) the content. They learn to evaluate the given content (Figure 5.6). When we put Kember's approach together with Bloom's taxonomy (Anderson & Krathwohl, 2001), we have another model for analyzing the quality of learning from remembering to become creative, whereas the first two categories, remembering and understanding, can be assigned to surface levels and the last categories, evaluating and creating, we assign to deep learning.

In our empirical studies and research experiences, there are many examples on how to design for learning expeditions. They show a range of different kinds of engaged learning activities; see Chapter 6. Our classroom observations and projects in educational institutions inform rich designs for a diverse set of learning activities, for example:

- Transformative learning: students transform existing math stories into new comics (using apps on the media tablet) to show that the math formula has been understood.
- Complex learning: students create a book review about a traditional textbook or chapter using the app Bookcreator, where not only written text but

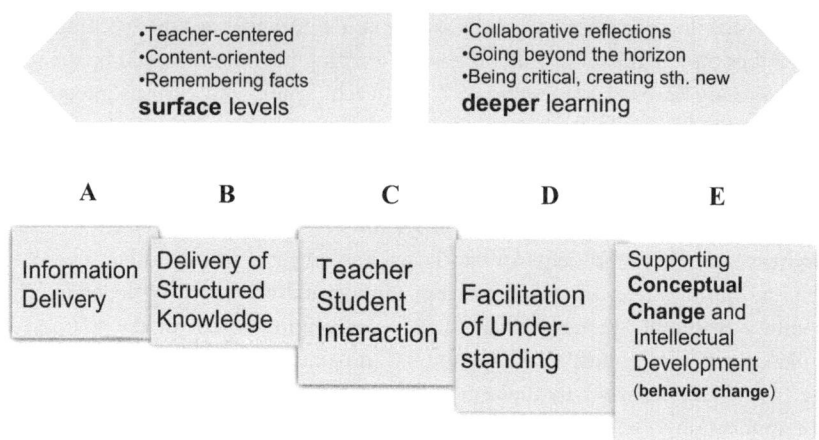

FIGURE 5.6 Kember's model of teachers' teaching concepts informing different levels of the learning quality (adopted from Johannes Wildt's slides, presented at Umeå University in Sweden, 2012)

also paintings, podcasts (recording one's own voice) and small videos are included.

- Peer-reflective reviewing: students write small texts from their research and discuss the quality of them in closed online groups (online discussion boards, Wiki-like systems, or social networking sites with commentary function)— in small student groups, every person comments to all; in bigger student groups, the teacher creates a scheme, e.g., four students in a group commenting to each other. Here, it is important that the students have some format, e.g., a form, for reviewing when they write a review the first time. Such a form includes items on formal issues and content issues.

- Collaboratively producing and reflecting of physics experiments: students create videos, podcasts or, with the app Explains Everything or Educreation, a stop-motion product instead of a pure written text to show what they have learned (the topics are delivered by the teacher, or the group discusses the themes on the topic in a first session). The teacher sets three deadlines, in the beginning, middle and just before the end, in order to *feedforward* the students' learning progress (as opposed to providing *feedback*). Guided reflections by the teacher and the peers are useful when reflecting on the current learning state, as well as becoming aware of possible problems and how to solve them.

Based on Kember's study, teaching has been seen for many years as a "delivery activity," as if one could deliver learning where textbook readings are at the center of learning. Many years ago, reading was the main activity; this is illustrated as SI (surface, individual) in Table 5.2. We went to schools to get access to

TABLE 5.2 Matrix for designing the quality of learning

	Individual learning (I)	*Learning in groups (G)*
Complex deeper learning (D)	Examples (DI) Multimodality, critical thinking, evaluating, producing something	Examples (DG) Peer-reflective learning, collaborative reflections, creating new knowledge in teams
Easy surface learning (S)	Examples (SI) Textbook readings, repetition of information, remembering, understanding	Examples (SG) Group learning: students split the tasks into individual subtasks

the books. Nowadays, we do not need to go to schools to get access to information. The information is all around us. Kember's empirical results also made it clear that teachers think that deep learning takes place as a conceptual change that he framed as the personal and intelligent development of a person. However, this does not show how to support such learning. Peer-reflective learning, collaborative reflections and designing experiments in groups might be some options, as illustrated in Table 5.2 as DG, deep learning in groups. Table 5.2 is derived from our empirical classroom studies in Denmark and Sweden (Jahnke et al., 2014).

5.2.5 Process-Based Assessment as Guided Reflections, Feedback and Feedforward

Traditional teaching is usually related to giving feedback at the end of a learning process and evaluating the product of learning made by a learner. This rather summative assessment approach lacks the process of monitoring the learning *progress*. To ensure deeper learning and learning expeditions, process-based reflection is the key principle of future designs for teaching and learning—and makes a difference to today's designs.

Process-based assessment is the teacher's design for creating feedback, feedforward and guided reflections on different levels such as self-assessment, peer-reflections and formative assessment given by the teacher during the learning process; the teacher has a plan for when to give feedforward and to whom.

Process-based assessment is the activity of creating and conducting guided reflections in different forms at different times during the learning process, such as peer- and self-assessment or feedback and feedforward by the teacher; it includes guided reflections, and has the purpose to show the learners 'where' they are in their learning (e.g., quality level), how to improve and how to continue in their learning progress. Process-based assessment has the purpose of supporting student engagement. Student engagement will be positively affected. Learners will be motivated to continue their learning. Chapman (2003) gives an overview on "alternative approaches to assessing student engagement rates . . . who wish to develop relevant assessment protocols that incorporate a combination of indices across the cognitive, affective, and behavioral domains."

Learning Is Relative

What teaching usually does is to give a grade to students and assess learning outcomes as an *absolute* result. This neglects that learning is *relative*. Different students have started their journeys from different points of departure, using different ways to achieve the teaching aim. Students have different preexisting knowledge; they are experienced in different contexts and learn differently. To take this into account, learning needs a form of assessment that can help students to grow during their learning process over time. This is what I call *process-based assessment* (adopted by Bergström, 2012).

Process-based assessment gives feedback to a learning state with the aim of *feedforwarding* students in the learning, to motivate them and to help them in phases when they are not successful. Process-based assessment helps students to progress during their learning processes, to become better, to improve instead of just giving a grade at the end. Process-based assessment is more than just helping students when they raise their hands; it is a process of structured facilitation using guided reflections.

It is not enough for the teacher simply to answer the questions for those students who have raised their hands. It is not enough for the teacher to go around a classroom or online and answer only those students who have raised their hands. It is not enough for teachers just to provide feedback by chance. The teacher needs a plan for process-based assessment activities with the focus on the students' future use of knowledge. Such a design includes activities for guided reflections on different levels (self-assessment; peer-reflective learning, teacher assessment) at several times within the learning process (at the beginning, in the middle, just before the end).

In a German lecture and seminar about mathematics, Hänze et al. (2013) tested in a semiexperimental research setting both traditional and process-based feedback mechanisms. The process-based teaching innovations primarily focused on better professional preparation of teachers, the design of the exercises with activating cognitive presence phases and meaningful feedback to the exercises. The teachers acted more like a coach focusing on "knowledge-building" instead of "knowledge-telling" (Roscoe & Chi, 2008). This assisted the learners. The study illustrates that process-based assessment has effects on the positive motivation of learners to learn. Motivation to learn and the initiation of learning processes depend on the learners' model of expectation and value aspects (Eccles & Wigfield, 2002). A teacher who uses process-based feedback focuses on an active performance and the problem-oriented controversy of learning objects, which relies to a large extent on support and counseling of individual learning processes (Schaper, Schloemer & Paechter, 2012).

Bergström (2012) defines process-based assessment differently from formative assessment. He argues that process-based assessment is not only the teacher's support for the learning process of students in continuing on their learning journeys: it is more than formative assessment. In a process-based assessment, everything can be negotiated—the process, the results, the learning aims. Such a negotiation takes place in a space or corridor of negotiation possibilities. The outer layer of the didactical conditions (Digital Didactics) provides such a space (go back to Figure 5.1), and the created curriculum, the organizational resources and the staff competences define a framework for negotiating the teaching and learning processes. For example, the curriculum provides a framework of what is allowed and what content is part and what is not part of teaching and learning. The problem is that once a curriculum is established, it serves as an "objective facticity" (Berger & Luckmann, 1967/1993), and it is hard to change it. It would be better for educational institutions to develop a curriculum that has more flexibility and is more dynamic.

5.2.6 Social Relations and Roles—Designing for Social Relationships

The social relations are often neglected in studies about teaching and learning in institutions. The design of social relations and social roles connects the elements of teaching, learning and assessment and makes the difference between surface individual learning and deeper collaborative learning (Jahnke & Liebscher, 2013). Roles have positive and negative effects on learning (Strijbos et al., 2003). Didaktik emphasizes the design of social relationships (e.g., Wildt, 2007). Without social relations, it is rather an instructional, teacher-centered and not a learning-centered concept. Learning without supporting social relations is just the repetition of existing information without the value and quality created by the social dimension.

Social relations embrace all kinds of human interaction and technology-mediated human interactions where the state of the social relationship between actor and situation is changing by interaction (read Chapter 2.3.2 Action and Interaction). Roles are then one form to 'see' the state of social relations between learners, and teacher and learners, in ways in which the social relations have been solidified.

From the outer circle (Layer 3 of the Digital Didactics, Figure 5.3), we have learned that formal structures can be a threat or can have a negative impact on developing learning innovations as forms of social practices. Formal structures like those developed in educational institutions over the last hundred years give a framework for human actions and coordinate different roles such as those of teachers, administration and learners but also can restrict interactions and learning: role-constrained learning (March & Olsen, 1975). Would it be better to have no structures? No. Social relations and structures are important for learning; without them, human interaction and learning are difficult to achieve. And even if we do not want any structures, we cannot wish them away. Wherever human communication is, there exists or emerge social structures in forms of expectations and other patterns.

In 1970 Jo Freeman wrote the "The Tyranny of the Structurelessness." The author makes it clear that pure informal structures or formlessness per se are not beneficial. Structurelessness can turn into chaos, where other social mechanisms such as power relations replace institutionalized structures. Social behavior, interactions and learning depend on the appropriate balance of both formal and informal structures. Institutionalized structures and defined processes try to support a balance in which all people have the same chance to participate. In contrast to work groups in educational institutions, where the group members are formally bound, learning networks consist of more informal than formal connections between members. Formal structures are characterized by conventional forms of behavior and established conventions, for example, behavior that is formally bound by a work contract or a formal role represented by a job/task description (e.g., formal moderator). Informal structures are rather casual, unofficial, loose and not triggered by any rules (e.g., activities of informal moderation).

Social structures are patterns and interrelationships of social elements, e.g., human behavior and relationships within sociotechnical communities that can be called roles. To observe the shape of roles offline and online, observable categories are required. According to the role model presented in Chapter 3, four categories are useful for understanding, analyzing and designing conditions for roles in learning expeditions:

- Teachers' and learners' positions within the community, relations to other members. Questions for designing learning are how to bring the learners from outside into the middle of the core members and what methods teachers can use for this.
- Teachers' and learners' tasks and purposes within the learning process. Questions for designing learning processes concern how to support different activities that enhance reflections toward role behavior.
- Tacit, implicit and explicit expectations of teachers and students. Questions for designing learning focus on how to solve conflicting expectations. Irritation by teachers, not to play the expected roles, can be useful to break through the established role patterns.
- Teachers' and learners' role performance; how they perceive themselves in which roles, and how the others perceive them. Questions for designing learning are how to give a structure for learners by having enough freedom to perform, how to support role changing, and what methods are useful. For

example, students are in consumer, producer, reflector, peer-reviewer and maker roles—and those roles are an explicit topic; the reflection of roles are on the agenda.

Designing for teaching and learning is not like working in a factory or sitting alone in the basement. When teaching has the aim of supporting deep learning such as a conceptual change (Kember, 1997; Roschelle, 1992), vivid interaction among participants is required. The heart of the Digital Didactics framework is therefore the design of social relations and roles. It is also the social connection between designs for performing teaching and designs for active learning. A positive, good, welcoming atmosphere among involved learners and teachers is a key for learning that allows and helps students to make mistakes and to learn from mistakes. The classroom and learning culture is one key to supporting students to grow in their competences to become critical problem solvers. The design of social relations helps to create such a welcome culture. For example, we all learn better when the given feedback is nice, critical-constructive and includes positive and negative issues, the sandwich model such as positive feedback, negative issues, and positive at the end to motivate the learner. Bad-formulated feedback affects the motivation of the learners in a wrong way (not all, there are some exceptions, but the majority of the learners).

Teachers can create such designs for developing social relations. There is just one challenge. The roles we have taken or are assigned do constrain our design thinking. We all have assumptions about the others and our own role—but these assumptions are almost always hidden and not clear to us or to others. For example, we have our beliefs as to what a good teacher does and what a good learner does. These beliefs change during a lifetime and across generations. These beliefs may even change during one class and one course. To make it clear, such dynamics of educational beliefs underlie social dynamics. Learners in the same classroom might have different and contradictory expectations about what a 'good' teacher and a 'good' learner are.

Unfortunately, there is no simple answer, and I cannot provide a recipe for what 'good' teachers and learners do. What 'good' is, is relative and depends on many things such as culture and values. However, I can report what innovative teachers in Denmark do, and I can share my experiences from teaching. Teachers in Denmark, for example, have created group activities in order to build social relations and have started guided reflections about teaching aims and metalearning (learning about learning). In one of the classes, the student group assignment was to find different QR codes outside the classroom; the QR codes led them to websites to answer questions about Danish grammar. The teaching objective in general was to improve writing skills. However, there was a second intention—the teacher went beyond the curriculum and created a metalearning process on learning how to learn. She asked the students at the end of the class about the learning activities: "What have you learnt, how was the group learning activity, did you like it or not, why or why not?" By doing so, the learners collected their opinions online in a closed system and voted and commented on it online. The results and comments were used in the next class to continue the discussion. In this way, the learners started a reflection about what they thought was a good learning activity and about their social relations to each other. It became also clear to them that different students have different opinions about a good learning assignment and activity. The teacher was engaged and designed for learning where the students were socially and personally connected.

The reflection on roles, perceptions and conceptions of role owners and roles of the counterpart can turn role-based constraints and role restrictions into a learning opportunity; but this means that role reflections must be integrated in the designs for learning.

5.2.7 Interactive Media: ICT Is More Than Just a Tool—Design Thinking in Education

One of the elements of a Digital Didactical Design is technology; there are many different technical devices and technological concepts outside in the world. What is the right one? What is the 'right' app when using a media tablet or any other web-enabled technology? This is the problem. There is no 'one size fits all.' So, how to find the right technology for a specific teaching method and learning situation? There is not the one and only right technology because one technology can be applied in different ways for different purposes. Robert McCormick and Peter Scrimshaw made it very clear when they wrote in 2001 the following:

> The approaches that focus on the computer–learner interactions, which represent the bulk of the research, do deal with teaching and learning issues. They often assume, however, that the software and the interaction with the learner are isolated from the surrounding pedagogy of the classroom or school. Research has shown that, even with highly 'self-contained' types of software such as Integrated Learning Systems, the success of the use of ICT is dependent upon the way in which the other elements of the classroom pedagogy relate to it (Wood, 1998). Such elements include other supporting classroom work, classroom discussion and how, if at all, students interact around the computer as they use the software (Wegerif & Scrimshaw, 1997). Recent publications in the area of collaborative learning involving computers have explored some of these issues (e.g., Littleton & Light, 1999).
>
> (p. 38)

I often hear from teachers and students, "We need suggestions from you about what are the correct technologies and apps (media tablets) to support student learning." Yes, good idea. But there are millions of apps, and different teachers prefer different apps for different reasons—their learning style or habits are just different. So, unfortunately, there is no simple answer to this question. Of course, I can provide ideas how I would start to find apps (for example, the "Pedagogy Wheel" and the "EdTechTeacher.org"), but every user has to adopt and adapt her style. In such situations, it is always useful to use existing discussion boards or other networks. Such a community helps, for example, to develop design thinking and discuss the criteria to find and evaluate technologies for different learning situations.

The problem we face is that we, often like teachers, educational developers, and designers of learning, think in a chronological way. We have here our curriculum, here is our course plan and now we add a kind of technology to make learning visible. Unfortunately, that is not how it works. There is no correct technology—the same sort of technology and mobile app can be used for and in different situations. We have to start somewhere, yes, but then learning takes place in "back and forth" and curves, not in a straight-ahead direction (Herrmann, 2009).

I rather suggest, in accordance with existing design-based approaches (Reeves et al., 2005; Design-based Research Collective) and design schools (e.g., Stanford, Umeå, Potsdam HPI), that we use a type of design thinking and apply it to the field of teaching and learning. Design thinking means that there is no straightforward problem-goal way; it is rather a back-and-forth way (Herrmann, 2012), leaving routines, trying something else with the support of colleagues at the workplace. Design thinking is a creative process: first, there are the phases of brainstorming and collecting ideas without judging them and, second, finding out what kind of ideas can be practiced, discarded and adjusted to a new design. Everyone can learn to become a design thinker. "All Design Is Re-design" (Platter, Meinel & Leifer, 2011; Kelley, 2009). The core of many models on design thinking is set forth in Table 5.3.

Their key principles are 1) create multidisciplinary teams; 2) designing happens in groups; two people are too few; 11 people are too many (what about football teams, are they not creative?); 3) flexible space ("all is on wheels"); 4) the process elements are Understand—Observe—Define point of view—Ideate—Prototype—Test; and 5) Iterations: "All design is re-design." "We do it over and over and over again."

Educational institutions might translate this idea to their teaching design practice. This model can serve as a start for developing an institutional strategy. In such a model, teachers are learners at the workplace. Teachers are designers for learning; they are *learning designers*. We even may use the words *didactical designers* and sociotechnical-pedagogical *process designers*.

From our studies in schools and teacher education using media tablets, we learned that there is a gap in translating the didactical and pedagogical models into a process plan for conducting teaching and learning in classrooms. There are didactical and pedagogical models, but teachers have not learned during their teacher education how to 'translate' the models into the practice of the classroom.

TABLE 5.3 Applying design thinking in education—teachers are designers for learning

Understand and define the problem	Do research, find ideas	Define it again, create ideas (ideate)	Create a prototype of the learning situation	Choose the powerful ideas	Implement the new learning way	Learn from it and do it again
What do you want to change in your teaching?	Find other teaching scenarios. What did other teachers do?	Rethink your teaching and learning model again, and redefine it.	Create a first plan and draft, including a process of what the students' learning activities are and create assignments (according to the DDD model).	You probably have too many ideas for such learning innovations.	Do it! Put the scenario into practice.	Reflect on your plan and practice.
Use the Digital Didactical Design model to analyze your class/seminar.				Just choose one of the powerful ideas and reshape the learning process, create a time plan and a process (what do the students do, when, why?) What results do you as a teacher expect?	Make a course diary (what was the plan, what did you change, why?).	Look back and analyze.
How to improve your teaching ways to support students' learning?	Find apps and teaching and learning examples.	Find first ideas to change from teaching models into learning expeditions.	How would you organize the next class when you have no restrictions, everything being possible?			What worked, what did not, why? Change it and do it again.
How to design sociotechnical-pedagogical processes?						

Cocreation, communication, collaboration
(in a team of diverse people such as teachers, designers, etc.)

Teachers follow the textbook instead of creating sociotechnical-pedagogical processes. The textbook usually guides the didactical design. Teachers have content knowledge (CK) from their subjects, they might have pedagogical knowledge (P) and also technology knowledge (T), but they do not have 'design knowledge.' These are known as TPCK (or TPACK) models (Koehler et al., 2007). Such models might be extended and add the dimension of how to translate the knowledge into a process design. Teacher education lacks in design thinking and design doing. I propose an advanced model called TPACK+D.

Such a design thinking approach also makes clear why some physical rooms feel more creative than others. Creativity emerges when knowledge and experience from different areas are merged into new ideas while overcoming solidified structures and overcoming established thought patterns. Creativity emerges when breaking through established patterns. Humor and flexible rooms (e.g., "all is on wheels"; instead of digital projectors, use interactive floors) are some ways of supporting such a breakthrough.

Characteristics of ICT—It Is More Than Just a Tool

In order to find a form of interactive technology, which educational actors need for those designs that support student learning, it is useful to know something about the different characteristics of technology. ICT is not just a tool; it is more than just a tool. ICT is not like a hammer; ICT is interactive and transformative. Whenever teachers and students use it, they create new spaces for more interaction and more communication. This affects teaching and learning.

Following Rammert (2003), technology might be differentiated in five categories: Passive, Active, Reactive, Interactive and Transactive. This is similar to the technology integration matrix (TIM) developed from the Florida State Initiative (http://fcit.usf.edu/matrix and http://fcit.usf.edu/matrix/matrix.php), which describes the levels of technology integrated into the curriculum (Jonassen et al., 2003; Allsopp, Hohlfeld & Kemker, 2007). Their five levels of technology are Entry (teacher "delivers curriculum content to students"), Adoption ("teacher directs"), Adaptation ("teacher facilitates students in exploring"), Infusion ("teacher provides the context and students choose") and Transformation ("teacher encourages the innovative use of technology"). On the other y-axis, they put five characteristics of the learning environment: Active ("students are actively engaged"), Collaborative ("students use tools to collaborate"), Constructive ("students use tools to connect new information"), Authentic ("students use tools to link learning activities") and Goal-directed (i.e., reflective) ("students use tools to set goals). "Together, the five levels of technology integration and the five characteristics of meaningful learning environments create a matrix of 25 cells" (Jonassen et al., 2003). The definitions and examples of TIM might be useful to start with when using technology for supporting learning.

The huge advantage of digital media and interactive technology such as Web 2.0 applications, web-enabled mobile devices, and apps is their "sociability" (Castell, 1996). They provide the potential to make learning visible. In Web 1.0, it was only possible to download information; nowadays, it is so easy to create new information online, on the fly, in a matter of seconds, and to communicate with millions of people online without knowing them via Twitter, Google+, LinkedIn, Instagram and many other applications. Such forms of digital media have pros and cons. Cyberbullying and cheating are two of the negative aspects; using private data for creating personal commercials is another problem. Uploading private photos without asking the person whose image is on the photo is also an ethical problem. In the coming years, governments need to create sophisticated Internet laws to react to such negative instances of human behavior and to create rules and norms for (re)acting online.

The advantage of ICT is access to the Internet, and this may help students to turn from consumers to producers into reflective makers. ICT can make a significant contribution to learning, especially in "making learning visible" (Hattie, 2009). Mårell-Olsson & Hudson (2008) illustrate different types of digital portfolios in which students develop the ability to "collect, organize, interpret and reflect on their individual learning and practice, and become more active and creative in the development of knowledge" (p. 73). The integration of mobile technologies in didactical designs and vice versa, however, is more complex than it seems (Kirschner & Davis, 2003). Koehler et al. (2007) show how complex the integration of content, technical and pedagogical knowledge is (TPCK/TPaCK model) (Banks, Leach & Moon, 1999). ICT implementation in teacher education is still under construction (Granberg, 2011) In addition, Loveless (2007) illustrates by the example of primary schools how the coevolutionary development of subject knowledge and didactics needs the support of "improvisation."

To find appropriate technology in order to design sociotechnical-pedagogical processes of learning expeditions, it is useful to develop first a set of criteria that is needed for a specific teaching and learning scenario. This set of criteria helps to assess different forms of technology for different teaching and learning purposes. There are different illustrations of what technology offers. First, the C-C-C triangle of communication, coordination and cooperation (Koch & Gross, 2006) provides a scheme for putting technologies into one of three 'C's': The designer asks if the technology supports communication, coordination, and/or cooperation and also asks to what extent it is useful for the teaching and learning scenario. Second, the Place-Time-Model provides a matrix for asynchronous and synchronous communication, as opposed to being at the same location or at different locations and at the same time or different times (O'Hara-Deveraux & Johansen, 1994). Third, the model by Meckel (2008) includes the functions of "share, express, connect." Learners share, express themselves and connect to others using different technologies. Fifth, the five-point model (see Figure 5.7)

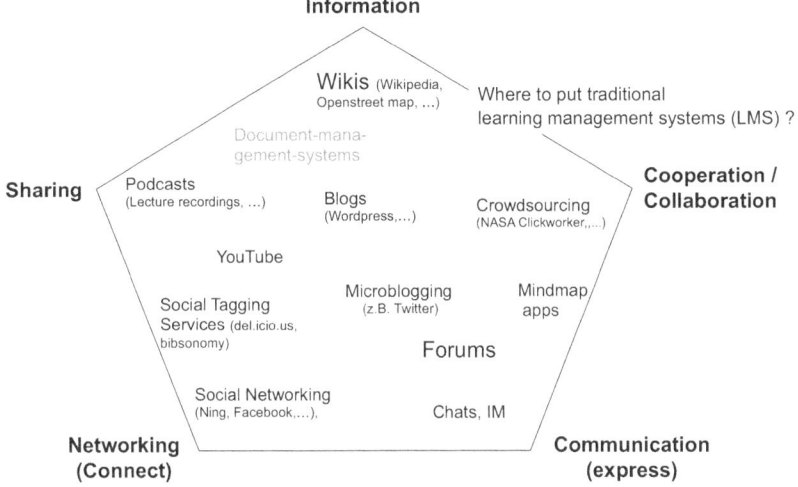

FIGURE 5.7 Examples of digital media and its different functions (crossovers in reality)

adds the function of sharing and providing information (formerly known as document-management systems).

Existing interactive media often serve more than just one function. It depends on how the user wants to use it and how the teachers introduce it to the learners.

There are many other attempts that categorize information and communication technologies (ICT). For example, an alternative option is to characterize them by their degree of "interactivity" (Burns, 2011):

- Learner interaction with an object or person in a way that allows learners to improve their knowledge and skills in a particular domain;
- Multiple forms of communication between learners around an object of study, a tool, or an experience;
- Learner control and program adaptation based on learner input (Sims, 2003);
- Reciprocal process of information exchange and sharing ideas between students and teachers; and
- Multiple forms of synergistic participation and communication that aid the development of meaningful learning.

McCormick and Scrimshaw (2001) made another useful differentiation of ICT: 1) as "efficiency aid," 2) as "extension device" (to extend learning such as having access to material on the Internet), and 3) as "transformative device" that turns learning into new forms, for example, learning expeditions (read their Table 1, pp. 51–52).

To some extent, the different categories might be useful for teachers to start creating designs for learning where they want to use different forms of technology. In reality, the user adopts ICT in new ways and it comes to "metamorphoses" (Orlikowski, 1992, 1996); this means that the user adopts ICT in a way that the software programmers, or the people who introduce it, have not anticipated before. Work and learning takes place in "situated actions" (Suchman, 1987).

The different theoretical understandings and categorizations on ICT show that web-enabled technology is more than just a tool; it is also a mediator that connects learners' communication and mediates human interactions. It gives access to communication and online places and spaces, but it also builds new spaces while using it.

Emerging Digital Didactical Designs When Linking Technology and Didactics

A highly relevant issue for enabling student learning is whether the technologies and mobile devices are linked to the pedagogical design or not (McCormick & Scrimshaw, 2001). The use of ICT and mobile technologies has various implications, ranging from being mere substitutes with only limited effects up to completely redefining the pedagogy (Puentedura, 2014). However, a focus on mobile devices alone cannot explain the emergence of new teaching designs and "is hard to convert into a pedagogy for teaching and learning since tools are always specific to tasks" (Wegerif, 2005, p. 155).

In the era of the Internet-driven world, in a networked world, teaching and learning practices are always technology based. But they do range from a low extent to a high extent, supporting different forms of learning where the quantity and the quality of the technology integration vary. For example, the sharing of documents, PPT-slides and literature via Intranets is one means of using technology.

A low extent of ICT integration can be seen when there is a low or nonadded value of using mobile devices for learning situations or if the value of the use is not evident; for example, the media tablet is a substitute for pen and paper or a printed textbook. A medium extent is there when the mobile devices are a substitute for other existing technologies that also could have been used, for example, a computer, a laptop or a digital camera. A high extent exists when the use of the mobile technology shows special characteristics or new functions and features that no other device can add at present, for example, special apps, a one-in-all device, or a multimodal device. The SAMR model by Puentedura (2014) has similar thinking. The model is useful for teachers at schools and universities in understanding the level of technology integration in their organization from a low to high extent of ICT integration:

- Substitution: "Technology is used as a direct substitute for what you might do already, with no functional change"—low extent of ICT use.

- Augmentation: "Technology is a direct substitute, but there is functional improvement over what you did without the technology"—low-medium extent of media ICT use.
- Modification: "Technology allows you to significantly redesign the task"— high-medium extent of ICT use.
- Redefinition: "Technology allows you to do what was previously not possible"—high extent of ICT integration.

Our study in Denmark (Jahnke et al., 2014) on teaching practices in a tablet-mediated learning culture shows that 24 in-depth observed classrooms integrated the media tablet into the didactical design to a high extent (R = 11); the other eight classrooms linked the media tablets to the pedagogical design to a medium (M = 5; A = 5) or low extent (S = 3). This indicates that some of the applied digital didactical designs enhance engaged and deeper learning better than the others do.

Studies on integrating technology, pedagogical and content/subject knowledge by teachers, known as TPCK models, show how these dimensions affect each other (Koehler, Mishra & Yahya, 2007). While the TPCK models are too vague for studying the ways in which teachers utilize Digital Didactical Designs in their *actual classroom practice*, studies on mobile learning focus on micro levels of learning from a learner's perspective and ignore that teaching is a *design project* developed and carried out by teachers. It is still underexplored and underresearched as to how the new situation of co-expanded spaces, created through the use of media tablets, affects a teacher's practice for enabling learning. Therefore, in our research (Jahnke, Svendsen, Johansen & Zander, 2014), we studied the integration of mobile technology in *teaching practices* in co-located settings where media tablets, teaching and learning spaces merged together into new co-expanded spaces.

From all our studies, we have learned that the approach of Digital Didactics is not just the addition of didactics 'plus' interactive media to traditional teaching concepts. Wherever teachers just added the digital media to an existing didactical approach, there was not much benefit for learning. The elements require rather an interwoven thinking and a reorganization of existing designs toward new digital didactical designs. It envisions new models of design thinking and new ways of teaching and learning for creating rich learning opportunities. It is a coevolutionary creation of didactics and technology into new forms of Digital Didactical Designs. From our studies in tablet-classrooms (Chapter 6), we explored the following key factors when teachers designed for tablet-mediated learning:

- Teachers create new practices to approach informal-in-formal learning in arena X across existing rooms. It is not the course-based model that is the foundation; rather, the learning expedition is the key to designing learning.

- Teachers combine traditional textbook readings with open, unstructured, informal learning space where "students are encouraged to experiment, play and explore topics" (Johnson et al., 2013).
- Teachers create new learning goals on the fly in a learning expedition within fast-changing surroundings.
- Teachers produce and create learning expeditions instead of reproducing existing course models.
- Teachers create designs that focus on learning as a process, including process-based assessment over time, and make learning visible.
- Teachers create designs for social relations, helping the students in their group learning (e.g., with project management methods or group facilitation methods).
- Learning in a group needs to be learned; from this viewpoint, the teacher is a 'process mentor' and a process designer for the dynamics of social relations.

5.3 It Is Not Technology or Didactics—Emergence of New Digital Didactical Designs

The younger generation (e.g., digital natives) have already created new forms of communication and knowledge sharing. We also see a change in the discussion cultures of daily-life groups. When facts are discussed, at least one person takes her smartphone and searches for the information online—unplanned learning takes place. With the mobile devices, which are almost everywhere, as each student has a smartphone, the pressure to rethink teaching practices and find ways to handle this omnipresent online presence is increasing. This is different than the earlier laptop age.

Today, mobile devices are small. In the future, we can expect devices such as smart glasses and smart watches with Internet access. They are so small and part of our normal clothes that if the user wishes, these devices can become invisible. A person can communicate in seconds. The devices need only seconds to start up. Such inventions bring innovations from daily life into schools and universities and trigger a rethink with regard to traditional teaching routines.

Teachers ask themselves: how can I handle the omnipresent online presence when students in my class google my lecture and scrutinize what I have said? From a didactical point of view, the reaction is 'Fantastic!' We all want students to think as researchers, to be engaged, critical and active. The problem remains that ICT use in schools and universities is far behind this social change. However, there are some innovative teachers out there, and we can learn from them, as shown here and in detail in Chapter 6.

The message here is that it is not one or the other—it is not a choice between technology and didactical approaches. To develop teaching and learning practices in a digital world, the innovative teachers look for tools and experience how they inspire them to create new forms of teaching, innovative pedagogies and Digital Didactical Designs. Our studies in Scandinavia illustrate that didactical designs cannot just be added to ICT or vice versa. Teachers have designed new forms of Digital Didactics to enable and boost student learning, and they provide the first ideas on how to define a learning expedition (Chapter 3). The cases show a new way of teaching that fosters new forms of learning, which we propose to name learning expedition and learning through reflective making. A learning expedition is a form of reflective cross-action on the two levels of 'making' and 'reflection' that stands for rather open-ended, problem-based learning paths and includes aims-oriented learning to master X or explore and understand the implications of N, in which the learning methods and instruments are very open and take place in CrossActionSpaces with reflecting peers where process-based assessment supports the learning progress.

Learning does take place in loops; it is not a straightforward way, but rather it has detours. When teaching is not only creating conditions for learning, it is the design of sociotechnical-pedagogical processes.

5.4 References

Allsopp, M. M., Hohlfeld, T. & Kemker, K. (2007). *The technology integration matrix: the development and field-test of an Internet based multi-media assessment tool for the implementation of instructional technology in the classroom.* Paper session presented at the annual meeting of the Florida Educational Research Association.

Anderson, L. W. & Krathwohl, D. R. (2001). *A Taxonomy for Learning, Teaching, and Assessing: A Revision of Bloom's Taxonomy of Educational Objectives.* New York: Longman.

Banks, F., Leach, J. & Moon, B. (1999). New understandings of teachers' pedagogic knowledge. In: J. Leach & B. Moon (Eds.): *Learners and Pedagogy.* London: Paul Chapman, pp. 89–110.

Barr, R. & Tagg, J. (1995): From teaching to learning. A new paradigm for undergraduate education. In: D. DeZure (Ed.): *Learning from Change. Change Magazine,* S198–200.

Berger, P. & Luckmann, T. (1993). *The Social Construction of Reality.* Frankfurt: Fischer (Original work published 1967)

Bergström, P. (2012). *Designing for the Unknown. Didactical Design for Process-Based Assessment in Technology-Rich Learning Environments.* Umeå, Sweden: Umeå University Press.

Biggs, J. (1996). Enhancing teaching through constructive alignment. *Higher Education,* 32(3), pp. 347–364.

Bloom, B. S. (1956). *Taxonomy of Educational Objectives, Handbook I: The Cognitive Domain.* New York: David McKay.

Bonderup Dohn, N. & Hansen, J. J. (2014): Is learning designs something you think, do, live with, react to, or conceptualize with? In *Designs for Learning Conference in Stockholm.* Retrieved May 8, 2014, from http://www.designsforlearning.nu/conference/program/pdf_webb/bonderupdohn_hansen.pdf

Burns, M. (2011). *Distance Education for Teacher Training Modes, Models, and Methods.* UNESCO Report. Washington, DC: Education Development Center.

Castell, M. (1996). *The Rise of the Network Society. The Information Age: Economy, Society and Culture.* Vol. 1. Cambridge, MA: Blackwell.

Chapman, E. (2003). Alternative approaches to assessing student engagement rates. *Practical Assessment, Research & Evaluation,* 8(13).

Cochrane, T. & Narayan, V. (2011). DeFrosting professional development: reconceptualising teaching using social learning technologies. In *ALT-C 2011 Conference Proceedings*, pp. 158ff.

Conole, G. (2013). *Designing for Learning in an Open World*. New York: Springer.

Duffy, T. M. & Cunningham, D. J. (1996): Constructivism: implications for the design and delivery of instruction. In: D. H. Jonassen (Ed.): *Handbook of Research for Educational Communications and Technology*. New York: Simon & Schuster Macmillan, pp. 170–198.

Eccles, J. & Wigfield, A. (2002). Motivational beliefs, values, and goals. *Annual Review of Psychology*, 53, 109–132. doi:10.1146/annurev.psych.53.100901.135153

Fink, D. L. (2003). *Integrated Course Design*. Idea paper #42. Kansas: Idea Center.

Freeman, J. (1970). The tyranny of the structurelessness. *Berkeley Journal of Sociology*, 17, pp. 151–165.

Granberg, C. (2011). *ICT and Learning in Teacher Education: The Social Construction of Pedagogical ICT Discourse and Design* (PhD thesis, Umeå University, Umeå, Sweden).

Hänze, M., Fischer, E., Schreiber, S., Biehler, R. & Hochmuth, R. (2013). Innovationen in der Hochschullehre: empirische Überprüfung eines Studienprogramms zur Verbesserung von vorlesungsbegleitenden Übungsgruppen in der Mathematik, *ZFHE*, 8(4), pp. 89–103.

Hattie, J. (2009). *Visible Learning: A Synthesis of Over 800 Meta-Analyses Relating to Achievement*. London: Routledge.

Hauge, T. E. & Dolonen, J. (2012). Towards an activity-driven design method for online learning resources. In A. D. Olofsson & O. J. Lindberg (Eds.): *Informed Design of Educational Technologies in Higher Education: Enhanced Learning and Teaching*. Hershey, PA: IGI Global, pp. 101–117.

Herrmann, Th. (2009). Design heuristics for computer supported collaborative creativity. In *Proceedings of the 42nd Hawaii International Conference on System Sciences* (HICSS), IEEE Computer Society, pp. 1–10.

Herrmann, Th. (2012). Kreatives Prozessdesign (*Creative Process Design*). Heidelberg: Springer.

Hinssen, P. (2010). The new normal—explore the limits of the digital world. Lanoo. Retrieved May 7, 2013, from http://www.goodreads.com/book/show/9517901-the-new-normal

Hudson, B. (2008). A didactical design perspective on teacher presence in an international online learning community. *Journal of Research in Teacher Education*, Umeå University, 15(3–4), 93–112.

Hyman, P. (2012). In the year of disruptive education. *Communications of the ACM*, 55(12), 20–22. doi:10.1145/2380656.2380664

Jahnke, I. (2010). Dynamics of social roles in a knowledge management community. *Computers in Human Behavior*, 26(4), 533–546. doi:10.1016/j.chb.2009.08.010

Jahnke, I. (2011). How to foster creativity in technology enhanced learning. In: B. White, I. King & Ph. Tsang (Eds.): *Social Media Tools and Platforms in Learning Environments: Present and Future*. Berlin: Springer, pp. 95–116. doi:10.1007/978-3-642-20392-3_6

Jahnke, I. & Kumar, S. (2014). iPad-didactics—didactical designs for iPad-classrooms: experiences from Danish schools and a Swedish university. In: Ch. Miller & A. Doering (Eds.): *The New Landscape of Mobile Learning: Redesigning Education in an App-based World*. New York: Routledge.

Jahnke, I. & Liebscher, J. (2013). Towards a didactical design using mobile devices to encourage creativity. *Enhancing Learning in the Social Sciences*, 5(1), 51–64. doi:10.11120/elss.2013.05010051

Jahnke, I. & Norberg, A. (2013). Digital didactics—scaffolding a new normality of learning. *Open Education Contributions to the JRC-IPTS Call for Vision Papers.* Part III: Higher Education, pp. 129–134.

Jahnke, I., Norqvist, L. & Olsson, A. (2014, September 16–19). Digital Didactical Designs of Learning Expeditions. In: C. Rensing et al. (Eds.): *Open Learning and Teaching in Educational Communities.* The 9th European Conference on Technology Enhanced Learning, EC-TEL 2014, Graz, Austria, LNCS Vol. 8719, pp. 165–178.

Jahnke, I., Svendsen, N. V., Johansen, S. K. & Zander, P.-O. (2014). The dream about the magic silver bullet—the complexity of designing for tablet-mediated learning. In: *ACM GROUP 2014 Conference Proceedings.*

Johnson, L., Adams Becker, S., Cummins, M., Estrada, V., Freeman, A. & Ludgate, H. (2013). *NMC Horizon Report: 2013 Higher Education Edition.* Austin, TX: New Media Consortium.

Jonassen, D., Howland J., Moore, J. & Marra, R. (2003). *Learning to Solve Problems With Technology: A Constructivist Perspective* (2nd ed.). Upper Saddle River, NJ: Merrill Prentice Hall.

Kelley, D. (2009). A designer takes on his biggest challenge ever. *Fast Company.* Retrieved September 19, 2014, from http://www.fastcompany.com/1139331/ideos-david-kelley-design-thinking

Kember, D. (1997). A reconceptualisation of the research into university academics' conceptions of teaching. *Learning and Instruction,* 7(3), 255–275.

Kirschner, P. & Davis, N. (2003). Pedagogic benchmarks for information and communications technology in teacher education. *Technology, Pedagogy and Education,* 12(1), 125–147. doi:10.1080/14759390300200149.

Klafki, W. (1963). *Studien zur Bildungstheorie und Didaktik* [*Studies of Education Theory and Didactics*]. Weinheim, Germany: Beltz.

Koch, M. & Gross, T. (2006, June). Computer-supported cooperative work—concepts, trends. In *Proceedings of the 11th Conference of the Association Information and Management (AIM),* Luxembourg.

Koehler, M. J., Mishra P. & Yahya, K. (2007). Tracing the development of teacher knowledge in a design seminar: integrating content, pedagogy and technology. *Computers & Education,* 49, 740–762.

Loveless, A. (2007). Preparing to teach with ICT: subject knowledge, Didaktik and improvisation. *Curriculum Journal,* 18(4), 509–522. doi:10.1080/09585170701687951.

Littleton, K. & Light, P. (Eds.). (1999). *Learning with Computers: Analysing Productive Interaction.* London: Routledge.

Lund, A. & Hauge, T. E. (2011). Designs for teaching and learning in technology-rich learning environments. *Nordic Journal of Digital Literacy,* 4, 258–272.

March, J. G. & Olsen, J. P. (1975). The uncertainty of the past-organizational learning under ambiguity. *European Journal of Political Research,* 3(2), 141–171.

Mårell-Olsson, E. & Hudson, A. (2008). To make learning visible: in what way can ICT and multimedia contribute? *Tidskrift för lärarutbildning och forskning,* 3–4, 73–90.

Marton F. & Säljö R. (1976) On qualitative differences in learning. *British Journal of Educational Psychology,* 46, 4–11.

McCombs, B. L. (2000, September 1–12). *Assessing the role of educational technology in the teaching and learning process: a learner-centered perspective.* In Proceedings of the Secretary's Conference on Educational Technology, Measuring Impacts and Shaping the Future Alexandria, VA, pp. 3–15.

McCormick, R., & Scrimshaw, P. (2001). Information and communications technology. *Knowledge and Pedagogy Education, Communication and Information*, 1(1), pp. 37–57.

Meckel, M. (2008). Aus Vielen wird das Eins gefunden—wie Web 2.0 unsere Kommunkation verändert [From many there will be the One—how Web 2.0 changes our communication]. *APuZ*, 39, 17–23.

Mehan, H. (1979). Learning Lessons. The Social Organization of Classroom Instruction. Cambridge, MA: Harvard University Press.

Norqvist, L., Leffler E. & Jahnke, I. (2015). Sweden and informal learning—towards integrated views of learning in a digital media world. A pedagogical attitude? In: T. Burger, M. Harring & M. Witte (Eds.): *Handbook for Informal Learning*. Weinheim, Germany: Juventa.

Northcote, M. (2009). Educational beliefs of higher education teachers and students: implications for teacher education. *Australian Journal of Teacher Education*, 34(3).

O'Hara-Devereaux, M. & Johansen, R. (1994). *Globalwork: Bridging Distance, Culture, and Time.* San Francisco, CA: Jossey-Bass.

Olofsson, A. D. & Lindberg, O. J. (2012). *Informed Design of Educational Technologies in Higher Education: Enhanced Learning and Teaching.* Hershey, PA: IGI Global.

Orlikowski, W. J. (1992). The duality of technology: rethinking the concept of technology in organizations. *Organization Science*, 3(3), 398–427.

Orlikowski, W. J. (1996). Improvising organizational transformation over time: a situated change perspective. *Information Systems Research*, 7(1), 63–92.

Platter, H., Meinel, Ch. & Leifer, L. (2011). *Design Thinking, Understand—Improve-Apply.* Heidelberg: Springer.

Prilla, M., Herrmann, Th. & Degeling, M. (2013). Collaborative reflection for learning at the healthcare workplace. In: S. P. Goggins, I. Jahnke & V. Wulf (Eds): *Computer-Supported Collaborative Learning at the Workplace—CSCL@Work.* New York: Springer, pp. 139–165.

Puentedura, R. (2014). SAMR model. Retrieved May 20, 2014, from https://sites.google.com/a/msad60.org/technology-is-learning/samr-model

Rammert, W. (2003). *Technik in Aktion: Verteiltes Handeln in soziotechnischen Konstellationen [Technology in action: distributed action in sociotechnical constellations].* TUTS Working Paper 2, TU Berlin University, Technology Studies.

Reeves, Th., Herrington, J. & Oliver, R., (2005, Spring). Design research. *Journal of Computing in Higher Education*, 16(2), 97–116.

Roschelle, J. (1992): Learning by collaborating: convergent conceptual change. *Journal of the Learning Sciences*, 2(3), 235–276.

Roscoe, R. & Chi, M. (2008, July). Tutor learning: the role of explaining and responding to questions. *Instructional Science*, 36(4), 321–350.

Schaper, N., Schlömer, T. & Paechter, M. (2012). Kompetenzen, Kompetenzorientierung und Employability in der Hochschule [Themenheft]. Zeitschrift für Hochschulentwicklung, 7(4). Retrieved October 14, 2014, from http://zfhe.at/index.php/zfhe/issue/current

Selander, S. & Kress, G. (2010). *Design för lärande—ett multimodalt perspektiv [Designing for Learning—A Multimodal Approach].* Stockholm: Norstedts.

Sims, R. (2003). Promises of interactivity: aligning learner perceptions and expectations with strategies for flexible and online learning. *Distance Education*, 24(1), 87–104.

Strijbos, J.-W., Martens, R. & Jochems, W. (2003). The effect of roles on group efficiency. In: B. Wasson, R. Baggetun, U. Hoppe & S. Ludvigsen (Eds.): *International Conference on Computer Support for Collaborative Learning 2003.* Bergen: Intermedia.

Suchman, L. (1987). *Plans and Situated Actions: The Problem of Human-Machine Communication.* New York: Cambridge University Press.

Vygotsky, L. S. (1978). *Mind in Society: The Development of Higher Psychological Processes.* Cambridge, MA: Harvard University Press.

Wasson, B. (2007). Design and use of collaborative network learning scenarios: the DoCTA experience. *Educational Technology & Society,* 10(4), 3–16.

Wegerif, R. & Scrimshaw, P. (1997). *Computers and Talk in the Primary Classroom.* Clevedon: Multilingual Matters.

Wegerif, R. 2005. A dialogic understanding of the relationship between CSCL and teaching thinking skills. *Computer Supported Collaborative Learning* 1, 143–157. doi:10.1007/s11412-006-6840-8

Wildt, J. (2007). On the way from teaching to learning by competences as learning outcomes. In: A. Pausits & A. Pellert (Eds.): *Higher Education Management and Development in Central, Southern and Eastern Europe.* Münster: Waxmann, pp. 115–123.

Wood, D. (1998). The UK ILS Evaluations: Final Report (Coventry, BECTa) 2000 Sutton Hoo Research Project 5/10/00. http://www.york.ac.uk/depts/arch/staff/sites/suttonhoo.htm

6

PROJECTS AND EMPIRICAL STUDIES TOWARD REFLECTIVE CROSSACTIONSPACES

Studying if "learning is better with ICT than without" is like studying "if learning is better with pen & paper than without"—it misses the Digital Didactical Design thinking.

(adopted from Anders Norberg)

I woke up in Berlin in March 2013 to attend a national conference on pedagogy and turned the TV on. I could not believe what I was watching. The daily news were reporting on a study in a high school in Germany where students received media tablets to study mathematics. Researchers wanted to find out if mathematics learning using media tablets is better than without. I was so surprised because the TV showed a normal class; it looked as if there were no changes at all in the teaching or learning or pedagogy. The scene had all the appearances of a traditional classroom where, instead of writing on a piece of paper, the students were using the media tablets. But they could have been using pen and paper, too. There would have been no difference. I was shocked. Would researchers ever consider carrying out such a comparative study just with a pen and paper instead of technology? No, because that would be odd.

It is not useful to carry out a study on whether learning in Classroom A with pen and paper is better or worse than in Classroom B without pen and paper. Learning is not better or worse because of the pen and paper; learning is better supported because of the revision of the Digital Didactical Design, where technology is integrated in the design. The new resource of a pen and paper and other forms of new technology provides different options for new forms of didactics and new ways of learning and how learners can express themselves. In other words, when using ICT or mobile technology, the didactic needs a change; otherwise, the potential of the new resource will be missed.

So why do researchers want to do such a comparative study with technology when it is pointless? My point here is that whenever we use technology for enhancing teaching and learning, then teaching cannot be performed in the same way as without such a resource. Because of the benefits and potentials of different resources, which the new resources provide, a different didactical design for learning opportunities is required. Whenever there is a new resource such as web-enabled technology, the entire Digital Didactical Design with all the five elements (Chapter 4) needs a reflection and probably a change or adjustment—otherwise, the new tool can limit learning, or there is no improvement in learning at all. The technology is just another element among others to design for learning. When constructively aligned, quality learning takes place.

MAKING MORE DESIGN-BASED RESEARCH STUDIES

Instead of making comparative studies, the Digital Didactical Design needs to be at the center of research. Then, the aim of a research project is to study and evaluate to what extent the Digital Didactical Design really meets the new designed teaching and learning goals. Such a study focuses on the benefits, challenges and problems that emerge with new designs and are viewed by different stakeholders such as teachers and students. An alternative option is the design-based research approach (DBR) that supports the development of new didactical designs and studies them using existing research methods (e.g., read PeTEX section below). DBR attracts many researchers with arguments that learning sciences could benefit from viewing it as a design science (e.g., Mor & Winters, 2011, Wang & Hannafin, 2005; Reeves, Herrington & Oliver, 2005; Sandoval & Bell, 2004).

In this chapter, I illustrate some of my latest empirical research projects. This will be an overview of the most important issues with regard to CrossAction-Spaces, Digital Didactical Designs and learning expeditions (as discussed in Chapters 2, 3, 4 and 5).

6.1 #InPUD—Example of an Early Form of Co-expanded Spaces in Higher Education

In empirical studies of social media in higher education, we studied learning in co-expanding spaces in its early years, starting in 2001. At this time, concepts such as Web 2.0 were not invented yet. In the years of Web 1.0, we applied a Community of Practice approach with the aim to support students to share, discuss and co-create knowledge about how to study computer science. We learned that students appreciate such an informal space that can be seen as an expansion to the formal study program.

During the years from 2001 to 2009, we studied InPUD (Informatik-Portal-University-Dortmund), a sociotechnical community (STC) that is part of a computer science study program in Germany. The prototype was launched in 2002. It included over 1,500 members from the approximate 2,000 students in the computer science department at that time. The study of InPUD illustrates a differentiated picture of an informal learning environment that has been added to the formal education. InPUD is not purely online. It is a mix of offline and online settings. Students and teachers meet in lectures or seminars. Therefore, we called it sociotechnical community. Created in 2002, InPUD showed the first characteristics of co-expanding spaces.

The STC, which supports study organization by offering access to social capital, was evaluated from its founding to its sustainable development and transformation phase in 2009. Qualitative and quantitative methods such as interviews, content analysis and online questionnaires were applied (Bryman, 2008).

InPUD shows results in three specific areas: the learners' satisfaction with the STC, the type and quality of use, and whether the STC is a helpful support for students to progress through their studies more effectively than without an STC. InPUD is a form of informal learning that helps students' cocreation of knowledge around organizing computer science studies.

6.1.1 Technology-Embraced Informal-in-Formal Learning Fosters the Conative Level of Learning

One finding is that the InPUD community indicates a special feeling of membership. This ambience is expressed in terms such as "we help each other" and "that's the sense of a community" (interviewees). InPUD activates the user's perception of having a specific form of social proximity, which is triggered by technology and the conative level of learning. The term 'conation' refers to a concrete action that is conducted by a learner; he not only *knows*, but he really *acts*; he is willing to do something and really does it (Kolbe, 1990). The concept of conation stresses what a learning outcome really is; a learning outcome is seen in changed behavior of the learners.

The conative level of learning is often neglected in formal schooling and teaching, where the cognitive learning of 'what' and textbook knowledge is focused on, without supporting the learners' ability to practice such knowledge in action. Traditional teaching neglects the designs for learning as an active process that includes reflective action (i.e., students as prosumers) but also neglects the creation of designs for social relations among students and between the teacher and the students. To make this gap smaller, solutions such as InPUD can be useful. An online discussion board can be a differentiator that supports the individual needs of the users.

> *Student services are different* . . . for higher education at least. While we all want to avoid creating a creepy treehouse, I think the real future for social networks in education lies in the realm of student services (and extended activities, obviously, such as clubs, sports, alumni groups, etc). I'm not convinced, even in higher ed, of efforts to mold a social network application . . . into an instructional space, but using those networks to provide

information that students need about services and activities—*in a way that isn't intrusive or creepy*—is a logical and growing service.

(C. Lott, January 2008, http://chrislott.org/tag/social-learning/)

6.1.2 Anonymity as Duality

An open question asked why InPUD members actively participate and why they write contributions online for the community. Most of the answers were "I ask questions where the answer was not clear to me" and "I need answers or solutions." Some interviewees also mentioned that they like to help other students: "I help other students since I hope they will help me later, when I need help," "that's the sense of a community, we help each other," and "only active members affect active, vivid forums." Other interviewees liked the opportunity to get in contact with others at unusual time slots ("direct contact possibilities at unusual times in the night") and stress the anonymity: "because of the anonymity, I can ask 'stupid' questions." During the data analysis of the open questions, two new reasons for active contribution were found. These are 1) 'criticizing deficiencies' and 2) 'gaining attention out of huge groups in higher education'—in more detail:

First, some members use the community for criticizing deficiencies or problems of the study program: "I want to show my opinion," "I can show my anger by using anonymity," "I can scarify deficiencies," and "When I'm annoyed about something or somebody, I can say it in the forum."

Second, other students use the community to get out from the huge group of learners in classes. Students perceive those large groups as an anonymous mass. So when writing something in InPUD, they want to show their individual faces and try to gain attention: "I post because I have to say something" and "Sometimes, I even want to say something." Some community members stressed especially the factor of awareness: "I think the professor will be aware of me when I'm active in InPUD. So, I'm not just a number for him but become an individual."

Anonymity has a kind of double function. Because of the anonymity, some students use the community to show their anger or to reveal aspects with which they do not agree. If it were not anonymous, students would expect negative sanctions or difficulties (e.g., bad grade)—although probably this would not be the case, they still expect it. On the other hand, some other members use the community InPUD to gain more attention and escape from the anonymity of large groups by saying something. By participating, some members expect that others will perceive their individual voices to be stronger than without using the online forum. They do not want to be just a number; they want to be perceived as individuals.

6.1.3 InPUD Organizes the Jungle of Information for Learners

InPUD is characterized by a relatively high number of members and its continuous growth over time. It has a core that provides input regularly. It also has lurkers, but there are different reasons for being nonactive (lurking or reading only). Most of the common reasons are: "questions and answers were already online," "communication weakness," "Forum as information source not as communication" and "too lazy, no time." The learners are more or less satisfied with the informal spaces. The study shows a significant change toward a positive development from 2002 to 2009. InPUD did improve the information and communication structure. The participants assessed some categories as being significantly better in 2009 than in 2002. Four items were significantly better assessed than in 2002: the STC helps its students to find solutions regarding "When to attend what courses," "How to combine several courses," "Who is responsible for what in the department," and "How to get in contact with other students." With respect to these items, the community is helpful and has changed the cocreation of information positively—at least from the perspective of the students. By using the community, students can find a way out of the information jungle. However, the aspect of 'completeness' is not included. The study indicates that the aspect of completeness could not be improved over time. The community has more information but not any information that a user needs. In addition, regarding the item "how and when to prepare for examinations," the community does not help qualitatively better than before (without the InPUD community).

6.1.4 InPUD Is an Example of an Early CrossActionSpace

The main research question of the InPUD study was whether such an informal communication space, which is a specific form of an online environment at a university, supports learning; if yes, in what ways. Informal learning here is understood as a form of learning where no teacher is formally assigned or included. Informal learning does not have formal teaching aims that are coming from outside. When there are explicit learning aims, these are developed by the participants themselves.

Although a STC, like InPUD, is embedded into formal university structures, students can use the community when they wish and ask what they need. Students can communicate about their problems, which helps them to *go through* their studies in a better-prepared way than before the STC's launch. The results confirm the assumption that CrossActionSpaces promote learning in formally organized education and illustrates the relevance of supporting informal-*in*formal learning (Jahnke, 2010, 2012).

Reasons? Explanations?

A sociotechnical community delivers opportunities for the individualization of learning in large groups. Online forums foster the *customization* of learning by providing a choice of learning opportunities. Despite huge classes (2,000 students), me-centricity and individualization of the learners are supported by an informal learning system. The open design (InPUD is without special login, just an e-mail is needed; low/no control by the university), the double function of the portal (information *and* communication), and the optional participation by keeping private identity but public access, fosters the success of the sociotechnical community.

Another explanation is the flexibility of a just-in-time communication (Jahnke, 2009). Its members can obtain information, can ask questions and can give answers when they want and when they need support about what *they* want to discuss. For the members, it is easier to get only the information as they need at a specific time. The evolved communication is individually customized to the members' needs and enables the participants to engage in their own and others' learning progress actively.

Such a portal (a combination of Web 1.0 and Web 2.0 conditions) provides a better information exchange than without such an infrastructure and creates communication spaces for supporting flexible, informal learning. The availability of web access from anywhere at any time for human communication makes it easier to engage students in learning and knowledge sharing and can also link weakly coupled learners. From a role-based approach, the results indicate that members in the InPUD community are able to create different role expectations but also different role-playing, which they need to complete the learning progress.

To summarize, according to the evaluation from 2002 to 2009—before launching the community and seven years later—the study shows significant differences. The case study pointed out some effects of an implemented sociotechnical community in higher education as follows. First, an STC makes it easier for a community member to obtain the relevant information that s/he needs at a given time. It can reduce the social complexity and information overload from the official organization. Second, an STC can be an appropriate communication space for learners because it supports me-centricity and individualized learning in large groups. Such a designed sociotechnical community is a valuable platform for learning in higher education; it particularly supports informal learning.

From that point of view, such an online forum is an appropriate platform for fostering learning in higher education. Such 'informal' learning spaces enrich the traditional teaching approaches by the use of interactive media that fosters a positive learning experience for learners. The addition of informal learning spaces expands formal education and leads to an all-embracing learning experience that activates learners on all levels, such as the cognitive, affective and the conative level—this is what I call technology-embraced 'informal-*in*-formal learning.'

6.2 #PeTEX—Remote Lab Learning in Engineering Education

In our study titled "Platform for Telemetric Experimentation and e-Learning (PeTEX)," funded by the European Commission (2008–2010), the aim was to design experimental online learning for engineering education (Jahnke, Terkowsky, Pleul & Tekkaya, 2010; Pleul et al., 2011). The development of the PeTEX prototype served as proof of concept for an online engineering education environment for knowledge co-creation, individual and collaborative learning, and competence improvement in the area of manufacturing technology at the intersection of higher education and workplace learning (Terkowsky, Pleul, Jahnke & Tekkaya, 2011; Auer & Gravier, 2009; Gomes & Bogosyan, 2009).

6.2.1 Learning Expeditions Designed as Reflective Cross-Actions

PeTEX is an example for learning walkthroughs and learning expeditions; I especially want to show some principles of the design. In early chapters, I argued that learning expeditions are mainly grounded on reflective cross-actions. Here I show what this means.

The unique feature of PeTEX is that it enables experiential research-based learning, where students conduct telemetric experiments in real time and use equipment that is physically present in welding, forming and machining. This component of learning provides access that was previously unavailable to learners in product engineering. PeTEX is the result of a two-year study including modeling, development, implementation and improvement in accordance by a design-based research approach.

The learning environment was the product of several evaluation workshops that iterated on the model in light of data from previous studies (Jahnke et al., 2010). External experts, including students and teachers from engineering education as well as experts from e-learning and pedagogical research centers, validated the online learning model. The research utilized a thinking-aloud method including video recordings, screen recordings, and participant observation conducted in a project with students. A positive result was that the prototype was adopted almost intuitively. However, the evaluation also showed that students overestimated the attractiveness of experiments. The word 'experiment' promotes different expectations, and learners expect different things, which can cause problems regarding the learner's motivation. In particular, students need an understanding and clearer idea of what 'experimental learning' is and which possibilities and different expectations are connected to such a learning method.

Although the learning management system Moodle appears to follow a rather teacher-centered design, it was possible to develop the distributed learning community by using social media tools to facilitate student interaction. PeTEX provides different entry points and approaches with which to start. The learning walkthrough depends on the learner. The concept is that PeTEX allows the application of different learning theories. If a learner wants to have first knowledge and content information, then PeTEX provides this in seven learning modules. Alternatively, if she wishes to first explore the experiment and then learns that the data did not make sense to her and therefore she needs to consult the content, she can explore this content after exploring the experiment. It also occurs that an advanced learner has all theoretical knowledge and is able to start with the experiments directly, but then she has something go wrong during the experiment and needs the learner community to discuss her observation so as to make sense of the data. PeTEX makes this learning approach possible for a wide range of people willing to learn more about manufacturing production in forming, welding and machining, for example, testing different materials for designing lightweight airplanes. Using telemetric experiments, PeTEX helps learners in manufacturing engineering to grow in their learning, connected to a real-world problem.

6.2.2 Reflective Cross-Actions for Different Learning Levels

In contrast to the advanced and intermediate level, beginners need a more structured networked scaffolding support from the learning environment. Scaffolding helps the learners to learn step-by-step according to their previous experiences. This support for the beginners is characterized by more instructions and more tasks given by the teachers. The following main elements occur:

- *(before the experiments)* According to the learner's level, she walks differently through the teaching material, learning objects and in particular learning activities (phase of individual learning).
- She prepares and conducts remote experiments in production engineering.
- *(after the experiments)* The learner writes a report about the experimentation and its results, using Moodle to upload the report online (phase of learning in groups).

The advanced level contains more complex self-directed exploratory- and problem-based learning walkthroughs, where the learner would have comprehensive means of navigating through the entire environment, with the opportunity to interact with all learning objects and to find solutions for complex problems. For example, the learner has the opportunity to start where she wants.

A beginner probably wishes to start with getting some content about the domain before she would be able to plan and conduct a real-time experiment and to understand the data she would receive back from the machine. Learning here is based on the assumption that a learner needs content and knowledge before conducting the experiments. However, a beginner is also able to start with the experiments first, and then she gets some data from the observation; at that point, she wants to understand what happened, and she would look into the learning modules to give meaning to the data.

A more experienced learner does not need to go through the content and is able to start with the experiment first. She also is able to give meaning to the data she obtained. Perhaps the experiment failed, and she needs the learning community to discuss whether others have the same experiences in order to understand what went wrong and why. PeTEX provides different angles with which to start and also different learning walkthroughs, depending on the learner.

The experimental learning model was presented in an evaluation workshop in order to get external hints for improvements, confirmations or discussions. One central result was that the experts, consisting of users such as students and teachers as well as experts from education and sociotechnical design, confirmed the whole learning model (Jahnke et al., 2010). The experts evaluated the model as being an attractive learning scenario. PeTEX is an example for rethinking and remodeling existing teaching and learning models toward creative lifelong learning cultures of participation (Fischer, 2011).

In more detail, the learning walkthrough covered a range of learner activities including preparation of remote experiments, for instance, creating hypotheses before they walked through the remote lab. After the experimentation, learners wrote a lab report about "what they have observed, analyzed and learnt." Such an assessment activity, called a "learning diary," was supported by peer-reviewing processes within the learning community and feedback given by the teacher. In the case of successful assessment, learners received a certificate.

6.2.3 Intertwining the Technical, the Pedagogical and the Social Dimension

This section introduced PeTEX, an experimental online learning model including remote laboratories for studies in production engineering. Adapting the design-based research methodology including formative evaluation and modeling methods, the generated pilot shows details on how to embed remote experiments into teaching and learning processes. The model is useful for supporting learner-centered learning pedagogically and helpful in clarifying what technical and social design issues for a learning scenario like PeTEX's lab didactics are needed.

The PeTEX model guides the steps of learners' activities and what the project team implements in order to yield attractive online learning processes, but an appropriate balance between teaching input, learning objects and conducting the remote experiments is important for student motivation and engagement.

On the one hand, the design of learning modules requires a standardized framework and modularization of course content, so that the learner can decide if he needs beginner, intermediate or expert level, and a balance between passive reading (listening, watching something) and active learning tasks (for approximately every 10 minutes of passive reading/listening/watching, an active task has to follow).

On the other hand, an appropriate balance between learning modules and experiments is needed. Results from the student users' study show that the time for course content should not be longer than preparing, doing experiments and writing the report because telemetric experimentation is the attractive part. The experiments are at the center of the learning walkthrough. In more detail, a discovery-learning approach with remote labs in engineering needs a special degree of creativity and freedom for learners so that the learner may create theoretical assumptions about the experiment (in the phase of preparation). A good experimental online learning model also supports failures or 'false assumptions,' and the reports written by the learners help to discover such false friends and new assumptions.

From the PeTEX case, we learned how to design including developing, introducing, and evaluating technology-enhanced learning. PeTEX also shows us the key elements for designing. According to this study, a 'successful design' depends on three factors.

First, elements such as technical systems, social/organizational structures and pedagogical/didactical concepts are relevant, in particular how these elements can be integrated into a design for supporting learning expeditions. A design for learning expeditions has to deal with complex interconnections, structural coupling and interdependency of these elements. It is not a surprise that these elements (pedagogical, social and technical) are the foundation of the Digital Didactical Design (Chapter 5).

- Technical systems and elements (e.g., learning management systems like Moodle or digital media): Is the technical system easily changeable (by users)? Can users adapt easily, or are changes only possible by external people, software engineers? Is social media sufficiently integrated into the pedagogical concept, or is it like a satellite without connection to the teaching/learning concept? What is the understanding about the technical concept (passive, interactive, transactive, autonomy, etc.)?
- Social/organizational structures: forms of communication and interaction, different roles of teachers and students; organizational issues.
- Pedagogical concepts: teaching aims and learning intentions; learning activities based on different learning models; (non)formal, informal learning processes; phases of individual/group learning; research-based, problem-based, scenario-based learning; support of competence development (which ones?); interconnections between instruction (e.g., rules from teacher) and construction (learners' learning processes); forms of assessment; etc.

Second, every design needs to reflect on the degree of quality. This degree shows how well the elements interact. For example, the greater the unity among the three elements of technical, social and pedagogical concepts, the more the users are satisfied and/or the better they share knowledge and co-construction of knowledge takes place, the better they learn.

Third, a 'successful design' also depends on what the user's role is. Different target groups, people in different roles, have different cognitive conceptions of success. Teachers, students, university managers, pedagogical experts, and e-Learning experts define 'success' in the same context differently. A 'successful' design includes all the different views or, at least, supports a shared understanding for all. In addition, different social systems such as universities and faculties with different cultures may use similar ideas of learning expeditions, but they probably adapt them in the details differently.

Those three dimensions drive the design process.

6.3 #DaVinci—Creating Conditions for Creativity of Learning Expeditions

Creativity has been studied for many years and by many different disciplines (Jahnke & Haertel, 2010; Adriansen, 2010; McWilliam & Dawson, 2008). What we know so far is that the position of the observer matters!

Our empirical study from 2008 to 2011 on creativity in education (Isa Jahnke, Tobias Haertel, Johannes Wildt) makes visible the pluralistic view and the differences in teachers' conceptions and students' understanding of creativity in learning processes. In the DaVinci project, granted by the German BMBF ministry, we asked teachers about student creativity.

The result is a conceptual framework of six facets that illustrate a diverse picture of the similarities and differences of what teachers have in mind when they talk about creativity and how they perceive their students' creativity in learning. The facets are shown in Figure 6.1.

According to the teachers, creativity is a bundle of different things and can be perceived, observed and clustered into six aspects.

Teachers answered the following item: "I can see that my students are creative when . . ." and they illustrated it with many different examples, which we cluster into six broader areas. We call them the Six Facets:

- Self-reflective learning
- Autonomous and independent learning (students make their own decisions)
- Showing engagement, curiosity and motivation
- Creating something (learning by making)
- Multi-perspective thinking (students show more than one perspective on the same topic)
- Totally new and original ideas.

In a follow-up online survey, we tested those six aspects and offered a seventh option—'does not fit.' It is quite remarkable that the option 'does not fit' was selected for nine answers only, which is about 0.5% out of all 1,844 answers.

This result indicates that the six aspects are capable of comprising almost all of teachers' concepts of creativity in higher education. Furthermore, all six aspects are about equally represented, which suggests that all six are equally important

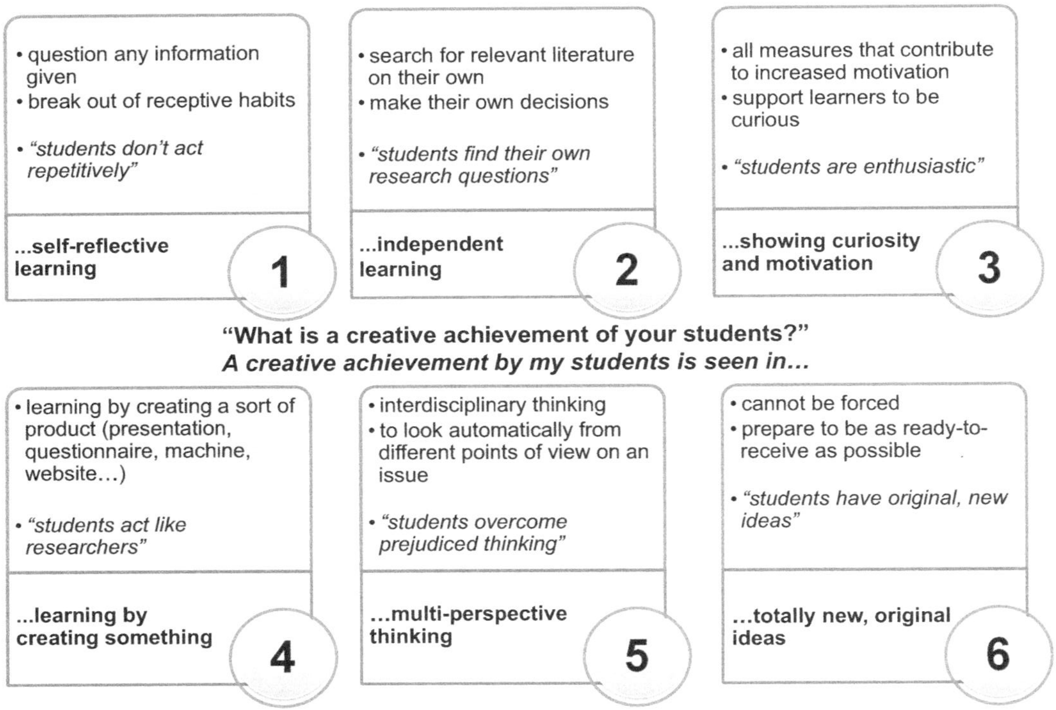

FIGURE 6.1 Six facets of how teachers conceptualize student creativity (Tobias Haertel, Isa Jahnke and Johannes Wildt, our slides presented at ICED2014)

across all disciplines. There is no single aspect that really dominates the concept of creativity or that does not matter.

The understanding by the interviewed university teachers of what a student's creativity is ranges from viewing it as a commonplace phenomenon, which can be influenced by a change in one's 'attentiveness'; as the development of one's own ideas, which generally could have already existed but are developed by the individual instead of simply being adopted; and as the creative linking of previously unconnected ideas or thoughts, up to considering creativity as the ability to see objects and relationships from different perspectives, to abandon habitual patterns of thinking and, finally, to create and implement entirely new ideas.

However, the study also indicates that university teachers have different ideas about creativity and what creativity is in their disciplines. Surprisingly, only a few students agreed that teachers were committed to fostering creativity in their courses (Haertel & Jahnke, 2011; Jahnke, 2013). It is also relevant that the teachers did not mention all of the facets at once. It did depend on their designed course. For example, some focused on Facet 4 and others on Facet 1. So, the study did not say that all of the facets are always needed. From our workshops with teachers, we learned, however, that the facets can be seen as a staircase. To achieve Facet 4 (creating and producing something), Facets 1 to 3 need to be considered. There is no learning by producing without self-reflection (F1), making decisions (F2) and curiosity (F3). In other words, when teachers design for Facet 4 but do not design conditions for Facets 1 to 3, the learning environment tends to fail.

Due to the fact that university teachers understand creativity in heterogeneous ways, which are in turn influenced by differences between the disciplines, ideological positions and various teaching situations, the six facets can be useful in revealing how student creativity can be encouraged. For university teachers in basic courses with hundreds of students, it is a valuable success if they create an appropriate teaching and learning design in order to foster their students' reflective thinking (Facet 1). Teachers in seminars with small numbers of students and large open spaces (e.g., design disciplines, like architecture or computer science) have a greater opportunity to foster the development of original, completely new ideas (Facet 6) in their classes. Nevertheless, Facets 5 and 6 are hard to imagine without reflective thinking (Facet 1) and independently working students (Facet 2). The six aspects are not separated but rather relate to each other.

The six-facet model can be used for teachers who ask two questions: 1) "I would like to encourage the creativity of my students—which aspect(s) can I support?" and 2) "How can I achieve that in my classroom/in my setting?"

This six-facet model of creativity in higher education can be used as a reflection tool for fostering creativity in higher education. We, and later mainly Tobias Haertel himself, conducted workshops for teachers titled "Through the Barricades" (for all disciplines) and "Rage Against the Machine" (for engineering teachers); both have been offered for years and at different universities. In some of the workshops, I was involved as co-organizer. More than 100 university teachers have already taken part and have used the model to reflect their own teaching. With the help of our approach, they have always been able to find ways of fostering their students' creativity in their lectures and classrooms.

6.4 #IPM—An Example of Challenges When Designing for Learning Expeditions

In this empirical study mainly conducted by Julia Liebscher on mobile devices, we explored the question of how technical devices can support students in terms of group coordination and work organization. In a course of Industrial Project Management (IPM) held at a European university, mobile devices (iPods) were used to support students during a project-based course. During a seven-week phase, students had the assignment to collaboratively work on a project from a business company (Jahnke & Liebscher, 2013). The IPM course offered iPods and field trips for students. The results were a surprise. The students did not use the iPods, or only very little, and the students preferred to meet face to face instead.

The mobile devices did not support learning. What happened?

We argue that the didactical design had a gap and limited the use of the mobile devices. The failure lay within the design. Two main factors can be named. First, the design did not support an anywhere-anytime didactics; second, the interpretation of students' needs were not correct or at least there was a gap. The study was based on observations, group interviews and conversations with teachers and students.

6.4.1 Why Didn't Students Use the Mobile Devices?

iPods Were Not Used During the Field Trips—Explanations
by the Students

The students argued that the devices were too small to work with for a long period. They also had technical problems. One major issue was no Wi-Fi. Thus, when the students were off-campus, they could not work on the project—at least they could not use the iPod sufficiently enough.

The students mentioned that because they had no difficulties in organizing their group coordination and communication, they did not need the iPods. However, they also added, they would have preferred a different form of support on the part of the technical devices. Instead of using the iPods for group coordination, they lacked support for their collaborative, creative, problem-solving processes. "It was very difficult to find out a) what the problem of the company was, b) how we (the students) wanted to proceed with the development of problem-solving, and that c) it would have been useful to assist us (the students) in developing creative new ideas and solutions for the project" (quote of a student participant).

The potential of the iPods and the didactical design were not matched with the students' needs. Instead of supporting their communication, aspects such as creativity, getting new ideas and collaborative problem-solving processes needed to be considered in detail.

iPods Were Not Used—Explanations by Didactical Designers

From a didactical design's perspective, there are different explanations as to why the students did not use the iPods. The instructions and assessments within the course only focused on the 'content,' such as professional knowledge development. Therefore, the learning activities were designed on the focus of cocreation of new knowledge but without explicitly designing for creative problem solving. The teaching aim of 'working together' was only implicitly integrated in the design and was more seen as a *side effect*, not formatively assessed or supported. It was not included in the design. Such a didactical design that focused on content and neglected to design for problem solving affected how the students used the iPods. When it was clear to them that it was not the cooperation process itself that was needed to be successful but only the solution and product at the end, there was no reason at all for them to use the mobile devices. The design had a lack in how to relate the technical devices appropriately to the learning activities, assessment and social roles.

When we go back to Chapter 5, where I describe the model of the "three layers," we can see that the IPM course was designed with regard to the inner layer of "content" and with regard to the second layer of "teaching aims," but all other elements were not clear designed with regard to how to use the mobile devices. A suitable integrated design was missing in which the use of the iPods and the pedagogical designs did not match in this course. There was an imbalance.

In other words, the digital didactical approach was not consistent for the students. For example, in addition to the iPod use, there was also a learning management system (LMS); it was not clear to the students when to use the LMS, when to use the iPods and how they both could be integrated to enhance learning.

The course revealed that the learning process of 'problem solving' was not sufficiently supported. The teacher designed collaboration as information *exchange*, but the students had to collaborate to solve the problem within their group. When creating a course that supports problem solving in a project-based approach, peer-reflective co-construction of new knowledge needs to be supported. The didactical design did support the teaching aim of "applying information," rather than "creating" (Anderson & Krathwohl, 2001). The creative process and the students' creativity, where the iPod could have been useful, were not supported and not integrated in the Digital Didactical Design. The students lacked support in their collaborative learning (to find a solution where the answer is unknown) and in their creative problem-solving process (planning and conducting a project requires professional knowledge but also requires creativity, which was not supported explicitly within the course).

6.4.2 The Potential of Mobile Devices—Access to Collaboration at Any Time, Anywhere

Creativity is not connected to a particular physical space or time, and it is often not available per se or ad hoc; therefore, mobile devices provide one great opportunity to capture creativity when it arises. Using mobile devices can create such conditions conducive to creativity, and creativity techniques can be offered, which can then be used when learners are able to deal with them, for example, right at the moment when the new idea arrives independently of location and time (e.g., in the supermarket, at the train station, or in a university course).

Mobile devices and specific apps can support the creative process of the students (Carell & Schaller, 2010), for example, as *enablers and stimulators*, if they stimulate creative thinking and access to the problem on an emotional level (e.g., import images/films to give inspiration; produce acoustic impressions of sounds supporting inspiration); as *tools*, when they support cooperation and have relevant functionalities to support collaboration (e.g., collection of information); and as *creative tools* to support collaborative creativity within a group (e.g., joint brainstorming, analysis, assessment and evaluation of new ideas).

This example of IPM gives us the opportunity to reflect on the Digital Didactical Design. It might be that the teachers and others had a clear design in mind and that they had ideas how to design for learning. However, they did not create the conditions in such a way that it was useful with regard to mobile devices and creativity.

Despite the strong idea of the project-based learning approach, it is not sufficient to implement mobile devices primarily to support student coordination and cooperation, and it is not sufficient to use mobile devices only for applying professional knowledge. In the digital age, students are well equipped to make contact with each other or meet. Instead of the technical infrastructures (anytime-anywhere), learning expeditions designed as creative processes and collaborative creativity need support, perhaps even more than the coordination activities.

6.5 #Tablet-Mediated Learning Expeditions in Schools

This study about innovative designs for teaching and learning in media tablet classrooms started in 2012 where we explored new forms of teaching and new ways of learning expeditions (Jahnke, Norqvist & Olsson, 2014; Jahnke & Kumar, 2014). We were in Denmark, Sweden and Finland and visited, observed and conducted interviews with students and teachers in more than 45 tablet-classrooms.

For example, Odder is a rural community in Denmark, which started a program of one media tablet per child for all seven schools from preschool to

Grade 9. Around 2,000 students aged 5 to 17 and 180 teachers received iPads. The decision was made due to their old laptops and the need to buy new ones. Instead of laptops, the politicians in Odder decided to use iPads. The head teachers and the local department of the teachers' union were consulted to secure their agreement; both groups agreed.

Qualitative and quantitative data such as larger school visits, interviews and classroom observations as well as three online surveys (Cohen, Manion & Morrisson, 2007) were conducted in 2012, 2013 and 2014; in total, we were in the schools for over six weeks (usually from 8 a.m. to 2–4 p.m.) over three years. A triangulation of data collection and methods was useful for the validity of such a qualitative study (Guion, Diehl & McDonald, 2002). We wanted to know the designs for teaching and learning when classrooms are enhanced by media tablets. To what extent, and how, do the teachers support learning in media-tablet classrooms? The use of web-enabled media tablets creates co-expanded spaces, and we wanted to know how the teachers design for learning under such conditions. We were curious and wanted to explore classroom practices from the perspective of Digital Didactical Designs (Chapter 5).

The teaching subjects ranged from language (Danish/Swedish/Finnish) and math to English, art and physics (sciences such as STEM)—we covered all grades and almost all subjects except sports. The classes ranged from 14 to 25 students in different grades and included preschool classes (grade 0), first grade math, first grade natural science, second grade math, competence cluster class from first until third grade language, competence cluster class from first until third grade history, sixth grade English, sixth grade music, seventh grade language, eighth grade language/arts, and ninth grade physics and chemistry.

We also visited 1:1 tablet classrooms in Swedish schools in 2014, which is part of a larger research project funded by the Swedish Research Council; in 2015, we have visited tablet classrooms in schools in Finland. We have over three years of experience with tablet-mediated learning; with this, we do not only rely on snapshot studies, but we encompass multiple times and loci where technology is shaped. This kind of triangulation method strengthens the findings. Here I want to share some of our 45 observed classrooms.

6.5.1 Classroom Studies—Learning Through Reflective Making?

Preschool Class

Students in the preschool class got individual assignments to make a book review of a traditional book. The learning activities included reading a book and then creating a review. They used Bookcreator to make that review. Since the students in the preschool class are young and just learning to read and write, the app was useful to support their learning in different ways. It allows inclusion of digital paintings, and students recorded their own voices and typed some words (Figure 6.2). In

FIGURE 6.2 Learning language skills by using digital paintings, student voice recordings and text

such a range of possibilities, every student could express herself in the way that she preferred. The classroom was not a typical classroom. Rather, it was an open space without doors that looks creative in terms of having different tools available, for example, books, sofas and whiteboards. The students sat on the floor on a nice carpet. When they did the individual assignment, they sat together in small groups and helped each other. The teacher went from group to group and student to student. Later, she gathered all students together and used the digital projector to show some of the created digital reviews.

Third Grade, Math

In this class, the young learners got the assignment to repeat and apply different math strategies of subtraction. The teacher showed two tasks on the whiteboard, such as 'A person has 17 dollars and buys goodies of 3 dollars. What is left?' Then, students in small groups used the Educreation app. This screencasting app supports voice recording and whiteboard functions at the same time. When a learner writes something and speaks into it, the app records the process of writing together with the words the learner said. It records the voice and the screen together, in the end, the students created short video lessons (approximately five minutes); see Figure 6.3. After a while, the teacher gathered all groups in front of the digital projector and showed the products of the groups. She discussed the quality with the young learners (what is good and what/how to improve). The

FIGURE 6.3 Screencasting app for documenting and reflecting math strategies

teacher also used the situation to discuss the different math strategies that the students applied in different ways.

Fourth Grade, Language

A similar approach of screencasting has been conducted in a fourth grade class of Scandinavian grammar. The students received an assignment that required them to explain to their peers the designation of nouns, verbs, and adjectives. They used the app Explains Everything to create small videos. Students created first a storyboard and then a showcase that included sound and visualization. The product was a brief animated video with students' recorded voices. When we were in the classroom, we saw that some of the students were not sure how to create such a video. The technical issues were not the challenge but rather the assignment "how to explain what a noun is"? And then they started to look into their books and what they learned over the last weeks, and they also searched on the Internet. That is an example of cross-action. Some student groups went outside the classroom, and the teacher even supported them doing so. He later explained to us that it is important that students learn not only inside the classroom but also in places where they feel differently and sometimes even not so comfortable. He wanted to have the students experience different places for learning. When all the student groups later showed their solutions to the class, they also got feedback from their peers and teacher about the quality of the developed product and solution.

Fifth Grade, Language

In a fifth grade language class, the students read first a traditional book. It was a comic book about a horror story in which a girl saves her friends with help by others. The learning activity was designed as a group action. They used the Booktrailer app that is part of iMovie. The students developed a three- to five-minute book trailer. The app supported them to reflect on their readings of the horror story; the patterns of horror stories; and the color, themes and other elements of a fiction story. The teacher used formative assessment methods in different ways. In the beginning, she asked all students to write down three questions and pass it over to the next student. Those questions and their answers now serve as criteria for creating the book trailers. To set such criteria in the beginning is crucial for learning because it is hard to paint a house when a learner does not know the criteria regarding how s/he would be assessed later. So, it is highly relevant for supporting the learning progress to make the assessment criteria clear and communicate the criteria to the learners in the beginning of a learning expedition. The teacher later also explained to us that this approach has been used several times. They even make a big event with a cinema and theatre evening where all other students of the entire school watch the book trailers. Sometimes, they even invite parents and other people to be part of the audience. The teachers are very happy about such a development because the students are more engaged and more motivated when they know that there is a real audience. They are also proud to show others their learning products.

Seventh Grade, Language, Peer-Reflective Learning

The teaching aim (learning intention) in that classroom was to improve writing skills. In this class, students received assignments to write a small paragraph from their childhood. The teacher used a closed Facebook group to which the students uploaded the small paragraphs. The comment function was used to give feedback. Every student gave and got feedback. Since it was technology enhanced, all feedback was visible. The peer reviews helped them to reflect and revise their first version. Several versions were allowed. The students learned two things. First, they learned how to give feedback. In the beginning, they just said "I like it"; the teacher commented that it is not enough to say 'yes' or 'no' or 'good' or 'not good,' but one has to give an argument why something is good or not good. In addition, the teacher also gave feedback. While doing this, the students could read all comments by the teacher, not only for their own entry but also for all others. Second, the students learned that comments by others and peers are helpful in the process of learning. They learned that different students have different opinions and how to handle the different feedback. When the students thought that their revised versions were the final version, they marked it or sent it to the teacher.

Seventh Grade, Language With QR Codes

In this class, improving grammar skills was the main learning intention by the teacher, but she also had a second aim. She wanted the students to reflect about their learning process. The teacher prepared QR codes and hid them in the backyard of the school. The students, organized in groups, had the assignment to search for the QR codes. The codes led them to a website where they got the task to answer questions about grammar (Figure 6.4).

The teacher combined outdoor learning with the traditional classroom. After about 30 minutes, all students were back in the classroom. First, the teacher went through the grammar questions and then the opened the discussion about learning. She asked, "Was it fun to be outside?" Almost all said yes. The second question was, "And, do you think you learn more when you have fun and when you are outdoors?" This discussion went differently. Some said yes; other were more critical. In some groups, they had a kind of leader that answered the grammar questions. Some students argued that it would be better when all would answer the questions; that is better for learning. The third part of the lesson was a collection of criteria, 'how students can assess the learning process'; these criteria were then uploaded to the Intranet, and the students had homework to reflect on those criteria and create answers.

FIGURE 6.4A QR codes outdoors for improving grammar language skills

FIGURE 6.4B QR codes outdoors for improving grammar language skills

Ninth Grade, Physics

In this physics classroom, the learning activity was to design new experiments based on the knowledge the students gained from previous classes designed as a collaborative learning activity: collaborative producing of physics experiments. The objective was to apply the recently learned knowledge and to show the teacher the learning outcome in the field of sound, light, magnetism and electricity. The teacher's only instruction to the students was, "Please, show me something essential about sound or light, and create an experiment about it—what is not in the books." He also asked them to document their process of planning and conducting the experiment.

While some students gathered and built groups and started to work on the assignment, one group of two students were not sure how to start. The teacher thus created a new assignment for their personal needs by asking them to create a joint mind map using the Popplet app. They brainstormed to collect their knowledge into one mind map to identify their personal gap in knowledge. That gap then served as the starting point to plan the experiment.

Other groups had some ideas and started with the experiment. In one group, there were seven students; in another group, there were three students. The students used the camera and video-recording features in the iPad and took photos. They also did a video podcast of the preparation of the experiment—see Figure 6.5. That was important because many experiments did fail and the video served then as a reflection tool. Some groups wanted the teacher to help them show the video and to understand what and why it went wrong. Other groups did the reflection without the teacher. The tablets were used to document the process of creating the experiment, searching for information using the digital textbook Pro Tuner app and later to upload their documentation to the school Intranet. Some videos were uploaded to a YouTube channel. The teacher went from group to group and gave feedback. The teacher said later that the entire design to plan and conduct an experiment is a formative assessment method. He said, "How do I know when the students have learnt something? When they can apply it to the real world." He also mentioned that he strongly focused on "informal teaching" and "allowing and fostering my students to make mistakes"; he would rather be in the background and let the students experiment. He liked to foster a role change, where students become the person who teaches other students and he acts like a process mentor who supports the personal learning needs of the students instead of telling them the facts. For example, we observed that the teacher asked the students to present their original idea of their experiment design on a blank sheet of paper, and so the students themselves got an "aha moment"; they suddenly saw that the idea was not clear enough and why the experiment went wrong. Such designs for learning are based on the idea that students test their theories through experiments within a given field (e.g., sound, light) and translate it to learn how it works in reality.

The examples show that tablets in schools are integrated for supporting learning through making. Students become prosumers, producers and makers of their learning processes.

FIGURE 6.5A Media tablets for collaboratively creating, documenting and reflecting physics experiments

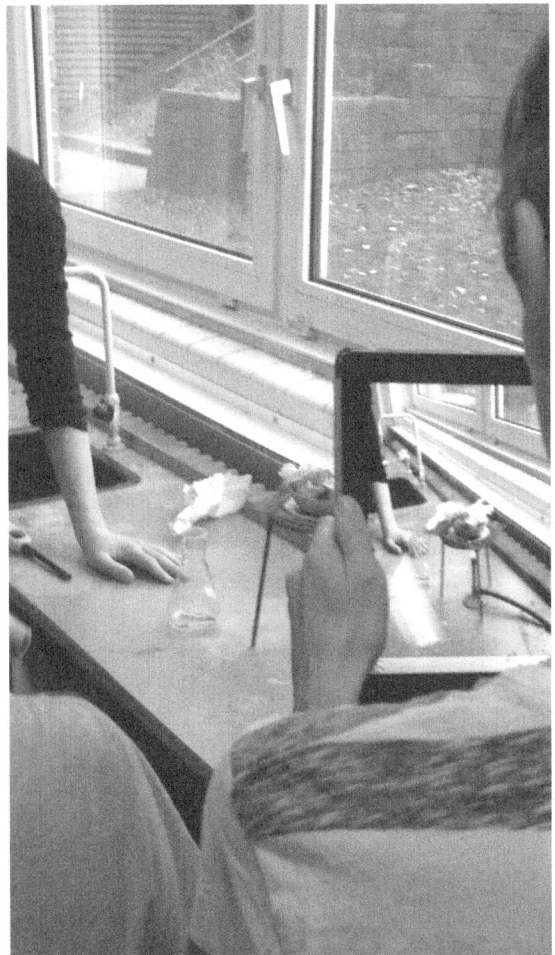

FIGURE 6.5B Media tablets for collaboratively documenting and reflecting physics experiments

6.5.2 Range of Learning Expeditions

Table 6.1 shows the range of the first 24 analyzed classrooms. Until today, we had observed 45 classrooms across three different countries; the range is on a matrix from surface and deeper learning and individual and group learning.

The reader might ask, "And do the students learn better or more in tablet classrooms?" The didactical designs have created 'other' and new conditions for

TABLE 6.1 Exploring types of learning expeditions—from surface, individual learning to deeper, group learning (adapted from Jahnke Norqvist & Olsson, 2014)

	Individual learning (I)	*Learning in groups (G)*
Deeper complex learning (D)	Transforming a math story (ID5)	Collaborative writing (ID10)
	Creating a multimodal book review (ID6)	Collaboratively designing of physical experiments (ID11)
	Creating chronological order (ID21)	Creating chemical experiments (ID18)
	Creating a multimodal story (ID 16)	Collaborative creation of a multimodal product (ID20)
	Finding animals across the globe (ID 22)	Collaborative production on "Explains everything" (ID23)
	Individual prod. of audio product (ID 1)	Creating a multimodal product from graphical novels (ID24)
	Creating a digital story/ proverbs (ID 2)	Collaboratively producing music (ID 7)
	Writing a non-fiction story (ID14)	Peer-reflective learning (ID 8)
	Individual timeline (ID 19)	Collaborative production of a video/ movie (ID3)
		Group discussions about math (ID4)
Surface learning (S)	Role-playing teacher-led (ID 13)	Group work outside of the classroom (ID17)
	Mind mapping existing knowledge (ID9)	Finding/discussing distances, GoogleMaps (ID15)
		Creating a digital presentation (ID12)

learning, for example, new ways for learners to express themselves. While using CrossActionSpaces, they become makers; they create meaning for what they do. The observed tablet-mediated designs support learning in terms of student engagement, student motivation, student reflection and teacher reflection.

From the innovative classrooms, we were able to derive a set of implications. In those, we see a new mind-set for designing learning processes toward learning expeditions. From our study, the applied teachers' designs-in-practice in media-tablet classrooms are characterized as maker pedagogy—we may call it learning through reflective making. Such technology-enhanced designs for learning expeditions are characterized by:

1. Activating student engagement and student motivation through producing and reflective making: The focus lies on cross-action where the teachers activate learner engagement through 'producing' and information seeking outside schools via Internet access. Learning takes place at different places inside and outside schoolrooms. Learning is not reduced to the place inside schools but includes forms of coproducing in different informal-*in*-formal spaces.

2. Involving more than one possible answer or strategy: students solve a complex problem where many different solutions are possible.
3. Documenting learning steps: making learning processes visible by documenting learning steps where students can express themselves in different ways.
4. Supporting choices of learning activities: students get support in applying different ways that are possible to build a product.
5. Supporting guided reflections during the learning process: e.g., teachers define criteria in advance and students know the criteria, which helps learners know how to improve the learning product while making and reflecting about it.
6. Enhancing the shift of roles: in some school cultures, students are expected to be consumers; but in Scandinavia, we saw that students are more likely the active participants where they are active and reflective makers. However, this support in shifting roles is not just 'there.' Students in our observed classrooms learned to be active because schools reward and benefit active learners in different ways. In order to become reflective makers, a shift in roles is required as an explicit part of a design for learning. That means that discussions are needed about what a 'good' learner does and does not do, what a good teacher does and does not do, and other informal and formal role patterns. Not only discussions but also the doing of role shifting is highly relevant to support a reflective maker culture and maker spaces.
7. Connecting the learning process to a real audience: bringing the real world into the schools either by using CrossActionSpaces or other forms (e.g., making a book trailer event and inviting people into schools to show the students' products.
8. Combining traditional resources (books, pens, whiteboards, etc.) and different apps: teachers and students use different apps that are not solely built for education and combine different resources together.

The innovative classrooms have one element in common that can be called the "maker culture" (Hatch, 2013). The term is borrowed from Hatch (2013); originally it comes from Do-It-Yourself cultures. Our research in Scandinavia shows how teachers in tablet-classrooms turn learning into a reflective "maker movement" in schools. The students produced, created and made products such as videos, movies, book trailers and digital paintings using bookcreators, educreation, short videos, screencasting products, and more to show what they have learned. During the learning process of producing and *making* (learning through making), the students applied existing knowledge needed to create new knowledge. They made, learned, reflected and shared. The difference to traditional learning designs is the great opportunity for the learner's own *expression*, what she or he has learnt.

Whereas the maker layer is obvious in our studies, the reflection layer is not always seen as such. Reflection about processes and products tends to focus on appearances, such as "it looks nice" or "it has nice pictures." However, making is not enough; criteria are needed so students know what a 'good' performance is, and these criteria help to support learning progress. Advanced, guided reflections are required that focus on skills and student ability development. The explicit design for reflections is available in some of the designs-in-practice, but there is still a gap to design for guided reflections and role shifting. In order to become a reflective maker, students and teachers' roles require a shift in their current understanding. Teachers are not only the experts; they are learning companions and mentors, while students need support to change their expectations from passive consumers to active makers and reflectors.

Future research is important that studies the reflection layer, the characterization and variety of process-based reflections, and how it can be designed for supporting the learning progress.

During a three-year study, we saw a development in the teaching practice where teachers become 'jugglers' of different elements. The complexity in classrooms increases through technical breakdowns, which affect their pedagogical plan (Jahnke et al., 2014) in the beginning. Later, teaching has turned from a *routine* activity toward a design project in teacher teams, in which the teachers are learners at the workplace (Goggins, Jahnke & Wulf, 2013). The designs for teaching and learning are shifting into a process design. Teaching is creating conditions for learning as a process.

We asked students in this municipality about learning situations and what turns a learning situation into a 'good' one (inspired by the photo-eliciting method by Cappello, 2005). They perceived that the value of learning might be clustered in seven different categories (N = 283 utterances by students). We did not ask them about the media tablets, but the students mention them in around 30% of all learning situations. So, what would happen if the schools took them away? Then 30% of the learning situations, which the students value as good (motivated and engaged), would be gone. Can schools afford this? (Norqvist, Jahnke & Olsson, 2014).

The study pointed to five different themes of Digital Didactical Designs in the classroom practice: 1) specific media-tablet didactics (MD), 2) Digital Didactics (DD), 3) weak alignment but benefit of media-tablet integration (BT), 4) potential for tablet didactics (PD), and 5) realignment of designs for learning (RE). Some teachers created new digital didactical approaches; they transformed their traditional classrooms into a creative learning experience for their students. Other cases showed potential for improvements. The applied designs-in-practice in the participating schools, as presented above, showed new ways of teaching and learning and new forms of Digital Didactical Designs in CrossActionSpaces.

6.6 References

Adriansen, H. K. (2010). How criticality affects students' creativity. In: C. Nygaard, N. Courtney & C. Holtham (Eds.): *Teaching Creativity—Creativity in Teaching*. Faringdon: Libri, pp. 65–85.

Anderson, L. W. & Krathwohl, D. R. (2001). *A Taxonomy for Learning, Teaching, and Assessing: A Revision of Bloom's Taxonomy of Educational Objectives*. New York: Longman.

Auer, M. E. & Gravier, C. (2009, October–December). The many facets of remote laboratories in online engineering education. *IEEE Transactions on Learning Technologies*, 2(4), 260–262.

Bryman, A. (2008). *Social Research Methods* (3rd ed.). New York: Oxford University Press.

Cappello, M. (2005): Photo interviews: eliciting data through conversations with children. *Field Methods*, 17(2), 170–182.

Carell, A. & Schaller, I. (2010): Kreativitätsförderung mit Neuen Medien in der universitären Lehre im Fach Informatik [Fostering creativity by new media—university teaching of computer science]. In: K. Meißner & M. Engelien (Eds.): *Enterprises & Communities in the New Web*. Workshop GeNeMe '10, Gemeinschaften in Neuen Medien, TU Dresden, 07/08.10.2010.

Cohen, L., Manion, L. & Morrisson, K. (2007). *Research Methods in Education*. London: Routledge.

Fischer, G. (2011, May–June). Understanding, fostering, and supporting cultures of participation. *Communications of ACM Interactions*, 18(3), 42–53.

Goggins, S. P., Jahnke, I., & Wulf, V. (2013). *Computer-Supported Collaborative Learning at the Workplace (CSCL@Work)*. New York: Springer.

Gomes, L. & Bogosyan, S. (2009, December). Current trends in remote laboratories. *IEEE Transactions on Industrial Electronics*, 56(12), 4744–4756.

Guion, L., Diehl, D. & McDonald, D. (2002). Triangulation: establishing the validity of qualitative studies. FCS6014. Retrieved March 24, 2014, from http://edis.ifas.ufl.edu/fy394

Haertel, T. & Jahnke, I. (2011). Wie kommt die Kreativitätsförderung in die Hochschullehre? In Zeitschrift für Hochschulentwicklung, *ZFHE*, 6(3), 238–245.

Hatch, M. (2013). *The Maker Movement Manifesto: Rules for Innovation in the New World of Crafters, Hackers, and Tinkerers*. New York: McGraw-Hill.

Jahnke, I. (2009). Socio-technical communities: from informal to formal? In B. Whitworth & A. de Moor (Eds.): *Handbook of Research on Socio-Technical Design and Social Networking Systems*. Hershey, PA: Information Science Reference, IGI Global, pp. 763–778.

Jahnke, I. (2010). A way out of the information jungle—a longitudinal study about a socio-technical community and informal learning in higher education. *International Journal of Socio-technology and Knowledge Development*, 4, pp. 18–38. doi:10.4018/jskd.2010100102

Jahnke, I. (2011). How to foster creativity in technology enhanced learning. In B. White, I. King & Ph. Tsang (Eds.): *Social Media Tools and Platforms in Learning Environments: Present and Future*. Springer, pp. 95–116. doi:10.1007/978-3-642-20392-3_6

Jahnke, I. (2012). Technology-embraced informal-*in*-formal learning. In: A. Ravencroft, S. Lindstaedt, C. Delgado Kloos & D. Hernandez-Leo (Eds): *21st Century Learning for 21st Century Skills*. Seventh European Conference on Technology Enhanced Learning. Berlin: Springer, pp. 395–400.

Jahnke, I. (2013, July–September). Teaching practices in iPad-classrooms: alignment of didactical designs, mobile devices and creativity. *International Journal of Mobile and Blended Learning (ijMBL)*, 5(3), 1–17.

Jahnke, I. & Haertel, T. (2010). Kreativitätsförderung in der Hochschule—ein Rahmenkonzept. (Fostering creativity in universities—a framework). In *Das Hochschulwesen*, 3, 88–96.

Jahnke, I. & Kumar, S. (2014). Digital Didactical Designs: Teachers' Integration of iPads for Learning-Centered Processes, In *Journal of Digital Learning in Teacher Education*, 30(3), 81–88. doi:10.1080/21532974.2014.891876

Jahnke, I. & Liebscher, J. (2013). Towards a didactical design using mobile devices to encourage creativity. *Enhancing Learning in the Social Sciences*, 5(1), 51–64. doi:10.11120/elss.2013.05010051

Jahnke, I., Norqvist, L. & Olsson, A. (2014, September 16–19). Digital Didactical Designs of Learning Expeditions. In: C. Rensing et al. (Eds.): *Open Learning and Teaching in Educational Communities*. The 9th European Conference on Technology Enhanced Learning, EC-TEL 2014, Graz, Austria, LNCS Vol. 8719, pp. 165–178.

Jahnke, I., Svendsen, N. V., Johansen, S. K. & Zander, P.-O. (2014). The dream about the magic silver bullet—the complexity of designing for tablet-mediated learning. *In ACM GROUP 2014 Conference Proceedings*.

Jahnke, I., Terkowsky, C., & Pleul, Ch. & Tekkaya, A. E. (2010). Online learning with remote-configured experiments. In: M. Kerres, N. Ojstersek, U. Schroeder & U. Hoppe (Eds): *Interaktive Kulturen, DeLFI 2010*. Proceedings of 8. Tagung der Fachgruppe E-Learning der Gesellschaft für Informatik e.V, pp. 265–277.

Kolbe, K. (1990). *The Conative Connection*. Reading, MA: Addison-Wesley.

McWilliam, E. & Dawson, S. (2008). Teaching for creativity: towards sustainable and replicable pedagogical practice. *Higher Education,* 56(6), 633–643.

Mor, Y. & Winters, N. (2011). Design approaches in technology-enhanced learning. *Interactive Learning Environments*, 15(1), 61–75.

Norqvist, L., Jahnke, I. & Olsson, A. (2014, September). The learners' expressed values of learning in a media tablet learning culture. In: C. Rensing et al. (Eds.): *Open Learning and Teaching in Educational Communities. The 9th EC-TEL2014, European Conference on Technology-Enhanced Learning*. LNCS Vol. 8719, Graz/Austria, Springer.

Pleul, C., Terkowsky, C., Jahnke, I. & Tekkaya, A. E. (2011). Tele-operated laboratory experiments in engineering education—the uniaxial tensile test for material characterization in forming technology. In: G. Alves & J. García-Zubía (Eds.): *Using Remote Labs in Education*. Bilbao, Spain: Duesto, pp. 323–348.

Reeves, Th., Herrington, J. & Oliver, R., (2005, Spring). Design research. *Journal of Computing in Higher Education*, 16(2), pp. 97–116.

Sandoval, W. A. & Bell, P. (2004): Design-based research methods for studying learning in context: introduction. *Educational Psychologist*, 39(4), 199–201.

Terkowsky, C., Pleul, C., Jahnke, I. & Tekkaya, A. E. (2011). Tele-operated laboratories for online production engineering education. Platform for e-Learning and telemetric experimentation (PeTEX). *International Journal of Online Engineering (iJOE)*, 7, Special Issue: Educon 2011, pp. 37–43. Vienna, IAOE.

Wang, F. & Hannafin, M. J. (2005). Design-based research and technology-enhanced learning environments. *Educational Technology Research and Development*, 53(4), 5–23.

7

CONCLUSION AND LOOKING FORWARD . . .

It is not possible to deliver learning like products to households, but in teaching we act "as if" this would work.

(adopted from Anders Norberg)

The first principle of true teaching is that nothing can be taught.

(Aurobindo Ghosh)

Berger and Luckmann (1967/1993) explained the social construction of reality, that the construction is manifested so that it is hard to change. Within the age of social media, this concept has changed into a sociotechnically constructed reality. There is no objective reality, but the complexity of societies does construct its own reality as if it is an objective fact; it is manifested in complex and hidden social and sociotechnical mechanisms—hard to wish them away. Nevertheless, new forms of learning are evolving, and this has effects and implications for established teaching and learning forms. Is there a gap between the Homo Interneticus (Krotoski, 2010) and the Homo Didacticus? What kind of Digital Didactical Designs for teaching and learning are useful to support meaningful, significant powerful learning designs in higher education and in schools?

What we have learned from our studies is that new Digital Didactical Designs include designs for the active co-construction of new knowledge; the designs, which we observed from innovative teachers, have a focus on processes and social relationships. Learning is supported through reflective cross-actions, including:

1. The design of technology-embraced, informal-*in*-formal learning that supports the *conative* level of learning, too (InPUD study);

2. The design for learning in a way that learning in unexpected, unusual (online) places across established boundaries is fostered (CSCL at work studies); and
3. The utilization of social media as a booster to intensify learning as a process strengthened through the design for creating social relations.

In the digital age, the paradigm of design for teaching and learning is shifting into a design that supports reflective CrossActionSpaces, where the social relations among the peers, as well as the teacher-student relations, are integrated into the Digital Didactical Designs for learning expeditions.

7.1 Empowering Teachers as Collaborative Designers—Organizational Change!

The Example of Denmark

In our projects in the Nordic countries of Denmark, Sweden and Finland, we studied Digital Didactical Designs of media tablets in classrooms. Larger school visits, interviews and classroom observations were conducted beginning in 2012.

Becoming part of the context and the program of Odder schools in Denmark, the researchers realized that the community does not only implement new technology. A task force and head teachers implemented a new philosophy and organizational management on how to handle new forms of teaching and innovations in schools and classrooms. Inspired by the approach of action research, where teachers become researchers to reflect on problems and to find solutions, the community implemented a model called 'LP' to reflect their practice on teaching; this began in 2009. This LP model focuses on "collegial cooperation between teachers and other pedagogical staff, who reflect on their teaching and carry it out in the best way possible for their students" (http://www.lp-modellen.dk; studied by the Norwegian professor Nordahl). The main concept is to foster collaborative reflections in the teachers' workplace. For this, teachers take a new role: they become designers and learners at work (Goggins, Jahnke & Wulf, 2013). The LP model consists of six steps, starting with "finding the problem" (try to write it down), "collecting information" (analysis) and then creating a strategy to improve the situation (strategy, evaluation, revision). The central question of such a model is: how do the teachers in Odder, Denmark, change the learning environments to improve teaching and learning? "We have to organize the meta-reflection," said the project manager in Odder. For that, the LP model is helpful: "the teachers learnt to reflect," and "they have now the tools for how to start and reflect." Odder is a very nice example that shows the relevance and importance of a school and a municipal strategy when launching new technology as social process—such a larger strategy is necessary to support a change toward digital didactical design thinking in education.

The Example of a School in Gainesville, Florida—Rebuilding Space/Place/Time

In 2012, I visited the Educational Technology Program at the University of Florida in Gainesville. During this time, two schools were visited that had implemented media tablets. The P.K. Yonge Developmental Research School at the University of Florida in Gainesville, is another very nice example of how schools may develop an alternative education model toward Digital Didactics. The school redesigned a building; in doing this, the school leaders and ICT-responsible person did not focus only on the tablet integration—instead, the main concept focused on rethinking education. One component was that the school did decide that the traditional model of 'one teacher per class' is an old model, and they designed a new one: all teachers have the same responsibility to the class. A group of teachers designed teaching and learning together. The school leaders and teachers created the slogan "school without borders"; the rooms do not have doors. In addition, the rooms had different sizes; they were not standardized nor did they contribute to conformity. The open spaces contributed to diversity, the diverse needs of learners and the teaching and learning objectives. The change for the teachers was also made evident in new, redesigned rooms and learning spaces. The teachers created a space in the center of the building where they obtained space and time for collaboration. Each week, they had some hours to prepare, discuss and reflect on teaching and learning. The school not only created a new mind-set for teachers as workplace learners and designers; they also built spaces and assigned time for reflection about teaching reality in classrooms—in other words, students, parents, visitors and new teachers could *see* the collaboration. The school assigned a materialized space for the activity of collaborative reflections.

7.2 Lessons Learned—Designing the Future

National tests such as PISA (Program for International Student Assessment; developed by the OECD) and different other rankings make the effort to show schools and universities where they stand and how good they are in terms of providing learning options for students. Students take tests on how well they perform in math, science, reading/writing skills, problem solving and more. The results of such tests and rankings show a range of different quality levels among schools and universities. The test results point to gaps in student learning. That is good; however, there are three major problems.

First, such tests and rankings measure only small portions of student learning and performance and do not and cannot measure the whole learning picture. Sir Ken Robinson made the problem very clear when he wrote, "Just because you can't count it doesn't mean it doesn't count" (on Twitter @SirKenRobinson, September 13, 2014). Exactly! Society and politics follow a "measurability belief."

"The entire society is permeated by the measurability belief" said Professor Sven Eric Liedmann on Twitter (@svenericliedman) in his keynote speech for #nu2014se, a national conference on higher education in Sweden. He added: "New Public Management is in a straitjacket for teachers. Stop focusing on hewn measurability."

I want to emphasize here that such tests do not provide the whole picture of teaching and learning. Of course, they show something but do not present the entire puzzle. What we can see from our studies is that the teachers in media-tablet classrooms build designs for deeper learning, such as learning expeditions, and use the potential of CrossActionSpaces. The students have changed from consumers into reflective producers and "makers." However, these new ways of teaching and learning are not reflected in national tests or institutional rankings, and this should be reflected in those tests.

Second, even if such tests and rankings show portions of gaps in schools and universities, the institutions themselves do not obtain any advice on how to close this gap. Schools and universities now sit there more or less alone and do not know how to make things better or how to improve teaching and learning. Here, the DDD approach (Chapter 5) provides an opportunity. The Digital Didactical Design model sees teaching and learning as process designs and starts with the teachers' applied didactical designs-in-practice by studying them; when made visible, the model shows what really happens in the classrooms. It illustrates benefits, the positive side and the gaps and problems. The data can be used to start a conversation and a dialogue with the schools, teachers and students about how they understand teaching and learning and how they want to improve the processes.

Third, such tests do reinforce the traditional concept of teaching and learning; they measure what the status quo is, and they do not reward schools and universities that try innovative pedagogy. Instead, bad test results reinforce them to go back to the old 'norm' rather than making a radical change in education. For example, some examples of PISA2015 show that they measure the information of a 'right' answer, but those answers can be found on the Internet or in online discussions. What is the point of such traditional learning concepts when we all have all of the information always with us in our pockets and handbags? We have access to the 'InfoSphere' via our tablets and smart phones. When trying to solve a problem, who would not ask the Internet or all the other online networks that are out there? The traditional learning approaches, for example, memorizing what is in the textbook to find a right answer, are meaningless in the near future. Instead, we need concepts where students want to learn, where they create and make things, or where they want to solve complex problems for which there are no answers available on the Internet so far; they then get support to reflect about their developed skills to improve learning progress.

7.2.1 Our World Is Full of Co-expanded Spaces— CrossActionSpaces

Our networked world is not only made of one space or several social and socio-technical systems, communities and networks. It is also a highly dynamic set of human inter- and cross-action that emerges into spaces for communication. Those spaces are made by social and antisocial communication (humans and bots). They are characterized by a higher tension between openness and constraints than in the nondigital world. CrossActionSpaces require teachers and learners to design for learning in other ways than in the nondigital age.

7.2.2 Learning Cannot Be Delivered—Traditional Designs Neglecting Designs for Partnerships

Traditional educational institutions act as if teaching can deliver learning like products and e-mails to households. The old learning is designed as if it were taking place without designing for social relations. Sure, all learning took place in groups more or less, but the teaching did not design for learnerships explicitly; it was not part of the design. This neglected the fact that individual and group learning is always socially framed. Social media can enable but also hinder learning; group dynamics, invisible assumptions and expectations by individuals affect each learning progress. In such complex situations, traditional teaching does not support students to reflect on group issues. But this could easily be done, for example, with coaching methods, supervision methods or basic trainings and exercises of how to give and receive feedback. The reflection on student roles is often not part of the learning designs—that makes it sometimes very hard to learn. And even if the student group succeeded, it is not always clear to them why they succeeded. Learning does not take place in isolated vacuum spaces; rather, it depends on social processes, structures and dynamics of formal and informal roles. The future classroom designs for learnerships and makes this element a central part of the design for learning.

7.2.3 Learning Is Reflective Multi-Cross-Actions in Relations

Roles enable but also hinder the connectivity of communication. There is no such thing as 'open world,' I provoke. Terms like 'openness' and 'open cultures' are fantastic, and politically they are allegedly useful in making clear that we all should be open-minded toward learning, technical systems should be open, and educational institutions are open in their courses for all learners. Here, I want to stress that openness often implies that there are no boundaries for learning at all. This is wrong. Where humans are involved, there are always boundaries, and new ones will be developed over time—it is a continuous process of coding and recoding. It is human nature to create social structures like assumptions and expectations, and expectations of expectations; without them, we could not arrange our daily lives. People make decisions what space to enter. In doing so, they include and exclude. There will always be boundaries—socially constructed and sociotechnically constructed. I wish to say that, instead of neglecting the existence of boundaries—or acting as if they do not exist—the better way would be to make them visible and to reflect about our role-constrained learning in order to develop learning progress and cross-actions for teacherpreneurs and learnerpreneurs.

7.2.4 Designing Conditions for Sociotechnical-Pedagogical Processes—Teaching Is Process Design

In the digital age, new CrossActionSpaces require designs for learning as forms of reflective cross-actions. Is there a significant difference in learning inside educational institutions and outside such systems? Yes, I argue: the teacher and Digital Didactical Designs can make the difference. A teacher in such a role will ask uncomfortable questions and usually brings a learner further than a student can come on his own (Vygotsky's studies, 1978, "Zone of Proximal Development"). The challenge is to redesign teaching practices in such a way that it enables opportunities and situations for deeper learning expeditions toward a student's conceptual change (Ho, Watkins & Kelly, 2001). Such an approach needs the constructive alignment of Digital Didactical Designs, interactive mobile media and creativity (Jahnke, 2013; Jahnke & Kumar, 2014). The challenge is to design both teaching and learning in educational institutions where the technology is not at the center of teaching but new forms of entirely new Digital Didactical Designs, which unfold learning expeditions as one example of reflective multi-cross-actions. Teaching becomes process design, where teachers are collaborative designers of processes that are sociotechnical-pedagogical processes as shown in Chapter 5 (process view).

7.2.5 Schools and HE Need Practices That Design for Learning Walkthroughs and Learning Expeditions

I argue for a critical-constructive view on sociotechnical-pedagogical processes in educational institutions that open the way toward unknown paths for teachers and learners. Two concepts might be useful to start with:

- The *learning walkthrough* presupposes a rather designed learning landscape more closely guided by teaching but with a greater variation and more student options for working and learning than the traditional course; while
- *Learning expeditions* are multiple cross-actions in relations that stand for more open-ended, problem-based learning paths, and/or for goal-oriented

learning, to master X or understand the implications of Y, where the learning methods and instruments are very open and take place in sociotechnical, multilocated communication spaces with reflecting peers where process-based assessment supports the learning progress.

When we adopt the concept of Digital Didactical Design (Chapter 3) and transform it to teaching in schools and higher education, it is important that teachers and instructors learn how to scaffold the process of peer-reflective learning, guided reflections and social partnerships. It is not enough just to give the students assignments and put them into a community; they need guidance and support in the form of micro-reflections and process-based feedback. Learning in a community, as Lave and Wenger (1991) proposed, is not enough anymore in a networked world. Guided reflections and social partnerships are a key to succeeding in a networked digital world. Based on the principles of learning in a community of reflecting peers, the nature of learning expeditions can be described as follows:

- Learning expeditions are multiple cross-actions in processes across established systems, communities and networks,
- in which learners walk through multi-existing co-expanded communication spaces but also create new ones,
- and such expeditions are grounded on research-based learning approaches,
- in which process-based feedback and feed*forward*, guided reflections and formative assessment are key principles of networked scaffolding and self-boosted learning,
- occurring in a community of reflective peers (guided reflections, self-reflections, collaborative reflections, and/or guided by a teacher).

7.2.6 Not All Learning Can Be Measured

The digital data age has the weakness that we act 'as if' we can measure learning. Is this really the case? What we measure are smaller pieces of information, which a learner remembers, understands and applies. The entire process of educational progress and the conceptual change of a person are not measurable. We can gather data to create a qualitative understanding about students' processes in progress, but we cannot measure it in total. The measurement movement has one problem. It affects new designs for learning. Instead of rethinking and creating a radical change in educational institutions, only such allegedly improvements will be made that one can measure—of course, not all act like this. It seems that the Nordic countries have some examples and want to go another way. Educational institutions align teaching and learning toward measurable items because there is pressure coming from somewhere (who drives this development?) that everything needs to be measured. Because people believe that we can measure all learning (which is not totally true), our educational systems turned into measurable items instead of developing competences, which is harder to assess. Nowadays, we live with the impression that what can be measured can be taught. This is wrong, and some schools in Scandinavia are trying to make a difference, as we illustrated in our empirical studies (Chapter 6). We have started to commercialize education—instead, we should start to create designs for deeper learning, where students are engaged and designing teaching that supports learners to become learnerpreneurs—quality not economy!

7.2.7 ICT Is More Than Just a Tool

Information and communication technology (ICT) is often described as a passive tool—like a hammer. This reduces technology to an external factor. However, ICT is more than just a tool; it is a mediator for communication. It affects communication. It is part of the communication. When using web-enabled ICT, it turns a social system such as a classroom, school, or university into new forms of communication where physical rooms are merging together with online spaces. Through technology, the future classroom evolves into CrossActionSpaces. The future classroom creates Digital Didactical Designs for using those spaces to engage the learners by connecting them to real-world problems.

7.2.8 Learning Analytics Is a Method and an Instrument to Control Students and Their Behavior—a Provoking Look

Learning analytics is a method to control student behavior. I provoke, sure. However, besides the benefits of such approaches, we need a look from an ethical viewpoint. From the view of ethics, Big Data and Learning Analytics restrict designs for social relations and roles; they can turn a social atmosphere based on trust into a climate of control, measurements, standardization and conformity. Instead of just instruments, we need communication on the different teacher and student roles from all involved people; then we will discover that students have diverse pictures of the role of a good teacher, as teachers have diverse views on that of a good student (as seen in studies about educational beliefs). Making this transparent and discussing the different, partly contradictory expectations is a first step toward a relationship that works for all. When using Big Data, a "right mindset" is required, as professor Viktor Mayer-Schönberger proposed in his keynote at the 2014 EC-TEL conference on September 18, 2014, in Graz, Austria. However, what is a 'right' mind-set, and who says what is 'right'?

Another crucial issue points to the data itself. Right now, society acts 'as if' only the data counts. But data is just a part or one little part of a bigger picture. Sometimes, even data can mislead the learner and the teacher. An example is a story that I observed many years ago. A high school student did seek advice for what to do after finishing high school. A regional job agency helped her to figure out what she liked and what she is good at. Using the results of that kind of test, the agent told her that she should not start with a study at a university but better would be an apprenticeship contract and finding work outside the academic world. "You should not study, you will not be successful", the agent told the job seeker. Fifteen years later I met the person again and she told me that she did follow the advice first. She worked for a year as a kind of secretary in an office. But after 8 months, she was borrowed and then wanted to try the university instead. She studied social sciences, and later, she even finished with a doctoral degree and became a professor. Had she followed the previous test results, she would still be a secretary instead of a professor. That example shows that data can make people do something they actually don't want or need to do. The person who is affected by data needs to learn to reflect on given data; what to do and what not to do with the data is key. Why is it so? Because, often such kind of data measures the status quo and neglects the development of learners. Therefore, when using data, a new data practice is needed that capture not only snapshots of a learner's status quo but takes into consideration multiply loci and times.

7.2.9 There Are No Simple Step-by-Step Models for Digital Didactical Designs

There are no simple step-by-step models for Digital Didactical Designs, but what helps is to empower teachers to think and act like Digital Didactical Designers. In a CrossActionSpace, teachers are juggling increased complexity within educational environments. Teachers' roles turn into those of learning designers, where teaching is shifting from a common routine activity to a design project. The innovative teachers become process designers for learning expedition. Teaching becomes a process design.

We all want to have easy models for how to design teaching and learning, easy-to-understand process models and a simple guide on how to design teaching practices for enabling engaged learning—we want a solution to everything (something along the lines of the answer '42' in *The Hitchhiker's Guide to the Galaxy* by Douglas Adams). A simple guide is not possible! Of course, we can learn about tools and approaches, but there is no simple step-by-step guide for how to make process designs. All design is redesign (read Chapter 5). What we can do is to make the framework and conditions visible, as I have done with the 'Digital Didactics' and 'Digital Didactical Designs' triangles in the earlier chapters, which provide a framework for understanding learning as MultiCrossActions in Relations. The Digital Didactical Design framework helps to explore further design thinking and provides a start toward designing teaching and learning in a networked world. An educational actor starts by reflecting on the teaching objectives toward educational technologies or toward learning activities; but in the end, all teachers will go through a phase of "back and forth, back and forth, and back and forth" (Herrmann, 2012) that looks like chaos to the outside observer. A design seems to be clear in the beginning; then there will be a vague feeling of insecurity in the middle, until a relatively clear plan emerges at the end. The redesign will be changed during the practice of teaching while applying the design. If it is a good design, the changes are small; if the design is just a draft and not well thought through, more changes will occur. "A plan is there to change," as my colleague Rainer Skrotzki often says. So, again, whenever humans wish to have a step-by-step guide (as I understand we all would like), we have to say that this is not available. All the easy plans are just theoretical models; they do not work in practice. Instead, we have to teach and learn in a design-thinking way to create Digital Didactical Designs for learning expeditions.

7.2.10 More Design-Oriented Research and Formative Evaluation Studies

In order to study Digital Didactical Designs in practice, evaluation studies and design-based research (Wang & Hannafin, 2005; "Action research," Avison et al., 1999) are two options.

Teaching happens in the 'wild life' out there, not in a controlled laboratory. From this viewpoint, it does not make sense to compare different classes, such as whether Class A with 'pen and paper' (example of new technology) is better than Class B without pen and paper. Scientists often carry out such comparative studies. In natural sciences, such studies might be useful, while in social sciences it is rather difficult because one cannot control all the thousands of variables, as is possible in a laboratory. It takes many groups in order to get such empirical, evidence-based data that are valid in general. Even then, scientists cannot be sure to have the correct results, because they might be true for this setting; but when new technology is involved, the results may not be true in the new setting. The problem is that there are studies that did not apply the comparative studies in enough groups; they did it just with one group and one control group, and the data was then used *as if* the results were true for all and *as if* the results were representatively valid for all learners—but this is not true to say for every comparative study. The problem is that people and society want to have such studies because they want to have such easy-to-communicate, study-based evidence, such as 'Group A is better than Group B.' And because this evidence is so easy to communicate, people believe in such data, although the results are only valid and true for this specific study. This need to believe in such studies leads to misunderstanding.

One alternative option is to carry out formative evaluation studies (Rossi, Lipsey & Freeman, 2004). The researcher asks in the beginning what the teaching and learning goals are, for example, surface learning, remembering the textbook or deeper learning, to develop critical-thinking skills and creative action. The researcher then studies whether the Digital Didactical Design applied by the teachers achieved its goals or not and to what extent. Different data in a triangulation can be used, such as the students' subjective views and their learning outcomes, stimulated recall method or 'the student diary method,' course observations and the teacher's view. When the study shows that the learning goals were not achieved, then the researcher and teachers make changes in the Digital Didactical Designs based on the data from the first study. After changing the Digital Didactical Designs, the teacher applies it in another course, and the researcher studies it again, similarly to the first phase. When applying such an evaluation and design-based research process, the data is useful to illustrate whether such designs do work in practice and to what extent the design was useful to support learning; the study also shows the challenges and problems in relation to the design. The evaluation takes place according to what goal the teacher and the curriculum want to achieve, which has been predefined in advance. Based on such evaluation studies, the studies inform what and how to improve the designs; on the outer layer (Figure 2, Chapter 1), they also report possible changes toward the curriculum, exams designs, academic staff development and institutional development.

All in all, I may sum up the content of the book by using a quote from Peter Bergström's PhD thesis (2012), "We lost contact with the students' learning process" (quote from his presentation on 24 Sept 2012 at Umeå University, Sweden); even more, I want to add that we have also lost contact with schools, teacher education and teachers' applied designs-in-practice. With this book, I hope we gain both back in better quality than before.

7.3 References

Avison, D., Lau, F., Myers, M. & Nielsen, P. (1999). Action research. *Communications of the ACM*, 42(1), 94–97.

Berger, P. & Luckmann, T. (1993). *The Social Construction of Reality*. Frankfurt/Main: Fischer (Original work published 1967)

Bergström, P. (2012). *Designing for the Unknown. Didactical Design for Process-based Assessment in Technology-Rich Learning Environments*. Umeå, Sweden: Umeå University Press.

Goggins, S., Jahnke, I. & Wulf, V. (2013). *CSCL@work, Computer-Supported Collaborative Learning at the Workplace*. New York: Springer.

Herrmann, T. (2012). *Kreatives Prozessdesign (Creative process design)*. Heidelberg: Springer.

Ho, A., Watkins, D. & Kelly, M. (2001). The conceptual change approach to improving teaching and learning: an evaluation of a Hong Kong staff development programme. *Higher Education*, 42, 143–169.

Jahnke, I. (2013, July–September). Teaching practices in iPad-classrooms: alignment of didactical designs, mobile devices and creativity. *International Journal of Mobile and Blended Learning (ijMBL)*, 5(3), 1–17.

Jahnke, I. & Kumar, S. (2014). Digital Didactical Designs: teachers' integration of iPads for learning-centered processes. *Journal of Digital Learning in Teacher Education*, 30(3), 81–88. doi:10.1080/21532974.2014.891876/

Krotoski, A. (2010). The virtual revolution. BBC. Retrieved July 1, 2011, from http://www.bbc.co.uk/programmes/b00r3qhg

Lave, J. & Wenger, E. (1991). *Situated Learning: Legitimate Peripheral Participation.* New York: Cambridge University Press.

Rossi, P., Lipsey, M. & Freeman, H. (2004). *Evaluation. A Systematic Approach* (7th ed.). Thousand Oaks, CA: Sage.

Vygotsky, L. S. (1978). *Mind in Society: The Development of Higher Psychological Processes.* Cambridge, MA: Harvard University Press.

Wang, F. & Hannafin, M. J. (2005). Design-based research and technology-enhanced learning environments. *Educational Technology Research and Development, 53*(4), 5–23.

INDEX

Note: Page numbers with *f* indicate figures; those with *t* indicate tables.

academic staff development 134
action 38; as characteristic of community 57
active learning 135
activity dimension of evolving structures 28
Actor-Network-Theory (ANT) 31–2, 58, 112
Adaptation (in AGIL) 76
AGIL 76
'aha!' moment 147–8
allopoietic communication, as element of technical systems 27, 33
alter ego 71, 73
anonymity 175
Aristotle 29
ascribed roles 98
Ashforth, B. E. 72
asocial media world 2–3
Augmentation, in SAMR model 165
autopoiesis 39
autopoietic system 35; social systems as 39

Badged Open Courses (BOCs) 125
Bailey, K. 23
Bales, R. F. 71, 99
Balog, A. 79
Banks, F. 138
Banton, M. 98, 99*t*
Barr, R. 112

Bateson, G. 40
behavior 38
behavioral expectations 83
Berger, P. 112, 201
Bergqvist, E. 116
Bergqvist, T. 116
Bergström, P. 155, 211
Bertalanffy, L. v. 30
Biddle, B. J. 71
Big Data 208–9
Bildung 137
biosocial roles 99*t*
blended learning 111, 115, 118–19
Blogs 26
Bloom, B. S. 151
Blumer, H. 72, 73*t*
Boshmaf, Y. 51
bots *see* social bots
Bot Traffic Report 3, 51
Bring Your Own Device (BYOD) 115
British Coal Mine 25
Brown, J.S. 113, 122
Bruckman, A. 26
Buchem, I. 115

C-C-C triangle 162
Chapman, E. 154
Cherns, A. 27
Ciborra, C. 58
class, role and 94

classrooms, future: crossactions and 11; CrossActionSpaces and 5, 6f; digital networked world and 10–11
co-aims 13
Coakes, E. 27
Cochrane, T. 134; initiative 62
co-expanded communication spaces 7, 9; multi-existing 7–8
co-located 2, 5, 62, 165
cognitive dimension of evolving structures 28
collaborative reflections 115
Collins, A. 25
communication 23; *see also* human communication; absence of, networks and 60–1; action and 38; behavior and 38; cross-actions and 38; forms of 46; human 24; interaction and 38–9; social systems and 23, 35–9
communication spaces 6–9; co-expanded 7; crossaction development and 9, 10f; described 6–7; human action in 8–9; multi-existing 7–8
communities 55–62; described 55–6; learning across, spaces 61–2; networks and 56–8; sociotechnical form of 60
communities of interests (COIs) 57–8, 125
community of practice (CoP) 55, 118, 122; benefits of 123; characteristics of 57; learning as form of 57; learning expeditions and 123–4; private identity and 123; public accessibility and 123
computer-human interaction 38
computer-supported cooperative work (CSCW), roles in 77, 86–7
computer-supported collaborative learning (CSCL) 77, 86
conation 174
conceptual change 12
connectivism 32, 34, 113–14
connectivity of communication 35, 39
constructive alignment 14
content-student-teacher relationship 133–4
context-oriented communication model 37
contingent communication, as element of social system 27
controlling 33
course-based learning, learning expeditions and 117–19
creative designs, learning expeditions and 121–2
creativity 182–5; *see also* DaVinci project

crossactions 8, 38, 106; classrooms of future and 11; communication development and 9, 10f; multiple 8–9
CrossActionSpaces 2–4, 205; characteristics of 9, 17; communication and 24; communication spaces and 6–9; components of 6–12; described 3–4, 5; human action as 8–9; InPUD as example of 176–7; learning in 4–12; networked worlds and learning in 130–1, 132; reflective learning and 115–16; requirements of 14; roles and (*see* roles); social roles and 18; sociotechnical systems as 22–62, 45–6; spaces and 6; teacher/student role structures in 3, 10–11, 13; *vs.* traditional classroom 5, 6f
Cultivating Communities of Practice (Wenger et al.) 55
cultivation 56
curriculum development 134–5

Dahrendorf, R. 71, 74, 76t, 98, 99t
DaVinci project 121, 182–5; Six Facets 182–4, 183f
Denmark, empowering teachers in 202
design 136
design-based research (DBR) studies 173
design in action, defined 13
design thinking 161; models of 160t; principles of 159; teaching as 12
deterministic communication, as element of technical systems 27
didactical conditions triangle 133f, 134–5
didactical design: described 137; extents of 14–15
didactical interaction triangle 133–4, 133f
didaktik 13, 19; defined 130; origin of 131; pedagogy and 131; use of 136
Digital Didactical Design (DDD) 13, 130–67; claims of 131; constructive alignment and 14; defined 131; described 135–8, 137f, 139f; design-based research for 210–11; design explained 136; didactical explained 136; different views on 138, 139f; elements of 13–14, 137–8, 137f; empirical studies and 141–2t; evaluation studies of 210–11; focus of 136; ICT and layers of 132–3, 133t; inner layer of 133–4, 133f; for learning activities 149–53, 152f, 153t; models for 209–10; new forms of 166–7; new normal idea and 131–2; outer layer of 133f,

134–5; overview of 130–2; process-based assessment and 153–5; reflecting learning practices and 141–2*t*; roles and 132; social relations and 155–8; study findings 201–2; tablet-mediated classroom example 143–7; for teaching aims 147–9; teaching and learning from, described 130–1; technology and 158–66, 160*t*, 163*f*; transforming, to five-layer pentagon 139, 139–40*f*, 141, 143; weaknesses of 42–3
digital didactical designing for learning 4; defined 13; teaching practice as 12–15
digital networked world: as CrossActionSpaces 4–5; learning in 10–11; social bots and 2–3
discovery learning 120
distance learning 111
do-it-with-others cultures 12
do-it-yourself (DIY) cultures 12, 17
dynamics of social roles 89
dynamic system, forms of 30–1

Eason, K. 27
Echo Chamber phenomenon 24
education: distribution of 111; ICT use and 110–11; reflective learning and 110–14
educational institutions, social systems and 48–50
Educational Technology Program, University of Florida 203
ego 71, 73
e-learning 119
ELIZA 52
empirical research projects 172–98; DaVinci project 182–5, 183*f*; designed-based *vs.* comparative 173; InPUD 173–7; IPM 185–7; overview of 172–3; PeTEX 177–82; tablet-mediated learning expeditions 187–98
Engeström, Y. 31
expectations: as dimension of roles 81*t*, 83, 88*t*, 90*t*; role-based 44
experiential learning theory 120
exploratory learning approach 120
extracommunicative behavior 37

Faraj, S. 26
50–50 structure of learning 125–6
Fink, D. L. 137
Fischer, G. 33, 113
five-layer pentagon DDD model 139, 139–40*f*, 141, 143

Florida State Initiative 161
Floridi, L. 17, 22, 45, 111
formal roles 100*t*, 102
Forte, A. 26
Freeman, J. 156
functionalistic perspective 71
future classroom 5

general systems theory (GST) 30
Gerhardt, U. 73, 98, 99*t*
Ghoshal, S. 27, 58
Giddens, A. 72, 91
Goals (in AGIL) 76
Goffman, E. 72, 73*t*
Gross, N. 98, 99*t*
Grudin, J. 47

Haertel, T. 184–5
Halfmann, J. 31
Halverson, R. 25
Hänze, M. 154
Hatch, M. 12, 17, 197
Haug, F. 71
Hauge, T. E. 137
Healey, M. 119
Herrmann, Th. 33, 37, 47, 78
high extent of support 15
Hinssen, P. 131
HitchBot 43
Hollenbeck, J. R. 81
Homo Didacticus 201
Homo Interneticus 1, 54, 201
Homo Sociologicus (Dahrendorf) 71
Howland, J. 14
Hudson, A. 162
Hudson, B. 137
human behavior, as roles 78–84; modifications/changes of 95*t*
human communication 24, 35–7; interpretation forms of 36
human-computer communication 38, 46
human-to-human communication 46
Humboldt, W. 50

ICT *see* information and communication technology (ICT)
Ilgen, D. R. 81
ILOs *see* intended learning outcomes (ILOs)
Imitation Game 52
Inclusive Learning Spaces 4
individual behavior 38
Industrial Project Management (IPM) 185–7; didactical designers explanation

for iPod non-use 186–7; mobile device potential 187; research project overview 185; student explanation for iPod non-use 185–6
informal communities 55–6; characteristics of 57
informal roles 100*t*, 102–3
information and communication technology (ICT) 1–2; advantage of 162; categories of 161–3; characteristics of 161–4, 163*f*; didactic design integration and 164–6; Digital Didactical Design and 132–3, 133*f*, 158–66, 160*t*, 163*f*; as efficiency aid 15, 208; elements of 33; as extension device 15; impact of 45; levels of 161; problems with 2–4; reflection and 2; roles and 77–8; as transformative device 15
InfoSphere 7
InPUD (Informatik-Portal-University-Dortmund) 113, 173–7; conative level of learning and 174–5; as CrossActionSpace example 55–6, 176–7; information/communication structure and 175–6; open question and 175; research project overview 173–4; Web 2.0 and 24, 26, 48
Instagram 162
installation 92; defined 31
instance, role and 94
Instruction-Response-Evaluation structure 6
Integration (in AGIL) 76
intended learning outcomes (ILOs) 13, 137–8, 137*f*, 149
interactionism theory, roles and 72–4, 73*t*, 90*t*
interactions 38–9; as social system type 34
Internet-based communication: as sociotechnical form 25; studies on 26
IPM *see* Industrial Project Management (IPM)

Jahnke, I. 17, 78, 118, 132
Jenkins, A. 119
Jesse, K. 24
Jonassen, D. H. 14
just-in-time communication 177

Kaptelinin, V. 31
Kember, D. 151, 152*f*
Khan Academy, peer-learning and 125

Kienle, A. 37
Klafki, W. 133
Koehler, M. J. 162
Kolb, D. 114, 120
Krappmann, L. 71, 72, 73*t*
Kukulska-Hulme, A. 114
Kushel, D. 24

Latent (in AGIL) 76
Latour, B. 31
Laurillard, D. 114
Lave, J. 57, 116–17, 122, 207
Leach, J. 138
learnerpreneurs 12
learners, consumers to critical-reflective producers shifting of 135–6
learning: connectivism approach to 113–14; as construction of new knowledge 117–18; as form of community of practice 57; forms of 110; as knowledge construction 135; measuring 149–50, 207–8; reflective cross-actions and 201–2 (*see also* reflective learning); research-led 119; research-oriented 119; research-tutored 119; role-constrained 105, 106; role-dependent 105
learning activities 137, 137*f*; didactical design for 149–53, 152*f*, 153*t*
Learning Analytics 208–9
learning cycle (Kolb) 114
learning designs: CrossActionSpaces and 11–12; do-it-yourself cultures and 12, 17; layers of 15–16, 16*f*
learning diary 180
learning expeditions 117–26, 206–7; community of practice and 123–4; course-based learning and 117–19; creative designs and 121–2; in digital era 110; future and, schools/universities of 124–6; in groups and communities 122–4; PeTEX model and 178–9; range of, in tablet-mediated classroom 195–8, 196*t*; research-based learning as 119–21
learning trajectory 118
learning walkthrough 110, 206; learning trajectory and 118
Leffler, E. 17
Liebscher, J. 185
Liedmann, S. E. 204
LinkedIn 32, 53, 162
Linton, R. 23, 71, 74, 76*t*, 98, 99*t*
Linux 45

Loveless, A. 162
low extent of support 15
LP model 202
Luckmann, T. 112, 201
Luhmann, N. 23, 31, 32, 34, 39, 40–1, 44, 45, 48–9, 69
Lund, A. 136, 137

Madrigal, A.C. 3, 51
maker culture 12, 197
maker movements 12, 17
March, J. G. 105
Mårell-Olsson, E. 162
Marra, R. M. 14
Marx, K. 30
massive open online course (MOOC) 39, 114
Mayer-Schönberger, V. 208
McCombs, B. 12
McCormick, R. 15, 138, 158, 163
McDermott, R. 122
Mead, George H. 23, 71, 72, 73*t*
meaningful learning 14
meaning-making 43
Meckel, M. 162
media-constructed social awareness approach 112
media tablets *see* tablet-mediated classroom
mediatization "media ecology" 112
medium extent of support 15
Merton, R. K. 74, 98, 99*t*
micromessaging services 2
mLearning theory 114
mobile devices 1
mobile learning 114–17
Modification, in SAMR model 165
Montgomery, J. 72
Moodle 45
Moon, B. 138
Moore, J. 14
multi-cross-action 109
MultiCrossActions in Relations (McAiR) 18, 61–2, 69
multi-existing co-expanded communication spaces 7–8
multiple interactions 105
Mumford, E. 27, 46

Nadel, S. 73
Nahapiet, J. 27, 58
Nardi, B. A. 31
networked scaffolding 115, 179–80

networks 58–9; communities and 56–8
new normal, the 131–2
Norberg, A. 115, 118, 132
normative 75
Norqvist, L. 17
Northcote, M. 138

objective facticity 112–13
Olsen, J. P. 105
online communities, as sociotechnical form 25, 27
online learning 119
online *vs.* offline worlds 111–12
open badges 115
open question 175
OpenUniversity (UK) 125
open world 3
operational closure of the deep structure 40
O'Reilly, T. 25
organizational and institutional development 134
organizations, as social system type 34
outside education 17

Pachler, N. 114
Parsons, T. 30, 74, 75–6, 76*t*
pedagogy, didaktiks and 131
PeTEX *see* Platform for eLearning and Telemetric Experiments (PeTEX)
PISA *see* Program for International Student Assessment (PISA)
P.K. Yonge Developmental Research School, University of Florida 203
PLACES 113
Place-Time-Model 162
Platform for eLearning and Telemetric Experiments (PeTEX) 120–1, 123, 177–82; learning expeditions and 178–9; learning levels, cross-actions for 179–80; research project overview 177–8; teaching dimensions and, intertwining 180–2
Plato 29
position, as dimension of roles 80*t*, 81–2, 88*t*, 90*t*
Preece, J. 27
Prezi.com 29
private identity 123
privileges, roles as 78
process: designs 112; learning as 109–10; research-based 120
process-based assessment 137, 137*f*, 153–5

Program for International Student
Assessment (PISA) 203
public accessibility 123
Puentedura, R. 164
purpose/function, as dimension of roles
80*t*, 82, 88*t*, 90*t*

QR codes 192, 192–3*f*

Rammert, W. 161
real world problems, defined 116–17
Redefinition, in SAMR model 165
reflection 2; in Digital Didactical
Design 13
reflective communication 4; learning
as 10
reflective learning 109–26, 205–6;
education and 110–14; learning
expeditions and 117–26; mobile
learning and 114–17; overview of
109–10; student/teacher roles and 117
relations 106
research-based learning 119; as learning
expedition 119–21; *vs.* research 119;
types of 119
research-led learning 119
research-oriented learning 119
research-tutored learning 119
Ritterskamp, C. 78
Roberts, T. 26
Robinson, K. 203
role-based access control (RBAC) 77–8
role-constrained learning 105, 106
role-dependent learning 105
role doing: development of 94–5; as
dimension of roles 81*t*, 83–4, 88*t*
roles 68–106; acquired/achieved types of
99*t*; ascribed 98; assigned and taken types
of 92–5, 100*t*; biosocial 99*t*; complexity
of, in educational institutions 101;
in computer-supported cooperative
work 77; concept of 35, 70–1; defined
23, 35, 69; descriptive categories of
99*t*; development of new 95, 95–7*t*;
didactical design for 155–6; Digital
Didactics and 132; dimensions of 80–1*t*,
80–4; duality of 44; expectations and
44, 81*t*, 83; formal 100*t*, 102; history of
71–2; human behavior as 78–84; impact
of, on learning 105; importance of, in
formal organizations 49–50; informal
100*t*, 102–3; institutional conditions
and 75–7; interactionism view of 72–4,

73*t*; learning expeditions and 117;
membership 41; multi-cross-actions and
84–6, 104–5; names of 101; networked
world and 91–2, 91*t*; overview of 68–70;
position and 80*t*, 81–2; purpose/function
and 80*t*, 82; role-based access control
and 77–8; role doing and 81*t*, 83–4; set
of, per person 100–1; sociocultural 99*t*;
sociotechnical actions in 79; structural-
functionalist perspective of 74–7,
76*t*; teacher/student, problems with
86–92, 88*t*, 90*t*; in technology/software
development 77–8; time dimension of
100; types of 98–103, 99*t*, 100*t*
role structures, online 3

SAMR model 164–5
Sandhu, R. 77
scaffolding 115, 179–80
Scholarship of Teaching and Learning
(SoTL) 62, 134
Scrimshaw, P. 15, 138, 158, 163
Second Life 45
SeeMe (Herrmann) 29
Sharples, N. 114
shitstorms 54–5
Siemens, G. 32, 113–14
situated learning, characteristics of
116–17
six-facet model of creativity 182–4, 183*f*
Skrotzki, R. 210
Snyder, W. M. 122
social bots 32; digital networked world
and 2–3; identifying 52–3; politics
and 3; as sociotechnical agents 50–4;
studying, questions for 53–4; Turing
Test and 52–3
social capital 5, 27–8, 60; trust and 28
social interaction *see* cross-actions
Social Life of Information, The (Brown and
Duguid) 110
socially framed 135
social networking sites 2
social networks 58–9; aim and objective
of 61; communication absence
and 60–1; communities and 56–8;
learning across, spaces 61–2; social
capital and 59–60; sociotechnical
form of 60
social processes, duality of 112
social relations 137, 137*f*; didactical design
for 155–8
social roles 18, 35; dynamics of 89

social systems 34–5; characteristics of 39–41; communication and 35–9; defined 25; educational institutions and 48–50; elements of 27, 35–44; learning across, spaces 61–2; structures of 43–4; types of 34
social system theory 23; advantages of 43–4
societies, as social system type 34
Society for General Systems Research 30
sociocultural roles 99*t*
sociotechnical actions in roles 79
sociotechnical community (STC) 173–4; *see also* InPUD (Informatik-Portal-University-Dortmund)
sociotechnical systems (STS) 22–62; communication and 35–9; communication spaces and, co-expanding 47–8, 48*t*; communities and 55–62; as CrossActionSpaces 45–6; defined 25, 26, 46–7; designing, for teaching/learning 41–3; examples of 27; failure of, reasons for 47; forms of 25; learning across, spaces 61–2; overview of 22–4; social bots and 50–4; social systems and 25–8, 34–5; system described 28–35; technical systems and 25, 26–8, 31–3
Socrates 29
Sommerville, I. 26
SoTL *see* Scholarship of Teaching and Learning (SoTL)
space perspective 6
structural dimension of evolving structures 28
structural-functionalist perspective of roles 74–7, 76*t*
structure, as characteristic of community 57
student-centered learning 118
Study of Man, The (Linton) 74
study program, future 125
Substitution, in SAMR model 164
symbolic interaction 69–71
system 6; aim and objective of 61; as characteristic of community 57; concept of 29–30; described 28–35; forms of 30–1; overview of 28–9; social 34–5; sociotechnical form of 60; technical 31–3

tablet-mediated classroom 6, 187–98; didactical design view of 143–5, 146*f*; fifth grade language 191; fourth grade

language 190–1; learning expeditions, range of 195–8, 196*t*; ninth grade physics 193–4, 194–5*f*; preschool class 188–9, 189*f*; process design view of 145–7, 146*f*; research project overview 187–8; seventh grade language, peer-reflective learning 191–2; seventh grade language, with QR codes 192, 192–3*f*; themes discovered in 198; third grade math 189–90, 190*f*
Tagg, J. 112
Tavistock Institute 25, 46
teachers, as collaborative designers 202–3
teaching, defined 131
teaching aims 137, 137*f*; described 147; didactical design for 147–9; intended learning outcomes and 149
teaching designs: CrossActionSpaces and 11–12; described 12
teaching practices, defined 137
technical systems 31–3; defined 25, 26; elements of 27
technology; *see also* information and communication technology (ICT): characteristics of 33; described 28–9; support 137, 137*f*; system-theoretical approach to 31
technology integration matrix (TIM) 161
technology/software development, roles in 77–8
textbook learning model 151
Thomas, E. J. 71
Tönnies, F. 56
TPCK models 165
transportation for education 110
trust, social capital and 28
Turing Test 51, 52–3
Twitter 3, 5, 32, 38, 51–2, 53, 85, 162; hashtag 8
Tyranny of the Structurelessness, The (Freeman) 156

Ungeheuer, G. 37

vandal hunters 26
van Ham, F. 24
Viegas, F. 24, 26
Vimeo channel 6
virtual worlds, as sociotechnical form 25
volatile, uncertain, complex and ambiguous (VUCA model) 55
Vygotsky, L. S. 131

Wasko, M. 26
Wattenberg, M. 24
Watzlawick, P. 37
wearable technology 1
Web 1.0 25–6
Web 2.0 25–6, 48, 53; roles and learning in 91–2, 91*t*; student roles and 88, 88*t*; teacher roles and 87–8, 88*t*; use of, as habitualized actions 112
Weber, M. 38, 56

Weizenbaum, J. 52
Wellman, B. 60
Wenger, E. 55, 57, 58, 116–17, 118, 122, 207
Whitworth, B. 91
Wikipedia 24, 26, 45, 59, 60
within education 17

Zone of Proximal Development (Vygotsky) 131